VOICES of MADNESS

FOUR PAMPHLETS, 1683–1796

EDITED BY
ALLAN INGRAM

FOREWORD BY
ROY PORTER

SUTTON PUBLISHING

First published in 1997 by
Sutton Publishing Limited · Phoenix Mill
Thrupp · Stroud · Gloucestershire · GL5 2BU

British Library Cataloguing in Publication Data
A catalogue record for this book is available from the British Library.

ISBN 0-7509-1210-3

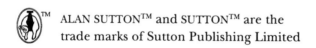

ALAN SUTTON™ and SUTTON™ are the
trade marks of Sutton Publishing Limited

Typeset in 10/11 Bembo.
Typesetting and origination by
Sutton Publishing Limited.
Printed in Great Britain by
Hartnolls, Bodmin, Cornwall.

To Neil, Jen, Joanne and Paul

Contents

Foreword

The distinguished historian G.M. Young once said the historian's job is to keep reading 'till you can hear people talking'. He didn't specifically have mad people in mind, but he might well have done. The mind of madness has been deeply misunderstood – indeed the procedures of psychiatric diagnosis in the past may tell us less about the 'diseases' from which patients were suffering than about in-built failures of communication between the 'madman' and those around him, including the psychiatric profession: the mad were talking a foreign language which few felt inclined to learn.

Despite Freud's attempt through psychoanalysis – early known as the 'talking cure' – to tune in to the consciousness of disturbed people through carefully listening to and interpreting what they said, other strands in modern psychiatry have been positively averse to the idea that madness has something to say and so should be listened to. William Sargant, perhaps the most celebrated psychiatrist in mid-twentieth-century Britain, strongly opposed the Freudian idea of listening to the mad and advocated powerful drug treatments which he said would 'cut the cackle'. In a similar manner, the distinguished psychiatrists and historians of psychiatry, Richard Hunter and Ida Macalpine, maintained that since 'patients are victims of their brain rather than their mind', psychiatry needed to reorient itself, switching 'from listening to looking'. Nowadays we are invited to 'listen to Prozac'. Such a strongly articulated disinclination to listen to the voices of madness may seem to many to be symptomatic of some mental aberration on the part of psychiatrists.

But even if we agree that listening is desirable, how is it to be done? The answer is indeed to follow Young's injunction – to keep reading 'till you can hear people talking'. For it turns out that there is a surprisingly large body of literature produced by the 'mad people' of earlier centuries. In particular, in the eighteenth century, with the growing practice of confinement in lunatic asylums, a patients' protest literature emerged alongside it. Cries went up from former asylum inmates vindicating their sanity and alleging victimization by sinister foes, in publications ranging from the poetry of James Carkesse just after the Restoration of Charles II, the pamphlets of Alexander Cruden, the great Bible concordance compiler

('Alexander the Great' as he called himself), indictments by lesser-known figures such as Samuel Bruckshaw and William Belcher – through in the 1830s to the harrowing *Narrative of the Treatment Received by a Gentleman* by John Perceval, son of the assassinated prime minister, Spencer Perceval.

Such writings are deeply fascinating for all kinds of reasons: they give us a unique ear upon unfamiliar discourses from the past. But most of them have long been unavailable. It is for this reason that *Voices of Madness* is so welcome, reprinting four engrossing bodies of writings by individuals commonly regarded as psychologically peculiar, and interpreting them from an introductory analysis. In these days of literary deconstructionism, the sheer ambivalence of the personal voice in these texts, and their ingenuity in the use of language and rhetoric, gives them an especially strong appeal. The inclusion of Hannah Allen's *Narrative* further gives us a rare chance to hear an early female voice. From the literary, the historical and the humanitarian viewpoints, these texts – far from being mere 'cackle' – are the voices of souls departed labouring under oppression. They have much to say.

Roy Porter
Professor of History of Medicine
The Wellcome Institute for the History of Medicine

Acknowledgements

I am grateful to all of the following for the various ways in which they have helped and supported this book into existence: Vanessa Corrick of the Bodleian Library, Jeremy Gregory, David Gray, Jane Shaw, Sarah Kane, Jane Lewis, Eve Pollard, Margaret Reay and Howard Wickes, whose scholarship leaves most of us standing.

Allan Ingram
Newcastle upon Tyne

Textual Note

The text of each pamphlet is taken from the first edition. I have retained the original spelling, punctuation and emphasis, correcting only the occasional obvious error. In the case of Bruckshaw's pamphlet I have reproduced the majority of his own footnotes, omitting those that give simply a cross-reference or very minor pieces of information.

Introduction

At one point in *The Life and Adventures of Sir Launcelot Greaves*, which was published in 1760–1, Smollett has his protagonist mistakenly confined in a private madhouse. As Sir Launcelot tries to settle down for his first night, he becomes aware of voices, starting up in different rooms of the house.

His ears were all at once saluted with a noise from the next room, conveyed in distant bounces against the wainscot; then a hoarse voice exclaimed: 'Bring up the artillery – let Brutandorf's brigade advance – detach my black hussars to ravage the country . . . I'll lay all the shoes in my shop, the breach will be practicable in four and twenty hours . . . .' 'Assuredly, (cried another voice from a different quarter) he that thinks to be saved by works is in a state of utter reprobation – I myself was a profane weaver, and trusted to the rottenness of works . . . but now I have got a glimpse of the new-light – I feel the operations of grace – I am of the new birth. . . .'

This dialogue operated like a train upon many other inhabitants of the place: one swore he was within three vibrations of finding the longitude, when the noise confounded his calculation: a second, in broken English, complained he was distorped in the moment of de proshection – a third, in the character of his holiness, denounced interdiction, excommunication and anathemas. . . . A fourth began to hollow in all the vociferation of a fox-hunter in the chace; and in an instant the whole house was in an uproar.[1]

The impact is effective, and simple: madness is a cacophony, with delusion striving to outdo delusion, and stereotype laid over stereotype – the religious weaver, the military cobbler, the obsession with calculating the longitude – to produce a witty, recognisable, structured, unthreateningly threatening version of chaos for the amusement of the novelist's readers. The 'voices of madness' are filtered through an ironic narrator, naturally interested in the uses to which he is to put them in his overall treatment of this episode in his protagonist's adventures. As a physician, Smollett no doubt had a more professional interest in the insane, but as a novelist they are made strictly subservient to the sane strategies of his own narrative.

The pamphlets printed in this volume turn Smollett inside out. Four mad individuals – or four people who were regarded as mad at least once in their life, one of whom, Hannah Allen, acknowledged it, while the other three vigorously denied it – claim the space to speak for themselves of their experience, of their treatment by others, and of their understanding of what has happened to them. As personalities they are obscure – Alexander Cruden is the exception here – and there is little surviving information about the rest of their lives. They are almost as anonymous as Smollett's voices from the dark, but instead of speaking only the stock lines and phrases necessary for the novelist's purpose, they reveal strongly individual histories, painstakingly recorded and robustly interpreted. Their focus, moreover, is unashamedly on individual experience, written largely without irony – this time William Belcher is the exception – and in the conviction that the integrity of the account will find sympathetic readers. If this allows an unintentional focus, too, on some of the obsessions and behaviour that led, in the cases of Cruden and Bruckshaw in particular, to their being defined as mad, it also gives insight into the function writing was being made to serve, not for entertainment or income but as self-assertion and self-renewal.

Ironically, the only one of the four not to have been confined in a madhouse was Hannah Allen, whose recognition of her madness, and of what she saw as the causes for it, is the whole point of her pamphlet. There are several reasons for this. As a woman, and particularly as a widow, her role within her immediate society was probably less conspicuous, certainly than Cruden, the bookseller and London-based Scot, and Bruckshaw, the Stamford wool merchant from Cheshire, and her behaviour was generally less in the public eye and more within the confines of her family circle. Also, coming from a reasonably prosperous middle-class background it was natural for her to be put in the care of a series of relations – mother, aunt, brother, family friend – while Cruden and Bruckshaw, living in rented lodgings and without relatives close by, had no such protection against outside forces. Their experiences were much more public, and, apparently, more damaging to their standing, than hers.

But there is also a difference in period. Between Hannah Allen's sufferings in the 1660s and William Belcher's from 1778 until 1795, not only did madness come to loom much more largely in the public imagination, but the mechanisms for treating it, including medical specialisation and provision of places of confinement, became much more expected and promoted. The eighteenth century saw a substantial professionalisation of insanity, and where Hannah Allen could be inconspicuously attended by a family friend and local clergyman, Mr Shorthose, Cruden was whisked off to Wright's private madhouse in Bethnal Green, prescribed for by Dr James Monro of Bethlem Hospital, and threatened with Bethlem itself as a last resort for his madness. Samuel Bruckshaw was carried across four counties to Wilson's dubious madhouse in Ashton-under-Lyne by order of the Mayor of Stamford, while William Belcher spent eighteen years in a private madhouse in Hackney before being released through the offices of Dr Thomas Monro, also of Bethlem Hospital. Far more people were making money out of madness than in Hannah Allen's time, and fewer families, apparently, felt obliged to care for their own within the privacy of their home.

Two particular issues relate to this: treatment and regulation. One of the striking facts arising from these pamphlets is how little the treatments for mad men and women changed over this entire period. Hannah Allen received relatively little medication, but her near contemporary, James Carkesse, who was kept at Dr Thomas Allen's madhouse in Finsbury in 1678, described the vomits, purges, and bleeding that remained standard through Cruden's confinement in the 1730s, Bruckshaw's in the 1770s, and Belcher's in the 1780s and '90s, as well as the poor and scant food, forced administration of medicines, beatings and chaining that appear in all three narratives. When Dr Thomas Monro, then physician at Bethlem, appeared before the Parliamentary Committee on Madhouses in England in 1815, it was to concede that the normal Bethlem regimen of purges and vomits was one he inherited from his father and grandfather and that he continued with it because he knew no better. Even though certain individual physicians, like John Woodward in the early part of the century, and George Cheyne during the 1730s and '40s, advocated individual, or even idiosyncratic, ideas on treatment, it was not until the founding of the Quaker York Retreat in 1792 that a serious challenge was made to the institutional regimen, though many enlightened and humane figures had written and practised over the previous hundred years.[2]

Regulation was also a seriously neglected field, particularly with regard to private madhouses. For much of the eighteenth century there was no requirement to register a private madhouse and, consequently, no attempt to inspect or even to list them. Many were very small, keeping perhaps only half a dozen, or even two or three, inmates for a basic weekly charge, and staffed largely by members of the owner's family. Others were owned and run by some of the most eminent psychiatric physicians, such as William Battie, who was instrumental, too, in founding St Luke's Hospital in opposition to Bethlem in 1751, the Monro family, dynastic physicians to Bethlem for most of the eighteenth century, and, in Leicester, Thomas Arnold, all of whom combined these profitable activities with their less remunerative public work. Some private houses provided a decent and caring service, while others, such as that experienced by Samuel Bruckshaw, were obviously scandalously abusive and neglectful. Not until 1774, with the passing of the Act for Regulating Private Madhouses, did it become necessary to register such establishments for licence, to undergo regular inspection, and to obtain, moreover, medical certification for the confinement of all but pauper lunatics. Neither Cruden nor Bruckshaw could have been confined as they were had the 1774 Act been in force – Bruckshaw, of course, missing it by a few crucial years. In practical terms, the Act almost inevitably achieved less than was intended, especially in the field of inspection. Indeed, some of the abuses reported to the 1815 committee suggest that obtaining a licence was only a formality and inspection little more than a figment. But at least private houses were on record, and, if nothing else, unlawful confinement did not figure significantly as an abuse in the testimonies recorded in 1815.[3]

These are matters of context, and help to place the following pamphlets within a medical arena and also within a social and, increasingly, a political one. But Hannah Allen, Cruden and Bruckshaw, while aware of context, also make a very personal appeal to their readers: 'Christian Reader,' says Allen in her preface, '*Peruse such Instances as these . . . with fear and trembling. How knowest thou but it may be thine own Case?*' Cruden and Bruckshaw make similar addresses, attempting quite explicitly to engage both the sympathies and the fears of their readers. How fragile a thing is sanity – or at least society's agreed definition of it. Bruckshaw's narrative, as he insists in his introduction, is 'beyond belief' in the oppressiveness and cruelty he underwent, yet it also happens so easily, and 'the oppression which crushes me to-day, may fall on my neighbour to-morrow, nor can any one assure himself He shall be able to escape'. To be taken for a madman is the ultimate in alienation, the most damaging of social stigmas, the most personally invasive of definitions, potentially the most remote and inaccessible of narrative positions, but it could be you! Irrespective of their various immediate contexts, of social standing, family, occupation, gender, religion, or of wider medical or political issues, all four writers aim at a common engagement with their readers: enter the reality of my life, understand my experience, think as I think, take me seriously. This is my voice: listen to it.

The reality of Hannah Allen's life stands out in this company, partly because she is the only woman, and partly because of religion. Hers is the only closed narrative – closed in the sense that the experience narrated is over, and not only over but accepted and explained. The assertion on the title page says it all: 'The great Advantages the Devil made of her deep Melancholy, and the Triumphant Victories, Rich and Sovereign Graces, God gave her over all his Stratagems and Devices.' The running title of the original edition, moreover, kept this in the reader's mind throughout the book: 'Satan's Methods and Malice Baffled.' To this extent hers is a much safer narrative than the others. She is confirmed as a 'choice Christian', just as she is now securely Mrs Hatt. That is one reality, and it is easily entered. Within this, however, the immediacy of her experience, the degeneration into melancholy, madness and attempted suicide of a young widowed mother from Derbyshire, exerts another, stronger, more threatening reality, posing questions about the nature of sanity, and of faith, and of the 'Gracious Dealings' of God.

Nothing is known of Hannah Allen beyond what is revealed in her pamphlet. She was born in Snelston, Derbyshire, daughter of John Archer, who died when she was two. Her mother's maiden name was Hart. They had family also in London, where Hannah stayed when she was twelve and later during her illness. Her marriage in around 1655 to Hannibal Allen, a merchant trading overseas, was arranged by relations, and she had one son by him before his death 'beyond sea' in 1663. Her lapsing into melancholy and despair was clearly stimulated in part by his prolonged absences and subsequent death, just as her marriage to Mr Hatt, which is the last fact known about her, marks the end of her period of suffering and her restoration to a cheerful trust in God. What we are given is a concentrated and painful account of the most intimate workings of Allen's mind for a very brief span of her life, the time in fact when she was Hannah Allen. Of Hannah Archer we know very little, and of Hannah Hatt only that she is secure in God and that she has written a pamphlet under her former name, some of which is based on materials – journal and letters – dating from that time. Three names, constituting a glimpse of detailed authenticity sandwiched between virtual anonymity.

In one way Allen's narrative can be slotted easily into the conventional Nonconformist pattern of spiritual autobiography, in which faith is discovered, or rediscovered, after a gruesome period of degeneracy, and many of the details would fit well into such a form – the temptation towards suicide, for example, and the rejection of offers of help and prayers from friends and clergymen. What makes this account so interesting, however, is the personal tone and detail of the writing. She is not merely tempted to commit suicide, she makes several remarkable efforts to do so, first by smoking spiders in a pipe with tobacco, and then by hiding herself under the floor-boards at the top of the house in order to starve to death. Later, she hires a coach in '*Aldersgate-Street*' in the City, taking care that the coachman is one 'with a good honest look', to drive her out to Barnet where she intends to 'get into a Wood and dye there'. Personality always resists what could be stock experience. Convinced that Satan will take her life during the journey to London, '*Mother,*' she asks, '*do you think people will like to have a dead Corps in the Coach with them?*' The voice is distinctive and authentic. Similarly, her self-loathing is expressed with a venom that is both biblical and individual: she quotes Jeremiah, '*The bellows are burnt, the lead is consumed of the fire; the Founder melteth in vain*'; she calls herself '*Dead Dog, Damn'd Wretch*'; she is '*Magor-Missabib*', again from Jeremiah; she is '*the Monster of the Creation*', adding, in an intimately personal touch, 'in this Word I much delighted'. There is a reaching out for terms and phrases sufficiently awful in order to allow her to express how she feels to herself.

These go beyond adherence to a convention and begin to take us to the heart of the relation between individuals and their language.

Allen's narrative is widely framed but narrowly focused. Her madness had profound implications for her spiritual salvation and for the nature of God's intentions, and the telling of it is made to signify an exemplary Christian triumph. At the same time, her experience was confined almost entirely within a small circle of family, friends and servants, and, in spite of being free to walk in the streets of London and to take coach rides, public notice of her behaviour and suffering was apparently negligible. Cruden and Bruckshaw, on the other hand, focused their experiences within the full scale of their London and Lincolnshire settings, interacting with a wide range of individuals, travelling, by foot or coach, through named and detailed streets and places, and crying out for validation. Cruden, limping along Whitechapel Road in the small hours of 31 May, his birthday, wearing one slipper and still carrying the chain that attached him to his bedpost, is emblematic: madness has taken to the streets, and is demanding recognition, restitution. Spiritual salvation is nowhere, and God's intentions, if of some account to both these men, are very much background issues compared to the outrageous injustice and oppression of which they complain.

In other words, with Cruden and Bruckshaw madness has gone public, and, just as Allen's title proclaimed the scale and setting of her pamphlet, theirs insist on the social and public interest their works hold: *The London-Citizen Exceedingly Injured*, with its assertion of the rights of the British subject, and *One More Proof of the Iniquitous Abuse of Private Madhouses*, staking out a reformist ground for what was actually an appeal for justice and compensatory damages. Madness was no longer a matter between the individual and God. Rather, it involved the fabric and structure of society, one's place and rights in relation to man and the law, and one's freedom of expression, access to language and its authenticating, persuasive qualities. Both these pamphlets stand in for the shortcomings of the law, and both are printed (as, later, was William Belcher's) 'for the author', in Bruckshaw's case 'to be had of him at No. 28, Poultry', between St Paul's and the Royal Exchange. The last resort of the injured, language at least is free, though publication has had to be paid for.

Alexander Cruden is the only one of these four pamphleteers for whom extensive biographical details are available, largely because he published in 1737, shortly before the events of *London-Citizen*, his *Complete Concordance to the Bible*, a meticulously detailed work of scholarship that brought him renown in his own lifetime and respect down to the present day. A serious-minded Presbyterian from Aberdeen, he was born on 31 May 1701, the second son of William Cruden, a merchant, and educated at Marischal College. His life was eventful, even prior to the Bethnal Green experience, for he was confined as deranged at his parents' request in the Aberdeen tolbooth after an ill-advised romantic infatuation. In his early twenties he departed for England, finding an appointment as reader in French to the Duke of Sussex, a position he almost immediately lost when it became clear that his knowledge of the language did not extend to its pronunciation. In London he worked as a corrector of the press, and eventually also opened a small bookshop near the Royal Exchange, from where he published the *Concordance.* Romantic involvement again brought trouble, though it is not clear from this pamphlet quite what the widow Mrs Payne's role was in the confining of Cruden, or why Robert Wightman, a man in his sixties who had only recently arrived in London from Edinburgh, took such an interest in her or Cruden's affairs and held such influence over so many of the participants, including Dr James Monro. Cruden, as well as suffering the cruelties and indignities described, also failed in his legal action against Wightman, having chosen to proceed on a misinterpretation of the law. Indeed, he took identical action against his own sister, Mrs Isabella Wild, some fifteen years later after a further confinement at a madhouse in Chelsea following a fracas in which he was involved in his by then self-appointed role as corrector of the nation's morals. On this occasion he had taken it upon himself to correct a young man's swearing 'with some severity', using the young man's own shovel to do so. Again, he lost the case and resorted once more to written self-justification with *The Adventures of Alexander the Corrector.* A genuinely pious, if fractious and showy, man, he died in prayer on 1 November 1770, and was found, still on his knees, at his lodgings in Camden Passage, Islington.[4]

If the parameters of Hannah Allen's intentions are religious, of Cruden's they are legalistic. His is an account laced through and through with the desire for evidence: the logging of times and places; who was present and who said what; statements from potential witnesses, especially about Cruden's behaviour and apparent state of mind; letters to and from, but mainly to, Robert Wightman; accounts of things opened, tampered with, or missing; time spent chained, or in the strait waistcoat; occasions on which he was beaten. Everything is arranged as if for a court of law, with Cruden as prosecuting counsel. Within this framework, however, there is also the resistless urge for self-expression, not least in Cruden's heavily adjectival style of writing. Allen's linguistic identity pushes against religious parameters, while Cruden's presentation of evidence is energetically injected with the sense of self-assertion. The constant use of words like 'barbarous', 'cruel', 'unjust', 'wicked' and 'malicious' applied to the behaviour of his captors and persecutors, and also of 'sensible', 'rational', 'serious', 'sound', 'solid' and 'quiet' with regard to himself, presents a meticulously adorned universe where not only are the facts not allowed to speak for themselves but that has Cruden, studiously passive and defiantly meek, at its very centre. Similarly, his obsession with packing all relevant, and not so relevant, information into a single sentence – 'A Tool of *Wightman*'s formerly an Apprentice to a Taylor, but lately a Coffin-breaker and Grave-digger in St. *Andrew*'s Burying-ground, and a few months before a pretended Physician of no figure, came in . . .' – is indicative of a powerful desire to leave nothing to chance. Every scrap of information has to become evidence and be marshalled into some kind of order, whether the syntactic patterns of English writing lend themselves to it or not.

It is neither possible nor desirable to say now whether Cruden was indeed mad, any more than it is of Bruckshaw or Belcher, or even of Allen, given the pressures on her to interpret her mental state in a particular way. What is possible and desirable is to observe that he was thought to be mad and to reflect, in that light, on how he presented his case to the world and to himself. Cruden's style is breathless, and his narrative is written with an urgency that is partly due to the very natural imperative of proving his sanity, but partly to the stresses involved in a very energetic man telling of his confinement, both inside Wright's private madhouse and within a cripplingly restrictive public perception.

Samuel Bruckshaw was also an energetic man, in business and physically. Indeed, at one point during his confinement a visitor to Wilson's madhouse tells the proprietor, 'He is naturally of a strong, healthy constitution, *which requires exercise*, why don't you let him come down into the family, *and take a little air?*' He was also, apparently, far more openly belligerent than Cruden, who was obviously gifted with a certain courtierly charm, especially with respect to women. Bruckshaw has no truck with women, or at least chooses not to narrate himself in female company. On the contrary, his is a brusquely masculine narrative, and his behaviour is far from meek or passive: he marches round to his former property, virtually forces entry, and tells Langton, the new owner, that he should 'consider yourself only as an intruder'; when Ely Buswell, constable, attempts to arrest Bruckshaw by seizing his collar, Bruckshaw instead seizes Ely by the collar and catches hold of his staff; he breaks out of a room where he has been locked in the town hall; and where Cruden insists on his compliance with even the most unreasonable demands Bruckshaw reports word for word the no-nonsense aggressiveness of his conversational style. Altogether, reading this narrative gives a convincing picture of the kind of behaviour that would have been taken as destructive of the peace, and possibly as mad, in a country town in the late eighteenth century.

Like Allen, information about Bruckshaw's life comes from his pamphlet and from another, *The Case, Petition and Address of Samuel Bruckshaw*, also published in 1774 and concerning the same events. He was probably born in Cheshire of a propertied family, but practised his business as a woolstapler – a buyer and grader of wool, purchasing from the producer and selling on to the manufacturer – at Bourne in Lincolnshire, from where he aspired to transfer to nearby Stamford in order to have the benefit of trade 'upon the North road'. This, by his account, made him powerful enemies in Stamford, but he also seems to have had a wide circle of friends and business contacts elsewhere in the country, including Cheshire, Manchester, Stockport, Halifax and London, as well as a brother, Joshua, and an uncle, Samuel Daniel, in Stockport, with whom he was on cordial if rather distant terms. Even more than Cruden, however, Bruckshaw's business life seems to have been ruined by his confinement as a madman and by his subsequent fruitless legal battle for damages. The fact that his pamphlet coincided with the Act to regulate private madhouses can have provided only a shred of comfort to someone whose career was apparently in tatters.

Bruckshaw, therefore, was another former 'madman' struggling to prove his sanity and anxiously collecting all possible evidence to forward his case, even to the extent of obtaining the signature of John Hopkins, the mayor responsible for his confinement, on a declaration of his suitability for employment. Indeed, the form of the narrative, as written by this self-declared 'unlearned sufferer', moves from strength to weakness as the struggle becomes more unequal, with Bruckshaw growing more and more dependent on law and legal functionaries. It eventually gives way under the weight of attached evidence. Legal opinion succeeeds legal opinion, and letter follows letter, concluding with a copy of Bruckshaw's last-throw petition to George III and a long appendix of documents relating to the case. After all the assaults on his personality, it was to be the frustratingly grinding process of the law that apparently broke Bruckshaw's stubborn energies, and the letting go of the narrative is a sure reflection of his gradual loss of hope.

But his account, like Cruden's, has all the redeeming features of obsessive self-justification, being written from an entirely single-minded point of view and loaded down with after-the-event interpretations. His arrest, for example, is the first occasion of physical assault committed on either side, and its narration is dramatic: 'seize him,' cries Langton, 'and take him before the Mayor'.

> Whereupon, Ely Buswell, seized me by the collar: in return, I seized Ely Buswell by his, demanding his authority, who up with his staff to knock me down, which I catched in my other hand; then Needham, the other constable, collared me, and they dragged me through the public streets just as the company were going to the race, to the Mayor's, who was upon the watch, and come out at the door as we arrived thus before his house, when I addressed myself to him, with, 'Mr. Mayor, do you permit your constables to act the part of ruffians? . . .' Whereupon, without asking the constables a single question, he ordered them to let me go, and they

instantly quitted their holds; all this happened in the public street, before the Mayor's door; I have no doubt, but that the aforesaid card was written with a design to send me irritated against Langton, to the said premises, as the constables were placed there ready for seizing me.

If Bruckshaw's preoccupation with spotting conspiracies at every turn is responsible for some reining back of his naturally direct and racy prose style, it also sustains the impression of individual conviction and robust coherence that carries him through the most personally intrusive episodes of his narrative.

Most intrusive of all, most destructive of the norms even of Bruckshaw's manners and behaviour, is his treatment at the hands of the Wilsons, and it is their almost comic portrayal that is perhaps the most memorable in all four of these pamphlets. The sinister, understated first appearance of these 'two strangers' with their 'air of great familiarity' is made to represent a whole underworld of threat, violence and bizarre linguistic self-assurance: 'Well, Mr. Bruckshaw, *how doone you*, Com yoo'sen go with us, t'see yoor friends i' Yorshire.' 'Wilson talk' has a startling impact, suggesting both regional authenticity and at the same time a kind of Dickensian surrealism. In particular, within the linguistic context of the narrative it immediately places as half human, as an alien life form, people who will shortly be capable of keeping Bruckshaw stripped, chained and deprived of sleep for a month in their 'breaking in garret', of beating and starving him, and of robbing him of his remaining possessions. Yet callous, brutal, pecuniary and cowardly though the Wilsons are, they also serve a second narrative purpose of wearing their offensiveness in their voices, in strong contrast to the conspiring middle-class villains of Stamford who speak an English that is apparently more correct than their actions, and in even stronger contrast to the London legal fraternity, whose inert but proper forms mask the self-interest, corrupt impenetrability and costliness that finally bring about the disintegration of Bruckshaw's narrative integrity.

The one writer who begins to throw doubt on the very notion of narrative integrity is William Belcher, which is doubly odd, given that the form of the first section of his pamphlet is 'A Letter to Dr. Thomas Monro', which implies a considerable degree of coherence, and that Belcher himself had published, and was to continue publishing (his last dated work is 1816), on both Latin and English grammar. In spite of having written as a grammarian, however, Belcher remains a shadowy figure, better known for his adopted 'mad' voice than for any events in his life. In fact, unlike the other three writers, Belcher's stance in this short pamphlet is that while he was certainly sane when first incarcerated in the madhouse in Hackney, he is not at all sure that he still is now that he has been released. Hence the 'Receipt To make a Lunatic' that constitutes the second section of his fragmented *Address to Humanity*. Unlike Allen, Cruden and Bruckshaw, he gives almost no specific details of his being taken for a lunatic, concentrating instead on snatches of his activities prior to his confinement: 'composing remarks on Johnson's Lives of the English Poets', using 'a farm of 100 acres entirely myself'. These, too, are not developed, but jostle for what little space there is alongside Belcher's reports of his treatment as a 'lunatic' – 'I have been bound and tortured in a strait waistcoat, fettered, crammed with physic with a bullock's horn, and knocked down, and at length declared a lunatic by a Jury that never saw me' – and his recurrent expressions of resentment at those who cheated him and profited by his sufferings, thus giving rise to his subscription, '*A Victim to the Trade of Lunacy*'.

This gives the pamphlet its odd mix of irony and anguish. There is enough genuine feeling here to give authenticity to the tributes to Thomas Monro for restoring Belcher 'from legal death', and the sustained attack on loss of liberty, property and civil rights for those entrapped in lunacy is coherently developed. Moreover, his case would seem to show at once how easily, and how soon, given that Belcher was confined in 1778, the force of the 1774 Act was able to be evaded. But from another perspective Belcher deliberately resists coherence. So many others, not least members of the legal profession, have cheated and misused him, so much has appearance and reality been carelessly at odds in their conduct, that he is no longer in a position to believe in the possibility of a coherent universe. Belcher seems to feel that he has been through so much that he might just as well give up now and join the other side: he cannot entirely become a lunatic, because he is not actually mad, but he can and does so cover the sanity in his tracks with irony as to block out personal investment in this most personal of statements and to look upon himself as almost the neutral recipient of the natural self-interest of those who prey upon the mad. From this perspective, not only are all values and intentions but pecuniary ones wholly drained, but language itself – terms such as 'friends', 'guardians', 'mind' and 'senses' – ceases to signify anything but the most casual of labels:

> N.B. The friends and guardians of a lunatic need very seldom be afraid that the state of his mind will be regarded as an object, unless they mean it should; but may depend on it that their will and choice will determine whether he is in his senses or not.

Better go along with lunacy than take on the army of 'managers, commissioners, attornies, counsel' as well as 'doctors, lawyers, committees, rent-gatherers, mad-house-keepers, ruffians, and various other respectable brutes' whose interest defines coherent understanding.

Belcher's attitude towards writing is moving to one extreme of mad language, and it is an extreme that he attempted to exploit more fully in his next publication, *Intellectual Electricity*, an extravagantly parodic scientific-religious pamphlet engaging in studiously crazed discourse. But at least two of these writers, Allen and Cruden, took language much more seriously during the time of their sufferings, both of them keeping journals or, in Hannah Allen's case, a 'Book . . . in Short-Hand' of 'the Promises, together with my Temptations and other afflictions, and my experiences of how God delivered me out of them', which make up part of their respective narratives. Their reliance on language and linguistic securities if anything increases as a result of their 'madness', not least in Cruden's case by his urge to have written evidence in the bank as proof of the sanity of his account. Allen, admittedly, goes through a period late in her illness when she cannot endure 'to hear the sound of reading, nor the sight of a Book or Paper', even striking 'the Horn-book out of my Childs hand'. Nevertheless, even then she finds security in repeating her favourite phrases, 'that I was a cursed Reprobate, and the Monster of the Creation'. When she emerges from her experience, it is with restored faith in the word, and, fittingly, she concludes her pamphlet by setting down the 'Promises', or biblical quotations, which were 'great supports and refreshments to me in the time of my various Temptations and Afflictions all along, till I fell into deep despair'. Bruckshaw, too, far from doubting the reliability of language and its forms seems to enjoy inserting appropriate quotations from Sterne, Shakespeare and Gay, as if the values they represent, at least, are secure. Moreover, it is under the weight of linguistic evidence that, ironically, his narrative at last subsides.

Far from retreating from language and its norms, the tendency of Allen, Cruden and Bruckshaw's writing is to reinforce the power of words and their regular arrangement, to set store by their communicative capacities, and even to take a degree of pleasure in the opportunities of their texts, a pleasure shared by Belcher for all his loss of faith in values. Moreover, all these writers assume readers who will read sanely and attach importance to the principles on which the texts are based. Again, even Belcher must at one level anticipate readers among the breadth of 'Humanity' who will be capable of unpicking the ironic portions of his pamphlet and restoring a sound narrative base to its fragmentariness. Everything testifies to the normal, to a desire to be restored to it, to be embraced once again by the protective certainties of the English language.

The voices of madness rarely sound mad, and if these writers come to us from the dark, it is not from the dark of the madhouse, from stereotyped compartments and the cells of repeated linguistic mechanisms. Rather, their darkness, like Malvolio's, is that of a social rejection that is still capable of being enlightened, they trust, by a written self-renewal demonstrating their capacities for moral perspective and linguistic choice.

A
NARRATIVE
OF
God's Gracious Dealings
With that Choice Christian
Mrs. *HANNAH ALLEN,*
(Afterwards Married to Mr. *Hatt,*)
RECITING

The great ·Advantages the Devil made of
her deep Melancholy, and the Triumphant Victories, Rich and Sovereign
Graces, God gave her over all his Stratagems and Devices.

O Lord! I am oppreſſed, undertake for me. Eſay
XXX. 14.
We are not ignorant of his Devices. 2 Cor. ii. 11.

London, Printed by *John Wallis.* 1683.

To The Reader

The Soul of Man hath a singular affection for its own Body, rejoycing in its Prosperity, and sympathizing with it in all its Maladies, Miseries, and Necessities. Hence if the Body be out of frame and tune, the Soul cannot be well at ease. As the most skilful Musician cannot make any pleasing melody upon an unstringed or broken Instrument.[2] The blood and humours are the Souls Organs, by which it doth exert its actions. If these be well temper'd and kept in a balance, Ordinarily there is an inward calm serenity upon the Spirit. Ordinarily I say: For in some cases the most chearful Temper may be broken down and overwhelmed either by the immediate impressions of God's wrath upon the Soul, or the letting loose of those Bandogs of Hell[3] to affright and terrifie it. This is no strange News to any one acquainted with the Scriptures, or the Records of the Church in its several Ages, or that hath been conservant with the most humble, serious and mortified Christians. Infinite Wisdom hath seen it fitting to keep his Saints from Hell for ever, by casting them as it were into Hell for a time. It being too much for the choicest Saints to have two Heavens, one in Earth, and another in Glory. Flesh is kept from Putrefaction by powdring it in Salt and Brine: and Gold loseth nothing of its Worth by being melted in the Furnace. To wave the broken bones of David, *the terrors and distractions of* Heman, *the groans, chatterings, mournings and pressing oppressions of* Hezekiah; *That Mirrour of Patience,* Job, *will tell us how much he suffered and that immediately too from God and his own God. He had as well as Father* Abraham, *an horrour of great darkness upon him. He was skared with Visions, terrified with Dreams, the poysoned Arrows of the Almighty were shot into his very Soul, the venom whereof drank up his spirits, and made him choose Strangling rather than Life.[4] Possibly he had his Temptations to Self-murder as well as some others fearing God under horrour. Hence you need not wonder at their impatiency, and in their agonies at blasphemous expressions. When I have heard from the mouth of an eminent and holy Minister of Christ, that once counted himself a Reprobate, undone and to be damn'd for ever, and was no longer able to subsist under the weight and burden of Everlasting and Almighty Wrath, (and who indeed can, if God should let it out upon him?)* That he hated God, yea hated him perfectly, because he was his Judge and Adversary, tho' a most loving and tender-hearted Father to his Saints; *When I read of miserable* Spira's *wishing himself above God; I do not in the least*

3

strange at such intemperate expressions, considering that God, and their Enemy doth blow the Coals, and it may be dictate the very words to them.

Christian Reader, *Peruse such Instances as these, and* this of a Now-glorified Soul presented to thee, *with fear and trembling. How knowest thou but it may be thine own Case? Let him that standeth take heed lest he fall. The peace, the comforts, the quiet, the joys natural and spiritual, they are all from Grace; you have no longer a Lease of them, no longer term of injoying them than the good will and pleasure of him that dwelt in the Burning Bush.*[5] *If God revoke his own gifts, hide his face, let loose the Tempter, awaken that sleeping Fury in thy bosom, let down but the smallest drop of his Wrath into thy Conscience, thy foundations will be shaken, and the mountain of thy peace will be hurled into a gulf of dismal sorrows.*

Learn then to hate Sin, all Sin bitterly and implacably, to avoid it universally and continually. Be humble and vile in thine own eyes, and walk humbly with thy God. Set upon a through Reformation. Because of Leviathan *'s*[6] *up-raising himself, the Mighty are afraid; by reason of breakings, the very Sinners purify themselves. God cautions Saints, and alarms Sinners by such flaming Beacons. If these things be done in the green Tree, what will not be done in the dry?*[7] *Keep no Idol, and beware of making inward comfort an Idol. This provokes God to Jealousy. The Christian's Life is not a life of Sense but of Faith. We walk by Faith, saith the Apostle, and not by sight.*[8] *Faith closing with the precious Promises, feeding upon the All-sufficient Merits of an unseen Jesus, bringeth in through the holy Ghost, peace, that peace of God, which passeth all understanding, into the Believer's Soul.*[9] *But then too, this Faith doth purify the Heart, expelleth all inward filth, conniveth, indulgeth not unto any the least sin; but puts the Soul upon skirmishing with it, and gets through the power of Christ, victory over it. Otherwise the troubles will return, as the Clouds after the Rain. The least briss*[10] *in the Eye shall create grief. The least core of bitterness in the Wound shall cause it wrankle afresh. The smallest leak in the Ship, not seen, will sink it; and as multitudes have been killed with Swords and Canons, so others with Stillettoes and Needles, with what the injudicious Worldling calls a Peccadillo, lurking in the Soul.*

Walk then, Christian Reader, *in thine integrity. He that walketh uprightly walketh safely. Live still in dependence upon thy Crucified Lord. All thy Springs are in him, all thy streams are from him. With joy shall you draw waters of Consolations, reviving Cordials from the wounds of thy dear and dying Saviour. Hide thy self always in the clefts of that blessed Rock of Ages,*[11] *and thou wilt find there as all the Saints have done in all Ages, a glorious high Throne of Sovereign Mercy for thy Sanctuary. The Secret of the Lord is with them that fear him, and unto such will he reveal his Covenant. Love the Lord Jesus intirely, supremely and transcendently; and remember that such as love him shall be beloved and saved by him.*

As to Scoffers and Mockers at such Relations, that Burlesque and Ridicule these great Instances of Divine Providence, I shall say nothing but that 'tis the Sin of our Age, foretold 1600 Years ago, accomplished in our Days,[12] *and an Exercise for the present, and possibly for surviving Saints. Here is the Faith and Patience of Saints, to keep the Testimony of Jesus, and walk Evenly in his ways in the midst of thorns and precipices, and when they are reputed the Worlds Monsters, and the Drunkards Song for so doing.*[13] *Laugh he that laughs last. The Saints are in heaviness through many Afflictions and Desertions for a little time; but Sinners shall be at last overwhelmed by them for evermore. Their joyful Comedy will have a most Tragick issue. Our blessed Lord hath inform'd his Disciples, that they should weep and lament, but the World should rejoyce; that they should be sorrowful, but their Sorrow should be turned into Joy, and their Joy no man should take from them.*[14] *But the wicked is driven away in his wickedness:*[15] *Before the Pots can feel the thorns, God shall take them away as with a Whirl-wind, both living and in his wrath.*[16]

Thy Soul-friend and
Servant for *Jesus* sake.

London Feb. 3.
1681.

Satan's Methods and Malice baffled, &c.

I *Hannah Allen*, the late Wife of *Hannibal Allen* Merchant, was born of Religious Parents; my Father was Mr. *John Archer* of *Snelston* in *Derby-shire*, who took to Wife, the Daughter of Mr. *William Hart* of *Uttoxeter Woodland* in *Stafford-shire*,[17] who brought me up in the fear of God from my Childhood; and about Twelve Years of Age, for my better Education, sent me up to London in the Year 1650, to my Father's Sister Mrs. *Ann Wilson*, the Wife of Mr. *Samuel Wilson*, Merchant, then Living in *Aldermanbury*,[18] and after some time spent there, and at School, I being not well in Health, had a desire to go down for a time to my Mother, being a Widow, (my Father dying when I was very young) where I staid almost two Years. In which time and a little before my going down, it pleased God to work in me earnest breathings after the ways of God, but the enemy of my Soul striving to crush such hopeful beginnings in the bud, cast in horrible blasphemous thoughts and injections into my mind, insomuch that I was seldom free day or night, unless when dead sleep was upon me. But I used to argue with my self to this purpose, Whether if I had a Servant that I knew loved me, and desired in all things to please me, and yet was so forced against his will to do that which was contrary to my mind, whether I would think ever the worse of him, seeing I knew what he did was to his grief. And by such thoughts as these, it pleased God to give me some support wherein his goodness did the more appear in casting such thoughts into my mind; I being young, and also bearing this burthen alone, not so much as acquainting my Mother with it, but by degrees these Temptations grew to that height, that I was perswaded I had sinned the Unpardonable Sin: With these dreadful Temptations I privately conflicted for some Months, not revealing it (as I said) to any one, thinking with my self that never any was like me, and therefore was loath to make my Condition known: I would often in my thoughts wish I might change Conditions with the vilest Persons I could think of, concluding there was hopes for them though not for me: that Scripture in the 57. of *Isa.* the two last Verses, did exceedingly terrify me, *But the wicked are like the troubled Sea, when it cannot rest, whose waters cast up mire and dirt. There is no peace to the wicked, saith my God.*[19] In this sad and perplexed state, upon a Sabbath day, my Mother having been reading in the Family in one of blessed Mr. *Bolton's* Books,[20] and being ready to go with them to Church; I thought with my self, To what purpose should I go hear the Word, since, as I thought, all means whatsoever for the good of my Soul were in vain, but the same time I carelessly turning over Mr. *Bolton's* Book as it lay on the Table, lighted on a place that directly treated on my Case; which it pleased God so to bless, that I was so much comforted and strengthened, that I recovered for that time from my Despairing condition, and so continued for several years with good hopes of the love of God in Christ towards me, yet still continually assaulted with Temptations, but with less violence than before. After my abode in the Countrey almost two years with my Mother, I returned to *London* to my Uncle and Aunt *Wilson*; by whom about a Year and four Months after, I was disposed of in Marriage to Mr. *Hannibal Allen*, but still lived with my Uncle and Aunt *Wilson* till after my Uncle dyed; and was about this time admitted to the Sacrament by Mr. *Calamy*, with good approbation: And in the time of his Life, I was frequently exercised with variety of Temptations, wherein the Devil had the more advantage I being much inclined to Melancholy, occasioned by the oft absence of my dear and affectionate Husband, with whom I lived present and absent about eight Years; and soon after he went his last Voyage, I went into the Countrey to live with my Aunt *Wilson*, who was now a Widow, and returned to live at *Snelston* with my aged Mother, she being Married again and living elsewhere; but in few Months after I heard of the death of my Husband (for he dyed beyond Sea) I began to fall into deep Melancholy, and no sooner did this black humour begin to darken my Soul, but the Devil set on with his former Temptations, which at first were with less violence and frequent intermissions, but yet with great struglings and fightings within me; as I would express it (to my Aunt) I am just as if two were fighting within me, but I trust, the Devil will never be able to overcome me; then I would repeat several promises suitable to my condition, and read over my former experiences that I had writ down, as is hereafter expressed, and obligations that I had laid upon my self, in the presence of God, and would say, Aunt, I hope I write not these things in Hypocrisie, I never intended any Eye should see them; but the Devil suggesteth dreadful things to me against God, and that I am an Hypocrite. At the first I began to complain that I found not that comfort and refreshment in Prayer as I was wont to do, and that God withdrew his comforting and quickening Presence from me.

When I had seen the Bible, I would say, oh that blessed Book that I so delighted in once! the Devil was strongly assaulting my Faith, and I seemed ready to be overcome, I answered the Tempter within my self in the bitterness of my Spirit; *Well, if I perish, God must deny himself.*

See the difference betwixt the voice of Faith, and the Language of Despair. At another time I cannot be saved because God cannot deny himself; The truth is, it had been most of all worth the Publishing my Expressions in the time of my Combating with Sathan at the beginning of my Affliction, but those passages are most of all forgotten. One hour my hope was firm, and the next hour ready to be overwhelmed.

This began in *Feb.* 63. but it grew worse and worse upon me nothwithstanding such means was used both by Physick and Journeys to several Friends for Diversion. The last Journey I took upon this account, was to a good Friend of mine, a Minister, Mr. *John Shorthose*, who was related to me by Marriage, who lived about Thirty Miles distance, where I still grew much worse, and my continual course there, was to be asking him Questions whether the truth of Grace could consist with such sins, for then I began to fear I was an Hypocrite, and that place I thought upon with much dread, in *Job* viii. 13. *The Hypocrites hope shall perish;*[21] nor had I any ease longer than I was thus discoursing with him, for though he often silenced my Objections, and I seemed for the present to be much satisfied, yet he was no sooner gone from me, but my troubles returned afresh, insomuch that his Wife would often send for him home when he was but gone into the Fields. While I was there the Devil would suggest something to this purpose to me, *That when I was gone from him, he would torment me.* After some stay there, I returned home again, where quickly I began to grow into deep Despair. It was my custom for several years before to write in a Book I kept for that purpose in Short-Hand, the Promises, together with my Temptations and other afflictions, and my experiences how God delivered me out of them, mixing therewith Prayer and Praises, which practice I continued till I was overwhelmed with despair, some few passages whereof are here inserted as they were written in my deep distress.

This Book in my Affliction I would oft say, would rise up in Judgment against me. As I was walking with my Cousin, Mrs. *Shorthose*, a Woman cursed and sware sadly; *Ah Cousin*, said I, *I have abhorred such Company all my Life, therefore I hope they shall not be my Companions to Eternity.*

This being the 20th. *Feb.* 63. is a time of great trouble and bitter Melancholy, and one great cause is for want of the light of God's Countenance; and for fear that if I should have any mercy shewed me, I should abuse it; and my wretchedly deceitful heart be drawn aside from God (for I am only fit for the School of Affliction;) and on the other hand, if God should send some further trials, I should sink under them; and my Life be made a burthen to me.

But (Lord) sure this is the voice of my wretched unbelieving heart; The Lord for Christ's sake, fit me for what ever thou wilt do with me, that I may have power again Sin and Satan, and enjoy the light of thy Countenance, and then do with me what thou wilt: Oh that I might prevail with my Lord, for Christ's sake, for graces suitable to every condition, and that I may be able to improve every mercy, and every affliction, to thy glory and the comfort of my poor Soul, and that I may be useful in my Generation and not be burthensom; Lord pity my state for Christ's sake, who hath never left me in my trials.

The sixth of *April* 64. The truth is I know not well what to say, for as yet I am under sad Melancholy, and sometimes dreadful Temptations, to have hard thoughts of my dearest Lord (The least assenting to which by his grace I dread more than Hell it self) Temptations to impatience and despair, and to give up all for lost; and to close with the Devil and forsake my God, which the Almighty for Christ's sake forbid: These Temptations were with dreadful violence. Besides, my Melancholy hath bad effects upon my body, greatly impairing my Health: Truly there is sometimes such a woful confusion and combating in my Soul, that I know not what to do; And now my earnest Prayer to my Lord is this, (which I trust for Christ's sake he will not deny me, though I cannot beg it with such earnest affections as I should, yet I hope my heart is sincere) that for my sweet Redeemer's sake he would preserve me from Sin and give me strength of Faith; and Self-denial and patience to wait upon him, and submit to him; and let him do with me what he pleaseth:

My God, I know thou hast (for ever adored be thy Majesty) appeared for me in many great and sore straits; for the Lord Jesus sake now appear in mercy for me; that I may have exceeding cause to bless thee for this thy mercy also, and give me an assurance that thou art mine, and that thou wilt never leave me, till thou hast brought me to thy Self in glory.

The 12th. of *May*, 64. Still my time of great distress and sore trials continues, sometimes the Devil tempts me wofully to hard and strange thoughts of my dear Lord; which (through his mercy) I dread and abhor the assenting to more than Hell it self; in a word, every day at present seems a great burthen to me; My earnest Prayer is, 'For the Lords sake, that if it be thy holy will, I might not perish in this great affliction which hath been of so long continuance, and is so great still notwithstanding means used, however for the Lords sake, let it be Sanctified to my eternal good, and give me grace suitable to my condition, and strength to bear my burthen, and then do with me what thou wilt; I know not what to say; the Lord pity me in every respect and appear for me, in these my great straits both of Soul and Body; I know not what to do, I shall be undone; This I write to see what God will do with me, whether ever he will deliver me out of such a distress as this; that I may have cause to praise and adore his name in the Land of the Living; 'Lord, comfort me and support me and revive me for Christ's sake'.

May 26th. 64. 'I desire (which the Lord help me to do) exceedingly to bless and praise thy Majesty that hath yet in some measure supported me under these dreadful trials and temptations, which do yet continue and have been woful upon me, for almost four Months together; For Christ's sake pity my case, or else I know not what to do; and do not deny me strength to bear up under my burthen; and for the Lord's sake grant, whatever thou dost with me, that one Sin may not be in me, unrepented of or unmortified; Do with me what thou wilt as to the Creature, so thou wilt subdue my sins, and chain up Sathan, and smile upon my Soul; Lord, I know not what to do, only mine Eyes are up to thee, the Devil still keeps me under dreadful bondage, and in sad distress and wo, but blessed be my God, that he doth not lay upon me all afflictions at once; that my Child is so well, and that I have so many other mercies, which the Lord open my Eyes to see; especially that Christ is mine, for the Lord's sake, and then I have enough.

After this I writ no more, but this and much more I writ before my last Journey aforesaid, for by that time I came back, I soon after fell into deep Despair, and my language and condition grew sadder than before. Now little to be heard from me, but lamenting my woful state, in very sad and dreadful Expressions; As that I was undone for ever; that I was worse than *Cain* or *Judas;*[22] that now the Devil had overcome me irrecoverably; that this was what he had been aiming at all along; Oh the Devil hath so deceiv'd me as never any one was deceived; he made me believe my condition was good when I was a cursed Hypocrite.

One night, I said there was a great clap of Thunder like the shot of a Piece of Ordnance, came down directly over my Bed; and that the same night, a while after, I heard like the voice of two Young Men singing in the Yard, over against my Chamber; which I said were Devils in the likeness of Men, singing for joy that they had overcome me; and in the morning as I was going to rise, that Scripture in the 10th. of *Heb.* and the last words of the 26th. Verse, was suggested to me from Heaven (as I thought) *There remains no more Sacrifice for sin;*[23] And this delusion remained with me as an Oracle all along; that by this miracle of the Thunder, and the Voice and the Scripture, God revealed to me that I was Damned: When my Aunt asked me, *Do you think God would work a Miracle to convince you that you are rejected? it is contrary to the manner of God's proceedings; we do not read of such a thing in all the Scripture.*

My Answer was, *Therefore my condition is unparalell'd, there was never such an one since God made any Creature either Angels or Men, nor never will be to the end of the world.*

One night as I was sitting by the fire, all of a sudden I said I should dye presently; whereupon my Aunt was called; to whom I said, *Aunt, I am just dying, I cannot live an hour if there were no more in the world;* in this opinion I continued a great while, every morning saying, *I should dye before night,* and every night, *before morning.* when I was thus in my dying condition, I often begged earnestly of my Aunt to bring up my Child strictly, that if it were possible, he might be saved, though he had such a Mother.

Many places of Scripture I would repeat with much terrour, applying them to my self; as *Jer.* vi. 29, 30. *The bellows are burnt, the lead is consumed of the fire; the Founder melteth in vain; Reprobate silver shall men call them, because the Lord hath rejected them;* Ezek. xxiv. 13. *In thy filthiness is lewdness, because I have purged thee and thou wast not purged; thou shalt not be purged from thy filthiness any more, till I have caused my fury to rest upon thee:* Luke xiii. 24. *Strive to enter in at the strait gate, for many I say unto you, will seek to enter in and shall not be able.*[24] This last Scripture I would express with much passionate weeping, saying, *This is a dreadful Scripture, I sought, but not in a right way; for the Devil blinded mine eyes, I sought to enter but was not able.*

When both my inward and outward distempers grew to such a height, my Aunt acquainted my Friends at *London* with my condition, for at *London* I had formerly had four loving Uncles, my Father's brethren; two whereof were then living, and a Brother of my own, that was set up in his Trade: These advised to send me up to *London*; there being the best means both for Soul and Body; in order to which Mrs. *Wilson* sent to intreat my Mother to accompany me to *London*; (for at that time she could not leave her Family so long) who accordingly came, but she found it a hard work to perswade me to this Journey; for I said *I should not live to get to the Coach, but I must go and dye by the way to please my friends:* I went up in the *Tamworth* Coach,[25] so that it was Twenty two Miles thither; *Tuesday* was the day we set forwards on; and on that day in particular, the Devil had suggested to me (the *Friday* before) *that I must dye and be with him*; and this the more confirmed me in my fear: My Aunt went with me that days journey, which was first to *Tamworth* on Horse-back, and from thence Nine Miles farther in the Coach to *Nun-Eton*,[26] which was a long journey, for one so weak and ill as I was. My Aunt complaining of weariness; *Ah,* said I, *but what must I do, that must have no rest to all eternity:* The next morning I would fain have returned back with my Aunt, but there we parted, and I went forward with my Mother, and a very sad Journey my Mother had with me, for every Morning she had no small trouble to perswade me to rise to go on my Journey; I would earnestly argue against it, and say, *I shall surely dye by the way, and had I not better dye in bed? Mother, do you think people will like to have a dead Corps in the Coach with them?* but still at last my Mother with much patience and importunity prevailed with me: As I passed along the way, if I saw a Church, as soon as I cast mine eyes upon it, it was presently suggested to me, that's a Hell-house with a kind of indignation; and this I thought was from my self, and therefore never spoke of it till after my recovery, for I thought if it had been known how vile I was, I must have been put to some horrible death: When I saw any black Clouds gather, or the Wind rise (as we went along) I presently concluded that some dreadful thing would fall out to shew what an One I was.

When I came to *London,* I went to my Brother's House in *Swithens-lane,*[27] where my Mother staid with me about three Weeks or a Month, in which time I took much Physick of one Mr. *Cocket* a Chymist[28] that lived over the way, but still I was, as I thought, always dying; and I yet wearying my Mother with such fancies and stories; One Evening my Mother said to me, *Well, if you will believe you shall be saved if you dye not this night, I will believe all that you say to be true if you do dye this night;* to this she agreed, and in the night about one a Clock (as we thought) the Maid being newly gone out of the Chamber to Bed, but left a Watch-light burning, we both heard like the hand of a Gyant, knock four times together on the Chamber door, which made a great noise (the Door being Wainscot;[29]) then said I, *You see, Mother, though I dyed not to night, the Devil came to let you know that I am damn'd;* my Mother answered, *but you see he had no power to come into the Chamber.*

Soon after this my Mother returned home into the Countrey, and left me in my Brother's house, who was a young Man unmarried, and had only a Man and a Maid, and he much abroad himself about his occasions; and now my opinion of Dying suddenly began to leave me, therefore I concluded that God would not suffer me to dye a natural death; but that I should commit some fearful abomination, and so be put to some horrible death: One day my Brother going along with me to Doctor *Pridgeon,* as we came back, I saw a company of Men with Halberds, *Look, Brother,* said I, *you will see such as these (one of these days) carry me to Newgate:*[30] to prevent which I studied several ways to make away my self, and I being so much alone, and in a large solitary House, had the more liberty to endeavour it; first I thought of taking *Opium*[31] that I might dye in my Sleep, and none know but that I dyed naturally, (which I desired that my Child might not be disgraced by my untimely end,) and therefore sent the Maid to several Apothecaries shops[32] for it, some said they had none, others said it was dangerous and would not sell it her: Once she had got some, and was coming away with it; the Master of the Shop coming in, asked what she had, and when he knew, took it from her; (this the Maid told me:) When I had sent her up and down several days, and saw she could get none; then I got Spiders and took one at a time in a Pipe with Tobacco,[33] but never scarce took it out, for my heart would fail me; but once I thought I had been poysoned; in the night awaking out of my sleep, I thought I felt death upon me, (for I had taken a Spider when I went to Bed) and called to my Brother and told him so, who presently arose and went to his Friend an *Apothecary,* who came and gave me something to expel it; the next day my Uncles and Brother (considering the inconveniency of that lonesome House) removed me to Mr. *Peter Walker's* House, a Hosier at the Three Crowns in *Newgate-Market;* (whose Wife was my Kinswoman) who received me very courteously, though I was at that time but an uncomfortable Guest.

In the time I was at my Brother's, I had strange apprehensions that the Lights that were in Neighbouring houses were apparitions of Devils, and that those Lights were of their making; and if I heard the voice of People talk or read in other houses, I would not be perswaded but that it was Devils like Men, talking of me, and mocking at my former reading, because I proved such an Hypocrite.

Madam,[34]

As for the time I was at my Cousin Walker*'s, I refer your Ladyship to them, or any Friend else that may assist you; only I have here set down several passages, as they came to my mind which passed there, which your Ladyship may make use of as You please.*

One time while I lay at my Cousin *Walker*'s, having promised a Friend that was very importunate with me to go to a Sermon with her; about two or three days after, the Devil began to terrifie me for making that promise, and suggested to me, *that I had much better break it than keep it, for I had enough Sermons to answer for already;* and sitting in great distress, contriving how I might put off my going, the Devil found me out a place on the top of the House, a hole where some boards were laid, and there I crowded in my self, and laid a long black Scarf upon me, and put the boards as well as I could to hide me from being found, and there intended to lye till I should starve to death; and all the Family and others concluded I had stoln out at the Door unknown to them to go lose my self in some Wood, which I much talked of; but when I had lain there almost three days, I was so hungry and cold, it being a very sharp Season, that I was forced to call as loud as I could, and so was heard and released from that place.

While she[35] was at Mr. *Walker*'s house, a Minister being desired to come and discourse with her, did come; and finding her in a more dejected state than any he ever saw, did oft visit her, and perceiving little visible good effect of his conferences with her, proposed to Preach a Sermon to her, that might suit her condition, hoping God might bless that Ordinance to her, that she might hear the voice of Joy and Gladness, that so the bones that God had broken might rejoyce; she consented to hear his Sermon, and when upon the day appointed he came to dispence the word, he found her writing the ensuing Lines to dissuade him.

Sir,

This is to beseech you as you would detract a few scalding drops of the fury of the Almighty from my poor miserable and ever to be abhorred Soul to all Eternity, that you cease your study upon any subject on my account, and likewise your Prayers, and instead of that pray to God to rid the World immediately of such a Monster, who am not only guilty of all the sins of the Devil, but likewise of such crimes as he is not capable of, which you will say is incredible, but woe and alas 'tis true.

This is all she had written, the Minister coming in unexpectedly prevented what she further intended to write.

Afterwards the Minister invited her to his House, where she was above a Week, but very loath to engage in any Duty: The Minister's Wife did sometimes importune her to pray with her, but could not prevail, she always excusing herself from her unfitness to take the holy and reverend Name of God within her polluted lips; *Dead Dog, Damn'd Wretch, she dare to speak to the great God;*[36] she expressed so great an awe and dread of the glorious and fearful Name of God, as discovered much grace in her most desponding state, to them that conversed with her. Some years after her recovery, she returning to *London*, came to the aforesaid Minister and his Wife, declaring to them God's great Goodness to her in manifesting himself to her Soul, and returned hearty thanks to them for their tenderness to her in her dejected state. From his Observation of the ground of her Trouble, he advises all Christians to mortifie inordinate Affection to lawful things. *Col. 3. 5.*[37]

I would say that *Pashurs* doom belonged to me, that I was *Magor-Missabib*, a Terrour to my self and all my Friends[38] (*Jerem.* 20.3.); that I was a Hell upon Earth, and a Devil incarnate; for that which I prayed against in hypocrisie, God had brought upon me in reality: for I used to have frequently in my Prayers such an expression as this (apprehending the vileness of my Nature) *if God should leave me to my self, I should be an Hell upon Earth, a Terrour to my self and all my Friends*; and because this was in Hypocrisy, therefore God had brought it on me in reality.

Sometimes when they had told me I had been Prayed for, I would say, *they did not pray for me, for I was not to be prayed for,* for the Scripture said, *That they who had sin'd the sin unto death, were not to be Prayed for.*[39] And when a good Friend of mine Mr. *Blake* came daily and unweariedly to see me; I would Ask him, *Why he yet came, seeing I rejected his Counsel;* And, *Christ bid his Messengers shake the dust of their Feet off against such.*[40] I would say *Because I have built my Fabrick upon the Sand so high, therefore my fall is so dreadful:*[41] When I was told of some that were possest with the Devil and were by Prayer dispossest, I would reply, *What tell you me of Possession, I cared not if I were possest with a Thousand Devils, so I were not a Devil to my self:* When some had told me that I had been Prayed for, I would Answer, *I was the less beholding to them, for it would but sink me the deeper into Hell. I* would often say, *I was a thousand times worse than the Devil, for the Devil had never committed such Sins as I had; for I had committed worse Sins than the Sin against the Holy-Ghost:*[42] some would answer, *The Scripture speaks not of worse sins, and can you be guilty of greater Sins than the Scripture mentions?* Yes, said *I, My Sins are so great, that if all the Sins of all the Devils and Damned in Hell, and all the Reprobates on Earth were comprehended in one man; mine are greater; There is no word comes so near the comprehension of the dreadfulness of my Condition; as that, I am the Monster of the Creation:* in this word *I* much delighted.

I would say, *Let him that thinks he stands, take heed lest he fall: I once thought my self to stand, but am miserably fallen.*

When *I* was forc'd to be present at Duty, *I* would often stop my Ears, my Carriage was very rugged and cross, contrary to my natural temper; Here *I* practised many devices to make away my self, sometimes by Spiders (as before) sometimes endeavouring to let my self blood with a pair of sharp sizers, and so bleed to death; once when the Surgeon had let me blood, *I* went up into a Chamber and bolted the Door to me, and took off the Plaister and tyed my Arm, and set the Vein a bleeding again;[43] which Mrs. *Walker* fearing, ran up stairs and got into the Chamber to me, *I* seeing her come in, ran into the Leads,[44] and there my Arm bled upon the Wall; *Now (said I) you may see there is the blood of a Cursed Reprobate.*

I pleased my self, often, with contriving how to get into a Wood and dye there; and one morning *I* cunningly got out from my Cousins and went into *Smithfield*,[45] where *I* walked up and down a great while, and knew not what to do; at last *I* tryed to hire a Coach but liked not the men there; then *I* went into *Aldersgate-street*,[46] and asked a Coach-man what he would take to carry me to *Barnet*,[47] (for then I meant to go into a Wood) but the man upon some small occasion sadly Cursed and Swore, which struck some Terrour into me, what thought *I*, must such as this be my Companions for ever? and so went away from him; and found one with a good honest look, and with him I agreed; and was to give him Eight Shillings;[48] who carryed me a good way beyond *High-Gate*,[49] and as *I* went along, *I* thought, am *I* now going to Converse with Devils? with such like Thoughts as these *I* was discouraged from going on; and called to the Coach-man, and prayed him to drive back again, and told him it was only a Melancholy Fancy: By these and several other ways *I* thought to put an End to my Life; but the watchful Eye of the Lord always graciously prevented me.

When *I* heard any dreadful thing cryed about the Streets in Books; *I* would say, *Oh what fearful things will be put out of me ere long in Books!* I would say, *I should be called* Allen *that Cursed Apostate.*[50] When I had tryed many ways to make away my self, and still saw God prevented my designs; I would say to my self; *Well, I see it cannot be, it must not be; God will have me come to some fearful End; and its fit it should be so, that God may glorifie himself upon such a wretched Creature.*

As I was going along the Streets, a Godly Minister passing by me; *Oh,* thought I, *with what horrour shall I see that face at the great day!* so would *I* think by many others of Gods people that *I* knew, either Relations or otherwise; *I* said, *I exceedingly wondred that such a Pious man as I heard my Father was, should have such a Child.*

I used to say, *I would change conditions with* Julian,[51] *and that he was a Saint in comparison of me; Nay, That the Devil himself was a Saint compared with me;* I would say, *That the hottest place in Hell must be mine; nay, did you know me, you would say it were too good for me; tho' I poor Creature cannot think so.*

When I complained of the those dreadful Sins I said I was guilty of; some

would Ask me, *If I would be glad to be rid of 'em, and to be in another Condition?*
Yes, said I, *so had the Devils; who do you think would not be happy? but I cannot*
desire it upon any other Account. I would say, *I now saw that my Faith was only a*
Fancy, and that according to an Expression of Mr. Baxters[52] *in a Book of his; That*
the Love I formerly had to God, was Carnal and Diabolical.

I would say to my Cousin *Walker, Tho' I am a damned Reprobate, yet from me*
believe (for sometimes the Devil speaks Truth) that there is a God, and that his Word
is true, and that there is a Devil, and that there is an Hell; which I must find by
woful Experience.

I would often Ask my Cousin *Walker, What those that came to visit me, thought*
of my Condition? he would Answer, *Very well;* I much wondred at it; and would
do what I could to discourage 'em from coming; yet if at any time I thought
they neglected me, I would be secretly troubled; as afterward I said.

I was wont earnestly to Enquire whether it was possible that the Child of
such a Mother as I could be saved; yet I would say I was without *Natural*
Affection; that I Loved neither God nor Man; and that I was given up to work
all manner of wickedness with greediness; *We see no such thing by you,* would
some say; I would Answer, Aye, but it is in my heart; *Why doth it not break out*
in Act? say they, It will do ere long; said I.

The Devil would bring many places of Scripture to my mind, especially
Promises; as I said, to Jear me with them, because once I thought I
delighted in them; but was miserably mistaken; which did much terrifie me.

I would with Dread think with my self, if the men of *Beth-she-mesh* were so
destroyed, I *Sam.* vi. 19. but for looking into the Ark,[53] what will be my
Condemnation that have so often medled with the Holy Ordinances of God,
as the Word and Sacraments; and now proved to be only a *Cursed Hypocrite,*
and nothing to do with them; I thought with my self then, I would not
partake of the Sacrament of the Lords Supper for a thousand worlds.

When any Friend desired me to go to hear the Word of God; I would
earnestly beg of them to let me alone, saying, I had Sermons enough to
Answer for already, and that it would add to my great Account; if they
offer'd to compel me to go, I would desire them to let me alone, and I
would go with them the next time, if I lived till then; but my aim was to
make away my self just before the time came, for I thought I had better go
to Hell sooner, than hear the Word still, and thereby encrease my Torment,
and heap up wrath against the Day of wrath, as I often exprest it.

I would sometimes say to my Cousin *Walker,* will you not pity me, that
must as sure as that there is a God, for ever burn in Hell; I must Confess I
am not to be pitied, for did you know me, you would abhor me, and say
Hell was too good for me; yet however pity me as I am your fellow-
Creature; and once thought my self not only a Woman but a Christian, and
tho' I was such a dreadful wretch as now it appears; yet I did not know it, I
verily thought my self in a good condition; and when you see me come to

15

my horrible End, which I am sure will be ere long; tho' you must loath me, yet I say, pity me.

Yes he would say, *if I thought it was true I would pity you, but I do not believe it.* I used to say, God could not save me, and the reason I gave was; that God could not deny himself.

I found within my self (as I apprehended) a scorning and jeering at Religion, and them that profest it, and a despising of 'em, when I came to the heighth of my distemper, the strugling and fighting that was in me continually at first (while I combated with Satan) left me: When I complained how vile I was, my Friends would tell me, *It was not I, but the Devils Temptations,* I would Answer, No, it is from my self; I am the Devil now, the Devil hath now done his work, he hath done tempting of me; he hath utterly overcome me: *Then why are you so troubled?* would some say; I would Answer, Have I not cause to be troubled, (think you) that am assuredly given up to the Devil and Eternally Damn'd. I would write in several places on the walls with the point of my Sizers, *Woe, Woe, Woe and alas to all Eternity; I am undone, undone for ever, so as never any was before me.*[54]

Upon some sudden occasion I would sometimes smile, but when I did; I would exceedingly check my self, and be the more troubled afterwards.

Mr. *Walker* endeavoured to get Mr. *Baxter* to come to me, but he still missed of him when he came to Town; No, (said I) God will not let Mr. *Baxter* come to such a Wretch as I am; but I had then a secret desire to see him, rather than any one else. And to my best remembrance my Cousin *Walker* told me that he asked me if I would believe better of my self, if Mr. *Baxter* told me my condition was safe; and that I answered, Yes.

When another Christian Friend Mr. *Mason*, brought me acquainted with any of Gods People, I would say, *Alass Mr.* Mason, *you'l dearly repent this; and how must I Curse you in Hell for all that you did in kindness to me.*

What is here writ of Mr. Blake *and Mr.* Mason, *is but to hint what may be said of my Carriage towards them.*

The next Spring which was in *May,* 1665. My Aunt *Wilson* came up to London, being restless in her mind till she saw me; when I heard that my Aunt was come to *High-Gate* to her Brother's House, and did not come to *London* till Monday, I often said I hoped to have seen my Aunt before I dyed; but now I shall not; this fire within me, will kindle and burn me before Monday; on Monday my Aunt came, I being taken with the first sight of her, went with her to dinner to a Friends house in the *Old-Jury;*[55] (Mr. *Hatt*'s House, who afterwards Married her.) but was at my old Language still every Day, That the Fire would kindle within me and burn me: the Sickness then encreasing, my Aunt resolved to take me down again into the Countrey, which I was very glad of; for there I thought I should live more privately, and be less disturbed; (for so I accounted of the kind visits of Friends.) A week before Mid-summer we set forward toward *Darby-Shire*, and an uncomfortable Journey we had, for by the way I would not eat sufficient to support Nature; when I was come to *Snelstone* again, I was where I would be; for there I could do what I pleased, with little opposition; there I shunned all Company tho' they were my near Relations; nor could I endure to be present at Prayer, or any other part of Gods Worship, nor to hear the sound of reading, nor the sight of a Book or Paper; tho' it were but a Letter, or an Almanack.

The Lady *Baker* was pleased to write me several Letters which I would not so much as look on, nor hear read by others, one being brought me, and I prest much to receive it, tore it in pieces. Nay I would strike the Horn-book out of my Childs hand;[56] but that would trouble me as soon as I had done it: I would wish I had never seen Book, or learned letter; I would say it had been happy for me if I had been born blind; daily repeating my accustomed Language, that I was a Cursed Reprobate, and the Monster of the Creation.

One Sabbath-day being disturbed about some small trifle, I fell into violent passion; weeping even to roaring, and cry'd out, I was made to be damn'd, God made me to that very end, to shew the power of his Justice more in me than in any other Creature.

My Aunt sometimes would tell me; that my expressions were so dreadful she knew not how to bear them; I would answer roundly, but what must I do then, that must feel them; I would often say to my Aunt, *Oh, you little know what a dismal dark condition I am in; Methinks I am as dark as Hell it self:* my Aunt would say, *Cousin, would you but believe you were melancholy it might be a great means to bring you out of this Condition; Melancholy*, would I say, *I have Cause to be Melancholy, that am as assuredly Damn'd as that there is a God; and no more hopes of me than of the Devils; I have more Cause to be Melancholy than they have*, it's a fearful thing to fall into the hands of the Living God. *Heb.* x.*vers.* 31.[57]

My Aunt would persuade me to seek God in the use of means, from that Argument of the resolution of the four Lepers, in the 2 *King.* vii. 4.[58] *I would Answer with scorn, I have heard that often enough.*

One fit my humour was such, that when Friends would have argued with me about my condition, I would not speak, but only give them some short scornful Answer and no more; but I would be sometimes in one temper and sometimes in another; my Aunt would take the advantage of my best humour, to talk with me then, and the main thing she designed in most of her Arguments with me was, to convince me of the fallacy and delusion that was in my Opinion; That it was so infallibly revealed to me that I was Damn'd; but alas all took no place with me; but when she began to speak with me of such things, I would generally fling away in a great fume, and say; *Will you not let me alone yet, methinks you might let me have a little quiet while I am out of Hell;* this was almost my daily practice while I was with my Aunt: I was usually very nimble in my Answers, and peevishly pettinacious[59] to please my own cross humour.

My Aunt told me she believed God would not have exercised me so with Afflictions, from my Child-hood, if he intended to reject me at last; I answer'd, *Do you not remember what Mr.* Calamy *used to say, That unsanctified Afflictions par-boyle the Soul for hell; Oh,* said I, *that I had gone to hell as soon as I had been born, (seeing I was born to be damned) and then I had not had so many sins to have answer'd for, then I should not have lived to be a Terrour to my self and all that know me; and my Torments in Hell would have been far less.*

When my Grandmother had told me of the depths of the Mercy of God in Christ: I would answer with indignation; *What do you tell me of a Christ; it had been better for me if there had never been a Saviour, then I should have gone to Hell at a Cheaper Rate.*

Towards Winter I grew to Eat very little, (much less than I did before) so that I was exceeding Lean; and at last nothing but Skin and Bones; (a Neighbouring Gentlewoman, a very discreet Person that had a great desire to see me, came in at the back-door of the House unawares and found me in the Kitchen, who after she had seen me, said to Mrs. *Wilson, She cannot live, she hath death in her face)* I would say still that every bit I did Eat hastned my Ruin; and that I had it with a dreadful Curse; and what I Eat encreased the Fire within me, which would at last burn me up; and I would now willingly live out of Hell as long as I could.

Thus sadly I passed that Winter, and towards Spring I began to Eat a little better.

This Spring in *April,* 1666. my good Friends Mr. *Shorthose* and his Wife, whose Company formerly I much delighted in, came over, and when I heard they were come and were at their Brothers house, half a mile off, and would come thither the Fryday after; *Ah,* says I, *that I dreaded, I cannot endure to see him, nor hear his voice; I have told him so many dreadful Lyes;* (meaning what I had formerly told him of my experiences, and, as I thought, infallible evidences of the Love of God towards me; and now believed my self to be the vilest Creature upon Earth) *I cannot see his face;* and wept tenderly, wherewith my Aunt was much affected, and promised that when he came he should not see me; (I would have seen neither of them, but especially my He-Cousin) On the Fryday, soon after they came in, they asked for me, but my Aunt put them off till after Dinner, and then told them, she had engaged her word they should not see me, and that if she once broke her promise with me, I would not believe her hereafter; with such persuasions she kept them from seeing me, but not satisfied them; for that Night Mr. *Shorthose* was much troubled, and told his Wife if he had thought they must not have seen me, he would scarce have gone to *Snelstone;* the next day they Supped at Mr. *Robert Archer's* House, Mrs. *Wilson's* Brother that then lived in the same Town, where my Aunt Supped with them; at the Table something was said of their not seeing Mrs. *Allen,* but after Supper Mr. *Shorthose* and his Wife stole away from the Company to Mrs. *Wilsons,* where they came in at the back-side of the House suddenly into the Kitchen where I was; but assoon as I saw them, I cryed out in a violent manner several times; *Ah, Aunt* Wilson *hast thou serv'd me so!* and ran into the Chimney and took up the Tongs; *No*, said they, *Your Aunt knows not of our coming; What do you do here?* said I, *We have something to say to you*, said they, *but I have nothing to say to you*, said I, Mr. *Shorthose* took me by the hand and said, *Come, come, lay down those Tongs and go with us into the Parlour*, which I did, and there they discoursed with me, till they had brought me to so calm and friendly a temper, that when they went, I accompanied them to the door and said; *Methinks I am loth to part with them*; Mr. *Shorthose* having so good encouragement, came the next day again, being Sabbath day after Dinner, and prevailed with me to walk with him into an Arbour in the Orchard,[60] where he had much discourse with me, and amongst the rest he entreated me to go home with him; which after long persuasions both from him and my Aunt, I consented to, upon this condition, that he promised me, *he would not compell me to any thing of the Worship of God, but what he could do by persuasion*; and that week I went with them, where I spent that Summer; in which time it pleased God by Mr. *Shorthose*'s means to do me much good both in Soul and Body; he had some skill in Physick himself, and also consulted with Physicians about me; he kept me to a course of Physick most part of the Summer, except when the great heat of the Weather prevented, I began much to leave my dreadful expressions concerning my condition, and was present with them at duty; and at last they prevailed with me to go with them to the publick Ordinance, and to walk with them to visit Friends, and was much alter'd for the better.

A fortnight after *Michaelmas*[61] my Aunt fetch'd me home again to *Snelston*, where I passed that Winter much better than formerly, and was pretty conformable and orderly in the Family; and the next Summer was much after the same manner, but grew still something better; and the next Winter likewise still mending though but slowly, till the Spring began, and then I changed much from my retiredness, and delighted to walk with Friends abroad.

And this Spring it pleased God to provide a very suitable Match for me, one Mr. *Charles Hatt*, a Widdower living in *Warwickshire*; with whom I live very comfortably, both as to my inward and outward man; my husband being one that truly fears God.

As my Melancholy came by degrees, so it wore off by degrees, and as my dark Melancholy bodily distempers abated, so did my spiritual Maladies also, and God convinced me by degrees; that all this was from Satan, his delusions and temptations, working in those dark and black humors, and not from my self, and this God cleared up to me more and more; and accordingly my love to, and delight in Religion, increased; and it is my desire that, lest this great Affliction should be a stumbling-block to any, it may be known, (seeing my Case is publish'd) that I evidently perceive that God did it in much mercy and faithfulness to my Soul; and though for the present it was a bitter Cup, yet that it was but what the only wise God saw I had need of according to that place, I *Pet.* i. 6. *Tho' now for a season, if need be, ye are in heaviness through manifold Temptations.*[62] Which Scripture did much comfort me under my former Afflictions in my first Husbands days.

These Promises which are here set down were great supports and refreshments to me in the time of my various Temptations and Afflictions all along, till I fell into deep despair, for from my Child-hood, God Exercised me with manifold Trials.

Isaiah, xliii. 1, 2.

BUT now thus saith the Lord that Created thee, O Jacob, *and he that formed thee, O* Israel, *fear not for I have redeemed thee; I have called thee by thy Name, thou art mine. Vers. 2. When thou passest through the Waters, I will be with thee, and through the Rivers they shall not overflow thee; when thou walkest through the fire, thou shalt not be burnt, neither shall the flame kindle upon thee; for I am the Lord thy God, the Holy One of* Israel *thy Saviour.*

Psal. xcvii. 11.

Light is sown for the Righteous, and Gladness for the upright in heart.

Isaiah, lxiv. 4.

*For since the beginning of the World, men have not heard, nor perceived by the Ear, neither hath the Eye seen, O God, besides thee, what he hath prepared for him that waiteth for him.

Lam. iii. 21, 26, 27, 31, 32.

The Lord is good unto them that wait for him, to the Soul that seeketh him; it is good that a man should both hope and quietly wait for the Salvation of the Lord; it is good for a man that he bear the Yoke in his Youth. Vers. 31, 32. For the Lord will not cast off for ever; but though he cause Grief, yet he will have Compassion according to the multitude of his Mercies.

Mic. vii. 7, 8.

Therefore I will look unto the Lord, I will wait for the God of my Salvation, for God will hear me; Vers. 8. Rejoyce not against me, O mine Enemy, when I fall I shall rise, when I sit in darkness the Lord shall be a Light unto me.

*This in the 64. of Isaiah, she used to press upon her self to wait upon God.

Psal. lxxii. 12.

For he shall deliver the Needy when he cryeth, the Poor also, and him that hath no helper.

Psal. xxxvii. 24.

Though he fall he shall not be utterly cast down, for the Lord upholdeth him with his hand.

I Cor. x. 13.

There hath no Temptation taken you but such as is common to man, but God is faithful, who will not suffer you to be tempted above that ye are able; but will with the Temptation, also make a way to Escape, that you may be able to bear it.

Phil. i. 6.

Being confident of this very thing that he which hath begun a good work in you, will perform it until the day of Jesus Christ.

James, i. 12.

Blessed is the man that endureth Temptation, for when he is tryed, he shall receive the Crown of Life, which the Lord hath promised to them that love him.

James v. 11.

Behold we count them happy which Endure; ye have heard of the Patience of Job, and have seen the End of the Lord; that the Lord is very pitiful and of tender mercy.

I John, iv. 4.

Ye are of God, little Children; and have overcome them, because greater is he that is in you, than he that is in the World.

THE END

THE

London-Citizen Exceedingly Injured:

OR A

BRITISH

INQUISITION

DISPLAY'D,

In an Account of the UNPARALLEL'D CASE of a *Citizen* of *London*, Bookſeller to the late Queen, who was in a moſt *unjuſt* and *arbitrary* Manner ſent on the 23d of *March* laſt, 1738, by one *Robert Wightman*, a mere Stranger, to a *Private Madhouſe*.

CONTAINING,

I. An Account of the ſaid CITIZEN's barbarous Treatment in *Wright's* Private Madhouſe on *Bethnal-Green*[2] for nine Weeks and ſix Days, and of his rational and patient Behaviour, whilſt *Chained, Handcuffed, Strait-Waſtecoated* and *Impriſoned* in the ſaid *Madhouſe:* Where he probably would have been continued, or died under his Confinement, if he had not moſt *Providentially* made his Eſcape: In which he was taken up by the Conſtable[3] and Watchmen, being ſuſpected to be a Felon, but was unchain'd and ſet at liberty by Sir *John Barnard* the then Lord Mayor.[4]

II. As alſo an Account of the illegal Steps, falſe Calumnies, wicked Contrivances, bold and deſperate Deſigns of the ſaid *Wightman*, in order to eſcape Juſtice for his Crimes, with ſome Account of his engaging Dr. *Monro*[5] and others as his Accomplices.

The Whole humbly addreſſed to the LEGISLATURE, as plainly ſhewing the abſolute Neceſſity of regulating *Private Madhouſes* in a more effectual manner than at preſent.

Brethren, pray for us, that we may be delivered from unreaſonable and wicked Men, 2 Theſſ. iii. 1, 2.[6]

LONDON:

Printed for T. COOPER at the *Globe* in *Pater-noſter-Row*, and Mrs. DODD at the *Peacock* without *Temple-Bar*, 1739.

To the Right Honourable The Lord H * * *[7]

MY LORD,

YOUR Lordship's great Benevolence, and kind Concern expressed to the Injured Person for the ill Usage he met with, is an Encouragement to lay the following Journal or Narrative of his great Sufferings, in a most humble Manner, before your Lordship.

THIS Affair, MY LORD, is now under the Cognisance of the Law. The following Narrative is humbly inscribed to Your Lordship, as being in one of the highest and most laborious Stations under his MAJESTY, whom GOD long preserve, and having given many Proofs of Your great Goodness and Regard to the Liberties of Mankind, Your Lordship, in perusing the following Journal, will find that there is a horrid and barbarous Inquisition at Bethnal-Green, which, it is humbly hoped, may be supressed by Your Lordship and other worthy Patriots, so that that growing Evil may be extinguished; Where honest, sensible and judicious Persons are by Malice, Envy, Revenge, and other unaccountable Motives hurried from their Habitations, their Lives endangered, their Health impaired, and their Substance wasted, their Credit intirely sunk, and they perhaps rendred for ever useless in their Generation; Where Injured Persons often suffer unheard, untried, and without having the least Hopes of Remedy, being deprived of Pen, Ink and Paper, and the Visits of Friends.

YOUR Lordship is humbly intreated to excuse the Liberty of this Address. That God may long continue Your great Usefulness, and bless you in all Respects, is the hearty Prayer of,

MY LORD,

Your Lordship's

Most obedient and

Most Humble Servant,

London, March 21, 1738–9.

The London-Citizen Exceedingly Injured; Or a Journal or Narrative Of Mr. C——'s Sufferings

At *Bethnal-Green*, by one *Wightman* and his Accomplices.

A Short Narrative is here given of the horrid Sufferings of a *London-Citizen* in *Wright*'s private Madhouse at *Bethnal-Green*, during nine weeks and six days, (till he made his wonderful Escape) by the Combination of *Robert Wightman* Merchant at *Edinburgh*, a stranger in *London*, and others, who had no right, warrant or authority in Law, Equity or Consanguinity, or any other manner whatsoever, to concern themselves with him or his affairs; and yet most unjustly imprisoned him in that dismal place. How unjustly and unaccountably they acted in first sending Mr. *C.* to *Bethnal-Green*, and how cruel and barbarous they were in their bold and desperate Design to fix him in *Bethlehem*, (after Mr. *C.* refused to sign their Pardon) that they might screen themselves from punishment, by covering one heinous crime with another more heinous, will appear by the following Journal of Mr. *C.*'s Sufferings.

After thirteen years acquaintance with Mr. *Bryan Payne*, Cornchandler in *Picadilly*,[8] and his Wife, where Mr. *C.* had officiated as Chaplain for some years on Sabbath-Evenings, and was used like their particular Friend, the said Mr. *Payne* died *August 9, 1737*. Some considerable time after his decease Mr. *C.* made his addresses to the Widow *Payne*, then a Gentlewoman of a great fortune, and was greatly encouraged by her, which increased his Affection. He was kindly received by her in the way of Courtship, and supping with her on *Monday* and *Tuesday* the 13th and 14th of *March*, at both those times he plainly expressed his great Esteem and Affection for her; and his addresses were received chearfully and pleasantly, without the least contradiction.

March 17. Mr. *C.* after he had been deeply engaged as Corrector at the Printing-Office in *Wild-Court*,[9] went about eight o'clock at night to visit Mrs. *Payne*, who entertained him most chearfully, and gave him scope enough to talk over his affair, which she received with a most agreeable air. He spoke to her what he thought was proper upon the affair in hand, but by some expressions she dropt Mr. *C.* began to suspect her Sincerity with regard to him.

March 18. Mr. *C.* being apt to think, that what Mrs. *Payne* said the night before, was chiefly for a trial of his love, and that it might be said of her,

Ardeat ipsa tamen, tormentis gaudet Amantis,[10]

wrote this morning a letter to her, and acquainted her that he designed to pay his respects to her to day at dinner-time. Mr. *C.* intended to get a plain Answer, and to know fully her Resolution from her own Mouth; and having done his business that morning at the Printing-Office in *Wild-Court*, he went afterwards to Mrs. *Payne*'s; and when he came thither, Mr. *William Crookshank* and *John Oswald*[11] were with her. Upon Mr. *C.*'s going into Mrs. *Payne*'s Dining-room she was not dressed, and went out without saying one word, which greatly displeased him; yet he tarried some time, being in hopes of her being quickly in a better disposition; but he being afterwards satisfied, that he had been mis-used by her in such a manner that no generous man could bear, he was greatly disobliged, and justly on the account of the great Encouragement she had given him in his addresses on former occasions.

Crookshank and *Oswald* were so officious, that they followed Mr. *C.* home to his lodging in *White's-Alley* in *Chancery-Lane*,[12] tho' he earnestly begged them not to go to his lodging, nor to speak any thing to *Grant* or his Wife of the affair relating to Mrs. *Payne*, fearing the weak people might misconstrue it: But those two weak and imprudent men, contrary to all justice and prudence, made secretly a false representation of Mr. *C.* and of this Affair to his silly Landlord and Landlady, who live in *Oswald's* house, and are only his servants. This false notion that *Crookshank* and *Oswald* instilled into the weak brains of *Grant* and his Wife, occasioned them from thenceforth to behave towards Mr. *C.* in a very foolish and contradictory manner. Whether these Persons misconstrued Mr. *C's.* actions to curry favour with Mrs. *Payne*, they know best. Mr. *Whatley* of *Gray's-Inn*,[13] and *Claudius Bonner*, a Compositor at the Printing-Office in *Wild-Court*, called this evening on Mr. *C.* at his lodging, and they have both declared that he behaved very sensibly.

March 19. Mr. *C.* being engaged to go this day to the Meeting-house in *Swallow-street*,[14] and being much offended at Mrs. *Payne* for her Haughtiness and bad Behaviour towards him, chose to sit in that Front-seat of the Gallery where Mr. *Payne* and Mrs. *Payne* some years before used to sit, that he might rather triumph over Mrs. *Payne* than show a mean or servile Spirit for the great Disappointment she had given him. It was owned by every body that he was very attentive in Publick Service. Mr. *Crookshank* had told him that he had been invited to dine this day with Mrs. *Payne.* Mr. *C.* desir'd at noon that he would not go to dine with her; *Crookshank* promised to grant him his Request, but he broke his Promise and went. After the Afternoon's Service in *Swallow-Street*, Mr. *C.* went home to his aforesaid Lodging; and *Wightman* and *Oswald* passed the evening with him in good Discourse, and regular Devotion perform'd by him in a decent and unexceptionable manner.

Monday, March 20. This morning *Wightman*, without being desired or expected, came to Mr. *C.'s* room, and advised him not to go to the Printing-Office that day, but to be let blood, and stay at home, which Mr. *C*, at last complied with, tho' with great reluctance. Mr. *C.* wrote a letter to Mr. *Ragg* the Surgeon, who came and let him blood: He was at home all that day in a quiet and calm manner.

Tuesday, March 21. He called in the morning on his Landlady *Grant's* Wife for some of his Papers committed to her care, but she for a great while made no Answer, 'till at last she said they might be about his bed: But while Mr. *C.* was making diligent search for them, *John Huet* a Blacksmith in the neighbourhood came up with a stick in his hand, in order to seize him as a Madman; which Mr. *C.* looked upon as the highest Affront and greatest

Provocation. Mr. *C.* took the stick from him, and forced him down stairs: But in a few minutes *Grant* and his Wife alarmed the neighbourhood as if he was a Madman, and so about a dozen of them came in, whom he obliged to go out, and then shut the doors. They rallied by the cellar-window, particularly a bloody Butcher came from below, who disfigured Mr. *C.'s* face with several blows: And while he was grappling with this diabolical Butcher, *John Duck* a Blackmore[15] and *John Anderson* a Coachman came up, rescued Mr. *C.* from the Butcher, and seized him. This cruel Butcher soon after gave him a severe blow, to the great effusion of his blood, with a stick on the head, without the least provocation, and then quickly disappeared, and no body can give any account of him. Mr. *C.* was amaz'd at this uncommon Treatment, and asked whether they were all become Madmen?

Duck and *Anderson* went up stairs with Mr. *C.* where he lay down on a bed, and Mr. *Ragg* the Surgeon came to dress his Wound. He examined if it had fractured the Skull, but happily it had not; for had it been a little deeper, it had been mortal. A Tool of *Wightman's* formerly an Apprentice to a Taylor, but lately a Coffin-breaker and Grave-digger in St. *Andrew's*[16] Burying-ground, and a few months before a pretended Physician of no figure, came in, who with great impudence insulted over Mr. *C.* but he greatly despised this silly man, and calmly and composedly desired *John Duncan* then in the room, to go to the learned and eminent Physician Dr. *Hulse*, to come and see him; but tho' *Duncan* promised to go, he never went. Mr. *C.* often called for a Constable, but tho' there was one at hand, he would not come, he not approving of their conduct. This was about twelve o' clock. He saw himself obliged to submit peaceably and patiently to their orders all that day.

Wednesday, March 22. Mr. *C.* stayed at home all day, cool and sedate, employing his time in reading: But the foolish people would allow none of his Friends to visit him, tho' some particular Friends called both yesterday and to day, and earnestly desired to go up to see him; yet *Wightman* hindered Mr. *Kelsey Bull* and Mr. *Frederick Bull*, two of Mr. *C.'s* particular Friends, from coming up to see him; and *Grant* and his Wife who stood at the door, were so impudent as to refuse Entrance to Mr. *John Cargil* another particular Friend, and made Mr. *C.* their Prisoner.

Thursday, March 23, Mr. *C.* sorting his Papers this morning in his room on the table where a candle stood, the foolish people made a great breach in the door, and knocked at it with such Fury, that they made the snuff of the candle to fall upon three loose sheets of paper on the table, and set fire to them; which Mr. *C.* to prevent any bad consequence, wrapt up together, and put them out at the breach of the door. This is all the ground that the malicious people had to say that Mr. *C.* designed to set the house on fire; which is abominably false.

This day *Oliver Robert* a Chairman came, as he said, from one *Robert Wightman* in *Spring-Gardens*,[17] and told Mr. *C.* that the said *Wightman* wanted to speak with him at his lodgings in *Spring-Gardens*; and *Roberts* taking with him *Anderson* the Coachman, decoy'd Mr. *C.* into a Hackney-coach; and till the Coach came to *Ludgate-hill* Mr. *C.* did not fully discover their wicked Design, for the Coach-windows were drawn up: Mr. *C.* had asked *Roberts* in *Chancery-Lane* which way the Coach was to go to *Spring-Gardens?* *Roberts* answered, Up the *Strand.* And when Mr. *C.* saw himself thus imposed upon, he expostulated with them in the following manner: 'Oh! what are you going to do with me? I bless God, I am not mad. Are you going to carry me to *Bethlehem?* How great is this Affliction! This is the way to put an end to all my Usefulness in the World, and to expose me to the highest Degree! Oh! what shall I do? God help me! I desire to submit to the Will of God.' *Roberts* then positively told him that he had Orders from the said *Wightman* to carry him to Country-Lodgings near *Bow*, which proved to be *Wright's* private Madhouse on *Bethnal-Green*, where he delivered him to *John Davis* the Under-Keeper of the said Madhouse, when Mr. *C.* requested *Roberts* and *Anderson* not to expose him by telling any body of his being brought to so dismal a Place: And *Roberts* particularly remembers that Mr. *C.* said, he hoped that God would make this great Affliction turn to his Good. *Roberts* also declares that Mr. *C.* always spoke sensibly, and behaved well, and much like a Gentleman.

The said *Davis* locked Mr. *C.* up in a room in the Madhouse, who was at first much dejected, but after going to Prayer was greatly comforted; and soon after *Davis, Samuel Wall* the Barber, *and Dorothy Mayleigh* Housemaid came, and spoke very civilly to the Prisoner, who this afternoon asked *Wall* if he saw any sign of Disorder about him? To which *Wall* replied, None at all as yet, but that he did not know how soon an alteration might come, which proved only a groundless suspicion.

That very afternoon the Prisoner desired Pen, Ink, and Paper, but *Davis* refused it to one in his Circumstances; yet the Prisoner acquainting *Davis* with the occasion, relating to his Shop under the *Royal-Exchange*, and promising to shew the Letter to *Davis*, the Housemaid brought him some Paper. This Letter was directed to *John Scot*, who had the care of the Prisoner's Shop, and was acknowledged by *Scot* and others to be a very sensible Letter, and much to the purpose.

Soon after in the evening the said *Scot* with Mr. *Robert Macpherson* and Mr. *John Duncan*, came to visit the Prisoner, who spoke to them very sensibly, and shewed no signs of Madness in his Conversation with them, as has been attested under the hands of the said *Macpherson* and *Duncan*.

After they were gone, *Wightman* and *Oswald* came to the Prisoner, who with very great temper seriously expostulated with *Wightman* about his presuming to send him to a Madhouse, that had no Power over him in Law, Equity or Consanguinity, but was his very slender acquaintance, and a stranger to all his affairs; and asked by what authority he had been so bold as to do so?

Wightman was confounded, and blamed *Grant* and his Wife, who, he said, were very weak silly persons: *Oswald*, like a self-condemned Person, was very silent, especially upon hearing that his Wife had been convicted of a gross Lye she had uttered to *Wright's* Wife in the morning, when she took the room for the Prisoner; and so *Wightman* and *Oswald* went away abruptly and without ceremony, instead of begging Pardon and releasing the Prisoner. *Davis* was present at this Conversation, and told *Wightman*, after he went out of the room, that he had not observed any signs of Madness about his Prisoner; but *Wightman*, who pretends to know that a person is mad from the Tone of his Voice, replied, that the Prisoner would be ill about three o'clock in the morning, but he proved a false Prophet. When the Prisoner went to bed about eight o'clock, *Davis* came and told him, that seeing he was in a Madhouse, he must allow himself to be used as a Madman, and submit to have the Chain on the bedstead lock'd upon his Leg, which the Prisoner patiently submitted to.

Friday, March 24. Davis told the Prisoner in the morning, that last night when *Wightman* and *Oswald* left his room, they went confounded up the first pair of stairs, as at a loss what to determine to do, and then went to consult with *Wright's* Wife, a most improper person indeed for advising the Releasment of the Prisoner.

The Prisoner desired *Davis* to tell his Master *Wright* to come himself and unlock the Chain, but *Wright*, who had not come home till five or six o'clock in the morning, told *Davis* that he would not do it for 500 *l.*

Thomas Lindon Apothecary[18] coming to visit a Patient in the Madhouse, the Prisoner desired him to feel his Pulse, who having felt it, declared it was regular and in order. Also *Job London* Apothecary, coming to visit the Prisoner by *Wightman's* Order, felt his Pulse, and declared it to be regular, as he afterwards acknowledged before the Lord Mayor. The said *London* brought physick with him for the Prisoner, by the Prescription of Dr. *Monro*, tho' the Doctor did not visit him till the 30th of this Instant *March*. The Prisoner prudently submitted to take the physick that evening. It is to be observed, that if Prisoners in this Madhouse refuse to take what is ordered them, there is a terrible iron Instrument put into their mouths to hold down their tongues, and to force the physick down their throats. The operation of the said physick awaked him about three o'clock in the morning, when he requested *Davis* in the next room to come and assist him; but *Davis* obstinately declined it, and instead of acknowledging his Barbarity, when he came in about nine o'clock, sternly made the Prisoner know that he was his Keeper; and to confirm his authority, not only kept the Chain on his Leg, but added to his Misery by chaining his two Wrists together with Handcuffs.

Saturday, March 25. This morning a Gentleman visited the Prisoner, and said to him, "*Be quiet and easy, for your King and your God is with you, and nothing can hurt you.*" This Expression the Prisoner often thought of, and, blessed be God, he experienced that it was so: And this day the Prisoner was for the first time visited by *Wright's* Wife, with whom he expostulated about his unjust and barbarous Confinement, but she answered him smoothly and cunningly.

In the afternoon *London* the Apothecary came, and took upon him to order *Davis* to put a *Strait-Wastecoat* on the Prisoner's Body, made of strong Tick, with long sleeves which came a great way below the ends of his Fingers; and so the Keeper clasped the Arms of the Prisoner upon his Breast, and his Hands round his Sides towards his Back, where his Hands were tied very firmly by Large strong strings of Tape.[19] The Apothecary seemed afterwards ashamed for ordering this *Strait-Wastecoat*, and even afraid it was a good Foundation for an Action against him: But the Prisoner having often told *London*, that he would not pay him a farthing for his Medicines, he thought fit to side with *Wightman* and *Oswald*, right or wrong, who had employed him, altho' once he put a letter from the Prisoner into the Peny-Post-Office[20] directed for *Scot* at his Shop, yet afterwards he told the Prisoner, he was ordered to do so no more; and doubtless by the People in the *Poultry*. The Prisoner did not think it prudent to fall out altogether with *London*, being afraid he would have poisoned his Medicines, he acting in some respects like a deceitful young man, being guilty of lying and profane swearing, one of *Wright*'s Companions, and too apt to concur in any thing with those who helped to consume his Drugs.

In the evening, the Prisoner endeavouring to slacken his Hands, and to get rid of the *Strait-Wastecoat*, by the help of the footpost of the bed, that was a few inches turned up with an acorn, was catched at it by *Davis* and *Wall*, who strongly fettered his Arms above the *Strait-Wastecoat*; and not permitting the Maid to feed him, he was obliged to eat his supper with his mouth like a Dog, as he did his breakfast and dinner the next day. Oh! what Difficulties he had to perform the Necessities of Nature in a becoming manner! which he did as well as he could in those unhappy Circumstances. The *Strait-Wastecoat* also hindered him from Sleep, and it was a great Mercy that this barbarous Usage did not throw him into a real Disorder.

There were but two of those *Strait-Wastcoats* in the house, which were made for a young Man a prisoner there, born Heir to an Estate in *Somersetshire* of about 1500 *l.* a Year, who by his sinful folly had catched the unclean Distemper, and from an unskilful hand had taken too much Mercury that got into his head, and had made him incurably mad.[21]

This day, Serjeant-Major *Cruden*[22] in *Dutchy-Lane* and his Wife, with two other Acquaintance, came, and most earnestly desired to see the Prisoner, but to no purpose, for *Davis* told them, he had Orders to allow none to see him without a written Order from *Wightman*, *Oswald*, or *Monro*: Nay, a Word of him from the window was denied, which made one of them say, that this Usage was worse than that of the Inquisition. Mr. *Cruden* on his return went to *Oswald* to demand an Order to visit the Prisoner, but he refused it, referring him to *Wightman,* tho' *Oswald* gave a Ticket to his own Maid and *John Duncan* to visit him next day.

The *Lord's Day, March* 26. *Davis* was deaf to all the Prisoner's Intreaties to take off the *Strait-Wastecoat;* and the Prisoner was much disturbed by the blasphemous cursing and swearing of a Patient in the Publick Parlour,[23] which made the Place a Resemblance of Hell: And the Prisoner's door being some time open, he said to some that came in, "*That the way to be mad, was to be sent to a Madhouse.*" And an Apothecary who hath been often at *Bethnal-Green,* declares, "That if Persons be not mad when sent to the Madhouse, *Wright's* People will make them mad if they can."

In the afternoon one *John Duncan* and *Oswald's* Maid were allowed to see the Prisoner by virtue of a written Order from *Oswald;* and they saw him in the *Strait-Wastecoat,* handcuffed and chained, and *Davis* would not loose him that he might be dressed. He intimated to the two Visitors his Design of making *Wightman* and *Oswald* suffer for their illegal and unjust Management.

The Prisoner having often called for *Wright's* Wife, she came about six o'clock at night, and took off the *Strait-Wastecoat,* to let his hands be free: But at eight o'clock at night *Davis* came, and clothed him with it, and chained him as before.

Monday, March 27. *Davis* loosened his hands, but handcuffed him, and the Prisoner was visited in the afternoon by a Woman-Patient in the White-house[24] that had liberty to go abroad, who treated him with some Tea.

At night *Davis* came, and tied him up in the *Strait-Wastecoat* as before.

Tuesday, March 28. About ten o'clock in the morning the Prisoner was the first time brought out of his room into the publick parlour among some of the Patients, when *Davis* took his hands from behind his back, but handcuffed him, and also chained his leg to the chimney-corner: But the Prisoner hating to be chained in the publick parlour with such disagreeable company, earnestly desired about noon rather to be chained in his own room, which was granted; and he sat in his own room, *wastecoated, handcuffed* and *chained* to his bedstead till night, when *Davis* came and tied the sleeves of the *Strait-Wastecoat* as before, with his hands behind his back; so that he could go to bed, only by entering at the bed's foot, the chain on his leg which was fixed to the foot of the bedstead, not being long enough to let him go to bed otherwise.

Wednesday, March 29. *Davis* did not open the sleeves of the *Strait-Wastecoat,* and the Prisoner was forced to stay in bed till the afternoon, when *Davis* perceiving that the Prisoner with his fingers had gradually made two holes in the sleeves of the *Strait-Wastecoat,* so large that he could get his hands out, *Davis,* in his sovereign Will and Pleasure, thought fit to take off the *Wastecoat,* but handcuffed him, and continued him chained to the foot of the bedstead. The Prisoner had a happy Deliverance, after he had wore that *Coat of Mail* about four or five days, and under all that barbarous Usage, the

Prisoner enjoyed much inward Peace and Tranquillity, which upon constant Prayer to Heaven God was pleased graciously to favour him with; for having neither Books nor Conversation he employed a great part of his time in Devotion; and being rid of the *Strait-Wastecoat* he slept well that night.

Thursday, March 30. Dr. *Monro* came in his Chariot[25] with *Wightman* to visit the Prisoner for the first time, tho' it was six days after he had ordered physick for him. The Prisoner not thinking it best to speak much to either of them, only expostulated about his unjust Confinement, and barbarous Usage, enough to convince them that he thought himself greatly injured. *Monro* ordered him to be blooded in the left foot, which was performed by *London* the Apothecary that evening, who took away so much blood that the foot was for some months after benumm'd.

Wightman told the Prisoner that he had made up an acquaintance with Dr. *Monro*, who became intirely *Wightman*'s Creature, and was devoted to his Service. *Monro* had soon told *Wightman* that he had done an action he could not answer for, in confining the Prisoner, and that it was in his power to bring him to trouble; therefore *Monro* contrived all ways to screen *Wightman*. *Monro*, *Wightman*, *Oswald* and others fell into a way of *Lying*, and, as if neither Men nor Christians, they must go on in it: But Integrity and Uprightness are the best means of Preservation. One wrong step often tempts lofty proud Men to take many more. The Prisoner desires all his Life to be thankful to God for his particular Care of him; for *the Snares of his Adversaries were broken, and he escaped as a Bird out of the Snare of the Fowlers.*[26] The Prisoner had great Serenity in his Mind, and trusted that God would bring him out of all his Troubles. Their wicked Devices against him were frustrated most providentially; *Hitherto shalt thou come, but no further, and here shall thy proud Waves be stayed.* Job xxxviii. 11.[27]

Friday, March 31. The above-mentioned *Thomas Lindon* Apothecary being at *Bethnal-Green*, came and felt the Prisoner's Pulse, and said it was feverish, tho' on 24th of *March*, as before observed, he had said that his Pulse was in good order, as *Job London* the other Apothecary had also said on the same 24th day, when these two strangers had no temptation to speak contrary to their real opinion: But supposing it to be true that the Prisoner's Pulse was feverish this 31st of *March*, no wise Man can wonder at it, who considers the above-mentioned Barbarity and cruel Usage of the Prisoner for seven days together.

The Prisoner's pockets having been rifled, he had no money, and therefore when he called on the servants in the Madhouse, they either did not answer him; or said, If you will be served, where is your money? But having now got a few shillings, and being now able a little to gratify the servants, he found it of some advantage; for this afternoon *Davis* unchained him from his bedstead, and allowed him to walk a little in the garden. There the Prisoner talked to a young Lady in the next garden, who had come to see an acquaintance in the Madhouse for the Women, and spoke so calmly, so sensibly, that the Lady said, she was surprised to see him handcuffed, which the Prisoner mentioned to *Davis* and the Housemaid: And the Prisoner now found it convenient to study to please the servants.

This afternoon the Prisoner being unchained was allowed to sit in the great parlour: Mr. *Turner* the Apothecary, Mr. *Kittleby* (whose son was a Patient) and the aforesaid *London* came in there, and conversed with him a long time. *London* talked about Books and Bookselling, and proposed to the Prisoner to change some books with him, and the Prisoner's conversation was very sensible, and mightily pleased *London*, as he himself declared; and this notwithstanding the strong Prejudices that *Wightman* and *Oswald* had instilled into this Apothecary. The Prisoner, before the said company, plainly told *London*, to acquaint those who had put him into the Madhouse, that if they did not speedily release him, he would demand legal Satisfaction in due time, and bring them to Shame and Punishment for the great Injuries done to him. At night *Davis* continued the Prisoner's handcuffs, and again chained him to the bedstead as usual.

Saturday, April 1. *Davis* came in the morning, when he pleased, to unchain the Prisoner, that he might get on his clothes, and allowed him to walk in the garden with his handcuffs: He employed himself that day in reading a book of Sermons, which he had borrowed from a Patient; and at night *Davis* continued his handcuffs, and chained him to the bedstead as usual.

The *Lord's Day, April* 2. *Davis* having unloosed the Prisoner's Chains in the morning, he went into the great Parlour with his handcuffs, where he met with a Patient Mrs. *Betty Atk——on* that was lodged there only for some particular Fancies, who otherwise seemed very rational and well: She went with him into his room, where they worshipped God together: And at night *Davis* being out of the way, the Housemaid was pleased to take off his handcuffs, and *Wall* chained him to his bedstead as usual.

Monday, April 3. This morning the Prisoner took a Vomit, as ordered by *Monro*, and prepared by *London*; but tho' he was unchained, he was again handcuffed by *Davis*. At night he was chained to his bedstead as usual.

Tuesday, April 4. *Davis* came and unchained the Prisoner, but continued his handcuffs. In the afternoon the aforesaid *John Duncan*, and afterwards *Oswald's* Maid, came to see the Prisoner, and saw him handcuffed in his room, with whom he talked as rationally as any Man, and at night *Davis* took off his handcuffs, but again chained him to the bedstead as usual.

Wednesday, April 5. In the morning *Davis* came and unchained the Prisoner, but handcuffed him, and telling him that a friend wanted to see him at *Wright's* dwelling-house, which is the *Great-Madhouse*, called the *White-house*, or the *Blind-Beggar's House*, it having been, as is said, possessed by a Blind Beggar in favour with *Henry* VII, *Davis* and *Caesar*[28] another servant guarded Mr. *C.* thither, where he was civilly received by *Wright* and his Wife, which Change in their Carriage made him somewhat astonished: For *Wright* carried him into the garden, and gave him a book to read in his parlour, a Paraphrase upon the Gospels and Epistles. *Wright's* Wife also shewed him several books. This Behaviour being mysterious to the Prisoner at first, he was apt to think they were sorry for detaining him so long unjustly; for *Davis* had told him in going along to the *White-house*, that he should not blame *Wright* for his Confinement, but those that sent him to *Bethnal-Green*.

It may be observed that *Wright* and his Wife seem to have such an insatiable thirst after Money, that if the most judicious and prudent persons upon earth were sent thither with a good weekly allowance, they must be their Prisoners either with *Handcuffs, Chains* or *Strait-Wastecoats*, or with *wheedling Pretences*; for *Wright's* Wife said that it is their way to execute the Orders of those that pay them, and send the Prisoner to the Madhouse. *Wightman* was to pay *Wright* a Guinea a week for the Prisoner; he drank his own Tea in the morning, had commonly Butcher's Meat to dinner, and Bread and Milk for supper; so that it's a question, whether the weekly Charge was to *Wright* over or under five shillings; and *Wright's* people are fond to have such beneficial Prisoners.

A *French* Gentleman, a Cornet in half-pay in the King's Service,[29] but not handcuff'd, who had been about three or four years a Prisoner in this *White-house*, was brought and recommended by *Wright* to the Prisoner's acquaintance. These two Prisoners conversed in *French*, and unmannerly *Wright* demanded to know the subject of their conservation, he behaving himself like the *Grand-Turk*, and treating those about him as his Slaves.

The Prisoner and others think the Cornet unjustly confined, being a very sensible and rational Gentleman, who told the Prisoner that his Mother in-law had confined him, lest he should have more Children by her Daughter his lawful Wife, but be that as it will it appears at present he wants no Confinement: The Cornet complained that Dr. *Monro* signed an Attestation of his being a Lunatick twice a year, that his friends might receive his pay. He said that the Doctor had a Guinea for each Subscription. No man can escape being called to an Account for his Actions at the Day of Judgment, tho' he may escape punishment from men.

Wright went to *London* before dinner, and the Prisoner conversed with the Cornet most of that day, dined with him handcuff'd, and played at Draughts with him and *Wright's* Wife in the afternoon; and behaved himself with uncommon Composure and Serenity. The Cornet and the Prisoner walked up and down, and beheld with Grief the many miserable Objects in the *White-house*, a Sight exceeding disagreeable to any man of a compassionate disposition, there being about forty or fifty Patients, some of them at four or five shillings a week. And *Wright* designed to confine the Prisoner in that *Great-Madhouse*, even tho' *Wightman* had engaged to pay a guinea a week for him: But the Prisoner fearing that that was to be *out of the Frying-pan into the Fire*, most earnestly begged of *Wright's* Wife to send him back to his former room in the private *Madhouse*; and in the evening with great difficulty prevailed with her, having told her that he would pursue *Wright* for detaining him so long unjustly a Prisoner in his Madhouse.

Thursday, April 6. The Keeper knowing that Dr. *Monro* was coming to visit the Prisoner, thought fit to take off his handcuffs and chains and the Doctor came between eight and nine o'clock in the morning, and *Wightman* with him: The Prisoner expostulated with *Monro* about his unjust Confinement, but *Monro*, like a bird upon the wing, made only a standing visit. *Wright's* Wife was this morning in the private Madhouse, and told *Davis* that the Prisoner had behaved very well at her house yesterday.

The Prisoner at night was chained to the Bedstead as usual.

Friday, April 7. In the morning *Davis* unchained the Prisoner, and by Dr. *Monro's* advice allowed him to walk in the garden, yet fearing his Escape he was again handcuff'd; for that fear was the reason of his handcuffs and chains.

Saturday, April 8. *Davis* unchained the Prisoner, but handcuffed him. About four o'clock *Scot* and *Oswald's* Wife came, and he prudently at this time received them in a very composed and decent manner, treated them with Tea, and conversed with them for about two or three hours, while he touching a little upon *Wightman's* bad conduct, said, he wanted to go to visit his friends at *Southgate*.[30] *Oswald's* Wife said that, if he was always as well as at that time, he might go any where. The Prisoner said that his Behaviour at *White's-Alley* was not like that of a Madman. *Oswald's* Wife answered, that he used to bear every thing, and not be provoked. *Scot* at this time spoke against the wretched Management of those who had sent the Prisoner to *Bethnal-Green*; but the poor silly young man was afterwards taught to speak otherwise.

Oswald's Wife coming from *Wightman*, then her Lodger, desired the Prisoner to write a letter to his Father,[31] for she said that *Wightman* was afraid he would not approve of his Conduct towards his Son; and the Prisoner replied, That no Man else in his right Wits could approve of it; that he had writ on *Thursday* last to his Father, and that if he was to write again, it would be in the same stile: But it seems this letter was intercepted, as many were afterwards. It is amazing that this *Virago* should after this long visit give credit to *Wightman's* Lies and Slanders against the Prisoner, namely that he was at certain times well, and at other times ill, which was one of vile *Wightman's* Calumnies: But the woman was loth to disoblige a good Lodger, and having, as it is said, by *Wightman's* Order, taken a room for the Prisoner at *Bethnal-Green*, whereby she became an Accomplice, she might be afraid of Punishment. This Woman is noted for being a scolding gossiping Woman, and has vigorously acted her part with the weapon of a false scolding Tongue. It seems that Mr. *Horton* thought this masculine Woman in the *Poultry* a dangerous and disagreeable Companion several years ago, for he expressly charged Mrs. *Horton* to keep no company with her.

Dr. *Rogers* of *Stamford* visited the Prisoner in the evening with Mr. *Colcot*

Master of the *Castle-Tavern* in *Holbourn*,[32] with whom the Prisoner talked very sensibly; and the Doctor desired *Davis* to take off the Prisoner's handcuffs, but to no purpose.

The Prisoner was at night chained to his bedstead as usual.

The *Lord's Day, April* 9. *Davis* having unchained the Prisoner, he was reading in his New Testament, when *Wright* the Gaoler of the Madhouse came into his room, viewed his hands and feet, and then quickly went away; soon after *Davis* entered the room, and told the Prisoner he had express orders to handcuff him which the Prisoner meekly submitted to.

The Prisoner was at night chain'd to his bedstead as usual.

Monday, April 10. The Prisoner being unchained by *Davis* was not handcuff'd till noon by *Wall*; and having received Pen, Ink and Paper from *Scot* the day before, the Prisoner wrote some letters to *Samuel Reynardson* Esq;[33] one of the six Clerks in Chancery, and several of his friends, which he delivered to one *William Hollowel* servant to *Matthew Jackson* the Barber on *Bethnal-Green*, with money to put them in the Peny-Post; but *Wall* soon after pursued the Journeyman by *Wright's* express Order, and took from him the letters and money, which the Prisoner did not know of till some months after his miraculous Escape. *Wall* says he delivered all the letters (being eight in number) to *Wright*. The Prisoner receiving no answer in a few days, and being afraid that his friends neglected to assist him in obtaining his liberty, wrote to some Persons of Distinction, but the letters were all intercepted. Mr. *Kelsey Bull* Linen-Draper at the *Bear* in *Cornhill*, and Mr. *Frederick Bull* at the *Tea-Chest* over-against the *Royal-Exchange*, kindly visited him this afternoon, when the Prisoner spoke to them very sensibly, and then told them of his barbarous Usage.

The Prisoner was chained at night to his bedstead as usual.

Tuesday, April 11. *Davis* having taken off the chain, the Prisoner was handcuff'd. In the afternoon *Scot* came to him with half a pound of Green Tea,[34] as a present from Mr. *Frederick Bull*, who had the day before been to visit the Prisoner. *Scot* owned that Mr. *Frederick Bull* declared to him, that the Prisoner spoke as sensibly as ever he had known him to do formerly.

The Prisoner at night was again chained to his bedstead.

Wednesday, April 12. The Prisoner was unchained by *Davis*, but was handcuff'd. In the afternoon Mr. *Henry Newcome* Master of the famous Boarding-School at *Hackney*,[35] with his Son, Mr. *Peter*, came to visit the Prisoner. After some conversation the Prisoner asked Mr. *Newcome* his judgment of him, who replied, "That if he had not seen him in this place, he should not have suspected him of the least Disorder, no more than when he saw him acting rationally in his own shop." Mean while Dr. *Rogers* came in, and after Mr. *Newsome* and his Son were gone, the Doctor and the Prisoner talked very rationally about their worldly concerns.

The Prisoner at night was chained to his bedstead as usual.

Thursday, April 13. Dr. *Monro* coming to *Bethnal-Green,* as was usual, the Prisoner was neither chain'd nor handcuff'd. About eight o'clock in the morning the Doctor came, and was courteously received by the Prisoner, who desired him to sit down. The Prisoner seriously reasoned the matter with *Monro,* why he ordered him physick six days before he had seen him, and why he took an account of his case, not from himself but from *Wightman,* a proud and self-conceited man; to which the Doctor replied, *That he understood his own Business.* But the question was about *Monro's* doing his business.

Monro said farther, That *Wightman* had desired him to ask the Prisoner, how he expected to get out of this dismal place? The Prisoner answered, That he came thither with submission to the Will of God, and he waited God's time for his Deliverance. *Monro* said, Do you expect that a Miracle will be wrought for your Deliverance? The Prisoner replied, That he had writ to some persons of the first Rank, and if they did not assist him, he would write to others, in order to be sound in the use of Means. *Monro* was so unmannerly as to enquire, To whom he had written? But the Prisoner told him, He knew that best himself. The Prisoner said to *Monro,* that he wanted to go to *Southgate* this day, and that no body had power to hinder him from going; and asked *Monro,* Who could hinder him? *Monro* replied that *Wightman* would, and so went off. This conversation between the Prisoner and *Monro* was in presence of *Wright.* Presently after *Monro* was gone, *Davis* handcuff'd the Prisoner for fear of his escaping and going to *Southgate.*

The Prisoner was afterwards informed, that the Rev. Mr. *Farmer* (who lodges at *Oswald's*) told, that *Monro* had said to Wightman and his Associates; *"That the Prisoner was a Man of Sense and Learning, and of a good Education, but that he was a great* Enthusiast; *and he believed that he thought that God would send an Angel from Heaven, or would work some Miracle for his Deliverance":* But the Doctor misrepresented the Prisoner, for that he is no Stoick, but believed in the Promise and Providence of God to be delivered in the use of Means.[36]

About two hours after *Monro* was gone, *Wightman* came while the Prisoner was at his devotion: He waited some time in the garden, and was afterwards received very coldly by the Prisoner: He spoke nothing till *Wightman* began, and soon told him, that he came to speak about moving him from this unhappy place to private lodgings. The Prisoner was glad to hear of it, and withal told him that he wanted to go to *Southgate.* To which *Wightman* replied in a passion, that, if he talked of *Southgate,* he would not release him at all, for he knew his Case: But the Prisoner answered, that God knew his Case best, and fell into a flood of tears. This was while one *Gracious Butts* was present, who came to call for *Wightman.* The Prisoner asked *Wightman* what authority he had over him? He answered, That he would afterwards account to the Prisoner for what he had done. *Wightman* told the Prisoner the reason of his being again handcuff'd, was his talking to Dr. *Monro* of his going to *Southgate*. Mean while *Wright* came in, and began to incense *Wightman* by insinuating that the Prisoner had talked against him to *Monro* that morning; but the Prisoner artfully prevented that conversation, fearing it might provoke *Wightman* to be the more averse to his Releasement, and earnestly desired to be released that day. *Wightman* said, that he would not release him at all if he was so peremptory, and that he had some preparations to make for his Releasement, which should be done as soon as possible. *Wightman* went away with *Butts*.

The Prisoner was chained at night to his bedstead as usual.

Friday, April 14. *Davis* came in the morning and unchained the Prisoner, who this day walked in the garden, and was visited about noon by one *John Robinson* an old acquaintance, who stayed with him about two or three hours, and hath declared that he behaved very sensibly. *Scot* came in the afternoon, and brought a letter to the Prisoner from his excellent and pious Friend the Rev. Mr. *John Willison* of *Dundee*, with a present of a book, called, *Plain Catechising*, which he had just published, and which the Prisoner read with much pleasure.

At night he was chained by *Davis* as usual.

This day is famous for the commencement of a Confederacy or Combination of *Wightman* and some of *Oswald's* friends to judge of the Prisoner's Case, to countenance *Wightman's* Proceedings, and to order what should be done with the Prisoner, as will appear by the next day's Journal. Cunning *Wightman*, and his Creature Dr. *Monro*, who had told *Wightman* of his illegal Management, willing to slip the collar off their own necks, had got Dr. *John Guyse*, Mr. *William Crookshank*, *John Cooke* Apothecary, and *John Oswald* Bookseller, to meet at *Oswald's* in the *Poultry*; when their Dictator *Wightman* informed them that he designed to set the Prisoner at liberty, and artfully desired their Concurrence in a sort of Decree, that the Prisoner should first sign a letter, importing that he should behave peaceably at his lodgings; and they yielded to decree the same: but like thoughtless men they did not demand to see the Letter that was to be sent by their Decree, as if they had acted by implicit Faith in *Wightman*, leaving the forming of it wholly to him.

Their blind Decrees made the Prisoner afterwards call this pretended Court *A* BLIND-BENCH, in a just contempt of those that had no power to decree any thing concerning him.

Saturday, April 15. *Davis* having unchained the Prisoner in the morning gave him some purging physick; and in the afternoon *Gracious Butts* came from *Wightman* with two letters dated this day. They were both writ by *Wightman*. One of them was directed to the Prisoner, wherein *Wightman* acquainted him, that the above-mentioned Persons had yesterday met at *Oswald's* in the *Poultry*, and had agreed that the Prisoner should go to private lodgings, provided he would sign the other letter, which was penn'd and writ by *Wightman*, and came at the same time by *Butts*. *Wightman* himself says in this letter, that the Prisoner comes not under the denomination of a Madman. If so, why did you, *Wightman* send him to *Bethnal-Green*? But *Wightman* some times forgets himself, tho' a Liar ought to have a good Memory; and some of his own letters will be good Evidences against himself. The Prisoner's pretended Disorder ebbed or flowed as it served the Interest and Ends of *Wightman* and his Creature *Monro*: But time will determine whether the Prisoner or those two persons acted the most disorderly or most illegal Part.

Wightman was Clerk to the Prisoner, and penned his letter for him, and drew up a pretty full Pardon for himself for Crimes that were past, and an Indulgence for any thing he be might guilty of afterwards. Among other shocking Expressions this that follows is remarkable: *"I shall not Blame you, nor any of my friends for any thing that has happened or may happen."* Tho' the Prisoner did not sign this letter, yet he thought it convenient not to send it back to *Wightman*, but has carefully kept it to be of use upon the Trial before the Court of the *King's Bench*.[37]

After the Prisoner had read those letters, he desired *Butts* to withdraw; and after being earnest in Prayer for God's Direction, he called in *Butts,* and bid him tell *Wightman* that he received him in a composed and calm manner, that he would give all possible assurance that he should behave himself peaceably at his lodgings, but that he had no reason to sign the letter, but many reasons to the contrary, and therefore absolutely refused to do it. *Butts* replied, that he hoped the Prisoner would excuse him; because, tho' he had brought a Hackney-Coach to carry him from *Bethnal-Green*, he had peremptory Orders not to carry him from thence without signing the letter, and so he went off. *Wightman* had also sent a letter by *Butts* to *Wright* to release the Prisoner, which Mrs. *Wright* opening sent to the tavern for her Husband; but all in vain, because the Prisoner had not signed the letter.

At night the Prisoner was chain'd as usual.

The *Lord's Day, April* 16. The Prisoner was unchained as usual in the morning. *Wright* came into his room about ten o'clock, and took him by the hand, kindly saying, that next *Tuesday* he should go in his Coach with his Wife to see Lord *Castlemain's* house. Some time after, *John Robinson* came, and stayed with the Prisoner the greatest part of the day. About four o'clock *Claudius Bonner* the Compositor with his Wife, came with a written Order from *Oswald* to see the Prisoner: and soon after Dr. *Rogers* and Mr. *Colcot* Master of the *Castle-Tavern* in *Holbourn* came in a Coach, with whom the Prisoner talked very sensibly. They stay'd a considerable time, and drank Tea with him.

At night the Prisoner was chained as usual.

Monday, April 17. The Prisoner was unchained in the morning, and after dinner the Rev. Mr. *James Wood* (who lives on *Bethnal-Green*) paid him a most respectful visit, to whom the Prisoner read *Wightman's* Letter, and told him of his positive and flat Denial to comply with the contents thereof; and Mr. *Wood* said that he was in the right not to sign it. Next day Mr. *Wood* acquainted his Friends in the City, that he had found the Prisoner in very good Sense and Reason, and that he thought he had been ill-used, and earnestly wished that means were found for his Deliverance, which language greatly chagrined *Wightman*, *Oswald* and other Accomplices.

In the evening *Scot* brought from *Wightman* the Prisoner's Account-Books, and the following Letter, spell'd and capital'd as in the Original.

To Mr. A. C.
> London 17 Aprile 1738.

Dear Sir,

Mr Scot *the bearer hereof brings you the Books, that you may settle Doctor* Rogers *Accompt, Which for Your ease I have draun out, and left the Ballance open, least you should have something to add for your trouble about his Bond, Which I have delivered him up, taking his Receipt as from You, by my hands – Whereof I doubt not your approbation – You'll observe an excrescence of 10 Bottles Gout-oyll accompted for more than you have gott, which I apprehend arises from a Mistake in the last Accompt, in accompting to him for 26 Bottles Retailed, whereas I find no more than 18 Bottles in the Book from 16 Octo. to 3 Jan. 1738 – Please write me an Order to pay Doctor* Rogers *Ballance after you have struck it.*

I am sorry you should Resolve to continue where You are, contrary to the opinion of all your good friends, Doctor Rogers *and Doctor* Stuckley[38] *not Excepted, it is to me a full proof that your disease continues in too great a Measure – I will not urge you to sign the Letter I sent you*; But I think, if you transcribed it *verbatim*, With your own hand, signed and sent it to me by the bearer you would do wisely and Wel, *and* in that Case *I would come my self to morrou morning early, and Cary you to your Privat Lodging Nigh* Hide park Corner – *I truly am*

> *Your faithful humble Servant*

> Robert Wightman

Ps. *If their is any thing in my Draught of your Letter that is disagreable, pray write one your self, possibly it may please Your other friends, and in that case it shall please me.*

Scot said that *Wightman* very much wanted an answer to this letter: But the Prisoner refused giving any answer to this cunning and artful letter, being determined to make him suffer the Penalties due by Law for his uncommon Crimes. A judicious Attorney observed, upon reading this Letter, that *Wightman* did not write to the Prisoner, as if he had thought him a Madman. It will appear plainly to the reader, that *Wightman* was only willing to set the Prisoner at liberty upon an Assurance of his Pardon.

At night the Prisoner was chain'd to his bedstead as usual.

Tuesday, April 18. The Prisoner was unchained as usual. In the morning *Wright* came into his room, and saw him engaged with his Account-books, and asked him what he was about? He told *Wright* that he was settling Dr. *Rogers*'s Account, and so *Wright* went off. Some time after Dr. *Rogers* came, and the Prisoner with solid judgment settled all that intricate Account to the Doctor's satisfaction, whereby it appeared that the Prisoner owed the Doctor only seven Pounds odd Money (whereas *Wightman*, in his Draught of the Account had brought in the Prisoner debtor for nineteen Pounds odd Money) for which the Doctor desired a Bill upon *Wightman*, which the Prisoner absolutely refused, but gave him a Bill upon *Scot*, which was punctually obeyed.[39]

The Doctor owned to the Prisoner that he thought him as sound in judgment as ever he had seen him in his Life; nor could *Wightman* think him a Madman, when he sent him his Account-books, and desired him to draw a Bill upon him.

Wednesday, April 19. *Davis* having unchain'd the Prisoner in the morning, brought him a Vomit by *Monro*'s Order: *John Robinson* came and saw him during the severe Operation; and at night *Davis* by *Wright*'s Order, again chained him to his bedstead.

This day the Rev. Mr. *Wood* came again to visit the Prisoner (before he went to *Bath*[40]) with the Rev. Mr. *Masters*, the Rev. Mr. *Mitchel*, and Mr. *Holland* Watchmaker and his Wife. Mr. *Wood* told *Wright*, that having visited the Prisoner the other day, he conversed with him an hour and an half, and found his behaviour to be very good and very sensible, and therefore blamed *Wright* for detaining him a Prisoner. Mr. *Wood* farther said to *Wright*, '*My Character is as good as yours at any time; and I can declare that the Prisoner can give as good an Account of his Actions, as you can do of yours.*' Upon which guilty *Wright* marched off, but quickly sent *Turner* the Keeper of his *Great-Madhouse* to tell Mr. *Wood* that if he did not forthwith go out of his Premises, he would find means to oblige him to make off: And so Mr. *Wood*, with his friends, prudently departed, as afraid of some scurvy consequence.

Thursday, April 20. *Davis* having unchained the Prisoner, Dr. *Monro* came to see him in the morning, with whom the Prisoner expostulated about his unjust Imprisonment, having never been disordered or mad. The Doctor, without returning any Answer, went off. This was the fourth and last visit he ever received from Dr. *Monro*. The Prisoner received this morning by the Peny-Post a joint Letter, dated *April* 19, from Dr. *Stukeley* and Dr. *Rogers*, (the only one that he received from any person by the Peny-Post) wherein these two ingenious Gentlemen acquainted him, that they had been with *Wightman*, who promised to come as this morning to pay off his lodgings, and *let him go where he pleased*, and *be at full liberty*. Guilty *Wightman* had promised, but did not perform that promise, fearing he could get no Indemnity from the Prisoner for his unjust and cruel Management.

The Prisoner wrote a respectful answer to those Physicians, and returned them hearty thanks for their great care and kindness, but told them that he was resolved to vindicate his own Character in a legal manner, as the only way to recover it.

The Prisoner was chain'd at night as usual.

Friday, April 21. The Prisoner was unchain'd in the morning, and towards noon the Prisoner's Servant *Scot*, with one Mr. *Macbean*, came to acquaint him that *Oswald* had been at the Prisoner's Shop with a message from *Wightman*, demanding of *Scot* to deliver up to him the Accounts of the Prisoner's Affairs, and of the Books in his Shop: But the Prisoner charged *Scot* by a written Order, not to obey the said Demand of *Wightman*, and by him sent to *Wightman* the following letter:

Mr. Robert Wightman,

Mr. Scot *surprises me by telling me that you want him to give up the Accounts of my Shop and Affairs to you. Pray, do I owe you any Money? Pray, what Right have you to make such a Demand? I know no more Right than a* Turk *or an* Indian. *As to your unaccountable and mad Steps in confining me in a Madhouse, I design, as God directs me, to vindicate my Character, and to bring you to due Punishment according to the Demerits of your uncommon Crimes. I know no Confusion my Business is in; if any want to see me about Business, they may write or come down to me at* Bethnal-Green. *I desire you may write me what conceited Pretences, or what sort of Reasons you can imagine for making this Demand. I believe before you be much older, your Heart will ake for your injurious Treatment of me. If you meddle with any of my Affairs, it shall be to the utmost Peril to yourself, and you may expect to suffer the utmost Penalties of Law. Pray expect you are to suffer, and to give an Account upon Oath about your meddling already with my Affairs. Dated at* Bethnal-Green April 21, 1738.

A.C.

The Prisoner gave *Scot* a packet of letters upon his promise faithfully to deliver them into the Peny-Post, but *Scot*, like an unfaithful servant,[41] delivered them to *Wightman*.

At night the Prisoner was chain'd as usual.

Saturday, April 23. The Prisoner was unchained in the morning, and took a dose of physick prescribed by *Monro*; and in the afternoon Dr. *Guyse*, and Mr. *Guyse* his Son, and Mr. *Cooke* the Apothecary, and *Oswald* came to see the Prisoner, and entred his room without ceremony, or giving the least notice by any of the servants, whereby he was much surprised, but had presence of mind to order *Oswald* to retire, and blamed the rest for bringing him thither, whom they must know to be wholly disagreeable to him. Dr. *Guyse* appeared to be too earnest to screen *Wightman* and his Bookseller *Oswald* from Punishment, and soon discovered his Errand by exhorting the

Prisoner to give *Wightman* a full Pardon; and knowing the Prisoner had a great esteem for him, the Doctor pressed it with much importunity and grave authority, even after the Prisoner had desired the company to call another cause, telling them that he thought it his Duty to vindicate his Character, and make *Wightman* suffer for the Injuries he had done him.

The Prisoner complained much to those three visitors of *Monro*'s conduct, and of his prescribing physick to him about a week before he had visited him, and of *Monro*'s never enquiring about the operation of his physick. Mr. *Cooke* said he supposed he might ask some of those questions at the Keeper. The Prisoner asked *Davis*, who told him that *Monro* had not asked him any questions. Pray, *Monro*, be pleased for the future, to shew some Concern for those you prescribe physick to, and enquire about its Operation, lest any body should say that you have not so much Concern for them as a Farmer hath for his Horses.

The Prisoner had ordered Tea to be brought in, and when the Maid was bringing the Tea, Mr. *Cooke* asked Dr. *Guyse* whether he would stay and drink some; but the Doctor refused it in a disrespectful manner, being chagrined that he had not prevailed with the Prisoner for obtaining *Wightman*'s Pardon. The Prisoner earnestly requested the Doctor to pray by him, which he refused.

The Prisoner having finished a letter to his Father, giving him an account of all the unjust and barbarous Treatment he had met with, and of his Design to pursue *Wightman* in a legal manner, Mr. *Cooke* received it, promising to forward it to the General Post-Office; but the Prisoner found afterwards, that those three visitors, with *Oswald*, opened the letter, and delivered it to *Wightman*. The Prisoner has been told that it is Felony wickedly and maliciously to intercept letters; if so, those four men are four Felons: But what this intercepting of letters deserves in Law, must be decided by Law. The Prisoner behaved courteously towards them; but as they came without ceremony, so they went off without ceremony.

After they were gone *Davis* told the Prisoner, that *Oswald* had asked him how the Prisoner conducted himself. To which *Davis* answered, that in his opinion he was very well, very quiet and very peaceable. Pray, *Oswald*, how can you answer to your own Conscience for your gross Lies to people in your shop, and for your assisting *Wightman* to call the *Blind-Bench* together, for going to Mr. *Gines* with *Wightman*, and being his Porter and Attendant from time to time when he was endeavouring to get his Neck out of the Collar, by injuring the Prisoner more and more, and wickedly aiming to send him to *Bethlehem*. To be sure Dr. *Guyse*'s Conduct made the Prisoner very uneasy, as was observed by the Housemaid, he not expecting it from his faithful and beloved Pastor.

The Prisoner was chained at night as usual.

The *Lord's Day*, *April* 23. The Prisoner being unchain'd spent the *Sabbath* religiously. He was visited by *John Robinson* and *William Simpson*, and in the afternoon by Mr. *Goodwin* of *Broadstreet* and his Son, to whom he told his uncommon Case. Having read to Mr. *Goodwin Wightman*'s Letter for his Pardon, Mr. *Goodwin* approved of the Prisoner's not signing it, for that it was a cunning letter. The Rev. *Hugh Colley* of *Mile-End-Green*,[42] with a Gentleman of his acquaintance, came in the evening and visited the Prisoner, who was of the same opinion about him with his friend Mr. *Newcome*, who had visited the Prisoner the 12th Instant. Mr. *Colley* asked, what sort of a man he could be that confined the Prisoner.

The Prisoner was chained at night as usual.

Monday, April 24. The Prisoner was unchained in the morning, but after dinner it was *Davis*'s sovereign Will and Pleasure to chain him again to his bedstead; but before he did it he gave the Prisoner a Blow on the Face, which almost beat out his Eye, and much disfigured his Face, of which he was not recovered for some weeks. Mr. *Turner* the Apothecary with his Wife and Mr. *Mind* the Engraver came this day into his room, and saw him thus chained and abused. The Prisoner delivered to Mr. *Turner* a packet to be delivered to *Scot*, in which there were three or four Copies of an Advertisement to be printed in the News-papers, giving an account of his unjust and barbarous Treatment, and of his Resolution to pursue *Wightman* for his unjust Conduct: But *Davis* would not let the Gentleman carry this packet off, but seized it and the money given him by the Prisoner to send it by a Porter; and it is supposed the packet was afterwards sent to *Wightman*.

The Prisoner was chain'd at night as usual.

Tuesday, April 25. The Prisoner was unchained in the morning by *Davis*, who declared his sorrow for the Blow he had given him. The Prisoner sent to acquaint *Wright*'s Wife with the Cruelty of *Davis*: She came to visit him, and seemingly was concerned at the severe Blow, therefore she ordered *Davis* no more to wait upon him, but put him intirely under the care of one *Anna Thomson*, that had been a Patient formerly, but was now a Servant in the private Madhouse. *Bonner* the Compositor at the Printing Office in *Wild Court*, where the Prisoner had been Corrector for five or six years, came again to visit him, with a written Order from *Wightman*; and the Prisoner putting confidence in him, shewed him a Copy of the foresaid Advertisement, but he went that night to *Wightman*, and, it is supposed, first acquainted him with it. *Wright*'s Wife gave this afternoon the Prisoner a visit, and he reasoned with her about the Injustice of his Confinement, and told her that he had been always in his Senses from the beginning of his Confinement. She was not so blind as not to see that he was not a fit Person for her house, and said at this time, "*Why don't you go to a Country-Lodging, for we desire not your Confinement for our small Profit?*" But why did not she open the Doors of the Prison, and let him go?

The Prisoner was chained at night as usual.

Wednesday, April 26. The Prisoner was unchained in the morning. *Scot* came early to acquaint him that *Wightman* sent for him last night, and had ordered him to demand the foresaid Account-Books, which the Prisoner refused to deliver, for *Wightman* nor no man else had any Right to demand his Property. The Prisoner not having fully discovered *Scot's* unfaithfulness, communicated to him several Copies of the foresaid Advertisement, desiring *Scot* to deliver them carefully to the several Printers of the News-papers; yet *Scot* basely delivered them to *Wightman*. *Wightman* was apprised of the Prisoner's Intention to publish him in the News-papers, and therefore sent a Letter by *Scot* this morning to *Wright* to seize all his Papers, and not to allow him to have Pen, Ink and Paper. Soon after *Scot* was gone, the Tyrant *Wright* came in with great Authority, and violently seized the Prisoner's Account-Books, Papers, Copies, Pen and Ink, and every thing he found. The Prisoner commanded the Villain to restore his Books and Papers, else it should cost him dear another time; but he was deaf to all the Prisoner could say. Then *Wright* ordered *Davis, Turner* and *Caesar* the Black to go and pull off the Prisoner's Shoes, and chain him strongly to the bedstead. The Prisoner charged the Ruffians to remember what they did, for they must answer for it another time: But they replied, We must obey our Master's Orders.

The aforesaid *Anna Thomson* had strict Orders given her to lock the Prisoner's room night and day, and to let none come to see him, but by an Order from *Wightman*. This cruel Treatment was to Prevent the Prisoner from either giving or receiving letters: And from henceforward the Prisoner was never unchained, until he made his amazing Escape *May* 31, so that every night he was forced to go in by the foot of the bed, and his Breeches were never off for the space of five weeks.

Thursday, April 27. The Prisoner still chained night and day, was told this morning by *Davis*, that *Oswald* and his Wife were at the door to wait upon him, but the Prisoner charged him not to bring them in, for he would not at all see them upon any pretence whatsoever: But his two Friends Serjeant-Major *Cruden* and his Wife came with an Order to see him, which by great importunity they had obtained from *Monro*, and stayed with him about three hours: *Oswald* and his Wife were only falsly and artfully said by *Davis* to be at the door, that his two Friends might not be admitted to see him; but happily the Prisoner knew Serjeant *Cruden's* voice, when he was intreating to come in, and expressed his ready inclination to see him. They were agreeably surpriz'd to find him intirely sedate and judicious, contrary to the false reports raised against him, and told them this morning by three false men *Wightman, Monro* and *Wright*. They told the Prisoner, that having asked *Monro* that morning, whether his Distemper was Lunacy? the Doctor said, no, but only a Fever on the Nerves.

The Prisoner gave his Friends a plain and pertinent Account of the

Barbarities he had hitherto undergone, and that he could easily get out, would he sign a Pardon for *Wightman* according to his earnest Request, but that he would never do it, thinking it a dishonourable thing. The Serjeant being much concerned for the Prisoner, and afraid of his Enemies entring into a Design to murder him, humbly requested him to comply with any thing to get out of that dismal place: The Prisoner replied, that he would sign no Paper, but what he would stand by, and that God would take care of him. The Serjeant said, that *Wright*, before he came in, had shewn him an Order from *Wightman* to seize the Prisoner's Account-Books, Pen and Ink, and every thing else. Mean while *Wright* came in, and taking the Prisoner kindly by the hand, told him, that he indeed had a Letter from *Wightman*, ordering him to do what he did the day before. The Serjeant and his Wife were moved at the Prisoner's present afflicted Situation, but were glad to see him bear it so patiently, and withal told him, that his cunning and powerful Enemies designed to send him to *Bethlehem* on *Saturday* se'nnight, as *Monro* had told them that morning.

This much affected the Prisoner, tho' he was glad of the Discovery which he found in a few days to be the Decree of the BLIND-BENCH, who had agreed to keep it a Secret from the Prisoner till they could get the Porters of *Bethlehem* to carry him from *Bethnal-Green* to *Morefields*;[43] but Murder will out. Mrs. *Cruden* stepping out into the garden, asked *Anna Thomson*, if the Prisoner was always as well and sensible as now; and *Thomson* answered, that she never saw him otherwise.

The Prisoner, by the Help of a Pencil and a piece of Paper from his Friend the Serjeant, wrote the names of many Friends, to whom he desired the Serjeant to go and acquaint them with his deplorable Case, that they might come and see him, and find means to extricate him out of that hellish Place, which the Serjeant carefully obeyed, tho' in vain; for people are naturally shy of concerning themselves with a person in the Prisoner's afflicted situation, some of them having been poisoned by *Wightman* and his Accomplices.

After the Prisoner's Friends were gone, whom he heartily thanked for their kind and seasonable visit; he being much cast down with the Thoughts of *Bethlehem*, as what would make him intirely useless, (few considering the Injustice of the Case) and render his Works and former Usefulness despicable, went to his usual Asylum the Throne of Grace, and prayed earnestly that God would discover ways and means for his Deliverance in due time, and would frustrate the devices of his Enemies.

Friday, April 28. The Prisoner being chain'd to the bedstead night and day as before, was only visited by his Keeper *Anna Thomson*, others being denied access.

Saturday, April 29. The Prisoner desiring *Anna Thomson* to bring him some Paper and Ink; she replied, she durst not do it, they having solemnly sworn her that she should do no such thing, else she could be no longer his

Keeper; and in the afternoon *William Hollowel* the Barber's Man on the *Green*, coming to shave him, the Prisoner gave him some money to bring him Paper and Ink, when he return'd with his Periwig; but the Ruffian *Davis* suspecting it, rifled *Hollowel* on his return, and seized the Paper and Ink.

The *Lord's Day, April* 30. The Prisoner being still chain'd night and day worshipped God alone, having none to join with him. In the afternoon *Oswald's* Maid and Apprentice came as Spies to visit him, and asked him about Serjeant *Cruden's* meddling in his Affairs: The Prisoner told them that he had impowered him so to do, but that he had not impowered *Wightman* and his Accomplices to meddle in any of his Concerns. The Prisoner observing the Apprentice to have a Bible in his pocket, with much difficulty prevailed with him to leave it. *Oswald's* Wife sent afterwards for it, but the Prisoner did not regard her.

Monday, May 1. The Prisoner being still chain'd night and day had no visitors, but comforted himself with his Bible and Devotions.

Tuesday, May 2. The Prisoner being chained night and day had no visitors, and could only converse with himself and his God.

Wednesday, May 3. The Prisoner being chain'd night and day was visited by *Hollowel* the Barber's Man, with whom he again prevailed to bring him some Paper and Ink, which he artfully conveyed to him when he brought his Periwig; and this day he wrote several Letters to his Friends, especially about the barbarous Design of sending him to *Bethlehem. Wright* came this day and told the Prisoner that *Wightman* had sent for his Account-Books. He answered, that *Wightman* had no Right to concern himself with him or his Account-Books, and that if *Wright* delivered them up to him, he would make him answerable. *Wright* thought fit for once not to obey *Wightman.*

Thursday, May 4. The Prisoner being still chain'd night and day, *Oswald's* Maid came in the morning, and earnestly requested to know who informed him of the Decree of the BLIND-BENCH for sending him to *Bethlehem*, but he gave her no satisfaction. After staying eight hours he asked her seriously, what signs of madness she had found in him? She could not instance any, but only foolishly mentioned his peremptory Refusal to see *Wightman, Oswald* and his Wife.

The Prisoner earnestly requested her to give him some discovery of the Design of sending him to *Bethlehem:* She replied, with much reluctance, that it had been decreed by the BLIND-BENCH, who had faithfully promised to keep it a mighty Secret from the Prisoner and his Friends; and that *Wightman* and *Horton* (one of the BLIND-BENCH,) had endeavoured to get the Officers of the Parish of St. *Christopher's*, where the Prisoner's Shop stood, to assist in getting him sent to *Bethlehem*, which she understood the Parish was to do.[44]

The Prisoner had writ several letters yesterday, and waited an opportunity of sending them: But he discovered that *Oswald's* Maid was not a fit person to be trusted with them. *Anna Thomson* told the Prisoner, after the Maid was gone, that the Servants looked thro' the lock-hole of the door, when *Oswald*'s Maid was with him, to see if he was writing, they suspecting the Maid would carry some letters for him. *Thomson* said, that they were to have searched the Maid narrowly, had not they been satisfied that the Prisoner did not write any letters at that time. The Prisoner this evening demanded his Account-Books of *Davis*, which *Wright* had delivered to him, and *Davis* thought fit to restore them.

Friday, May 5. The Prisoner being chained night and day rose betimes to write a letter to the Governors of *Bethlehem*, and also one to the Officers of St. *Christopher*'s Parish, and some other letters. The letter to the said Governors was as moving and affecting a letter as could be penned, for he was perhaps more afraid of *Bethlehem* than of Death, and this letter could not fail to make an impression upon Men of Humanity and of natural Compassion. He sent on purpose for *Hollowel* about noon to shave him, and with much ado persuaded him to conceal the packet of letters in his Breeches, and carry it to the Peny-Post on *Bethnal-Green*, which came safe to Serjeant *Cruden* who took care of the inclosed.

In the evening *John Duncan* came to visit the Prisoner by an Order from *Oswald*'s Apprentice. The Prisoner bid him tell *Wightman* that he intended to pursue him to the utmost for the many Injuries he had done him, and desired him to call upon Mr. *Harwood* the Attorney to be so good as to come and see him. *Duncan* told the Prisoner that he would do well to be cautious to whom he intrusted his Letters or Comissions, for he had reason to believe that every body betrayed him. The said *Duncan* told the Prisoner that *Oswald*'s Maid was not to have liberty to see him any more because she had declared that the Prisoner was well.

Saturday, May 6. The Prisoner, being still chained night and day, devoted this morning and every *Saturday* morning to Prayer and other religious Duties. He was uneasy and cast down in Spirit, fearing the Porters of *Bethlehem* should come to fetch him thither, and acquainted *Davis* with his Concern, who told him, that he need not be afraid of their coming to day, for that they usually come betimes in the morning, having their Orders over night.

Serjeant *Cruden*, at the Prisoner's earnest Request, writ to many of his Acquaintance about his unjust Imprisonment and barbarous Treatment, which greatly chagrin'd *Wightman, Oswald* and other Accomplices. *Wightman*, in his profound Penetration, penn'd a threatning and false letter to send to Serjeant *Cruden*, and desired the favour of *Scot* to sign it, wherein *Scot* told Serjeant *Cruden*, "*That his Conduct in writing to Mr.* Gines *and Mr.* Hitch, *and declaring that the Prisoner at* Bethnal-Green *was not in disorder, and was ill-used in being placed at* Bethnal-Green, *was very much resented by* Wightman *and others.*" *Scot* in this letter falsely asserts, that Serjeant *Cruden* had said, that the Prisoner at *Bethnal-Green* was disordered. In this letter there were several Queries, namely, *"Do you discern the Consequences of such Conduct? Is it not to declare, that Dr.* Monro *and several others are Rogues and Fools?"* If they be Rogues and Fools, they ought to be punished for their Roguery and Folly, and time will discover whether it be so or no. *Scot* says, *"Do you think they will bear with it, and not call you to an Account?"* *Scot* says that *Wightman* will call Serjeant *Cruden* to a severe Account, but the Serjeant was not at all afraid of him, and would not be terrified or wheedled into a Compliance, as others had been.

Serjeant *Cruden, May* 6, answered *Wightman*, and not *Scot*, and justly despised his Threatnings, and writ as follows; *"Last* Saturday, April 29, *I received a very threatning Letter from one* John Scot, *that looks after Mr.* C.*'s Shop, setting forth my bad Conduct in writing to Mr.* Gines *and Mr.* Hitch *that Mr.* C. *is not disorder'd, and is ill-used in being placed at* Bethnal-Green, *is very much resented by Dr.* Monro *and you. I writ, at my Friend's Desire, not only to them but to a great many more of his Acquaintance. As I found him restrained from the use of Pen, Ink, and Paper, I wrote to all of them to the same purport. I intimated to the Persons I writ to, that he was very well in his Senses during the time I was in his Company, which was from nine in the morning till past twelve o'clock. As for what* Scot *writes* [or rather *Wightman*] *of my being satisfied that Mr.* C. *was much disorder'd by the Report of Dr.* Monro *before I saw Mr.* C. *as also by the Report of Mr.* Wright *the Keeper of the Madhouse, I must certainly conclude him mad. But when I came into his Company, I found him quite otherwise, both as to talking and acting during the three hours I spent in his Company. I thought him as rational as ever I saw him during the time of our Acquaintance, which is about seven or eight Years. I find by your Letter to him of* April 17, *that you judged him capable of adjusting Accounts betwixt Dr.* Rogers *and himself. As for his transcribing or signing the Letter you sent him, he is determined not to do it."* Serjeant *Cruden* desired an Answer to this Letter, but *Wightman* never did nor never can answer it, even with the help of his Friend *Monro,* who has ventured every thing to screen *Wightman* from punishment. *Samuel Wall* above-mentioned said that *Wright* and his Wife often give Orders to their Servants, without any regard to Truth, to say of some Prisoners to any that want to see them, that they are very ill, and not fit to be seen; But *Wightman* and *Monro* ought not to have been false Men, as *Wright* and his Servants are.

The *Lord's Day, May* 7. The Prisoner being still chained night and day, was only visited by his Keeper *Anna Thomson,* and spent the *Sabbath* religiously alone.

Monday, May 8. The Prisoner still chained night and day had no visitors, and passed a great part of his time very agreeably in the exercises of Devotion, having such uncommon Peace and Serenity in his Mind, that *Bethnal-Green* was in some respects rather a Palace than a Prison.

Tuesday, May 9. The Prisoner still chain'd night and day had no visitors, and passed his time as usual.

Wednesday, May 10. The Prisoner still chain'd night and day had no visitors, but *Hollowel* that shaved him. *Hollowel* was strictly charged by *Davis* to carry out no letters, and, if he should receive any from the Prisoner, to deliver them to him.

Thursday, May 11. The Prisoner being still chain'd night and day, had no visitors, but passed his time agreeably alone.

Friday, May 12. The Prisoner being still chain'd night and day, had no visitors, and passed his time as usual.

Saturday, May 13. The Prisoner being still chain'd night and day had no visitors, but *Hollowel* that shaved him. The Prisoner every morning dressed as well as he could, that he might appear clean and decent, and in no respect resemble the poor Prisoners on *Bethnal-Green.*

The *Lord's Day, May* 14. The Prisoner being still chain'd night and day, spent the *Sabbath* religiously alone.

Monday, May 15. The Prisoner being still chained night and day had no visitors, and was much employed in writing letters which were barbarously intercepted.

Tuesday, May 16. The Prisoner being still chain'd night and day had a short visit from *Wright* about noon, who came in when the Prisoner was writing letters, but he artfully and speedily concealed every thing in his bed: *Wright* said, *"Why do you not make up matters with* Wightman *and get from hence, and be thankful for being well?"* The Prisoner said very little to him, for he mightily wanted him to be gone, his Letters, Pen and Ink being only concealed by the curtains of the bed being drawn.

Wednesday, May 17. The Prisoner being still chain'd night and day had no visitors but *Hollowel* that shaved him.

Thursday, May 18. The Prisoner being still chained night and day, Dr. *Monro* coming as usual to visit his Patients, and the Prisoner hearing his voice in the adjacent room called upon him; but the Doctor replied, "That he had nothing to say to the Prisoner, nor any thing to do with him."

Mr. *Kelsey Bull* and Mr. *Frederick Bull,* who had been last week denied access by *Wright's* Wife for want of a Ticket from *Wightman,* now came with one about noon; for it was common with *Wright's* Wife either to swear the Prisoner was not there, or that he could not be seen without an Order from *Wightman;* particularly Mr. *Rouse* the Attorney, Mr. *Oliver* the Printer, &c. were denied access, tho' they were sent for by the Prisoner, and earnestly begged to see him.

The Prisoner told these two kind Gentlemen, that he had lived above three weeks past, cut off from Company and Conversation, chain'd night and day to the bedstead, being robb'd of his Account-Books, Letters and Papers, and with the utmost difficulty had obtained a little paper and ink, nay more, that he had been often afraid of being assassinated in the night-time. The Prisoner intreated the favour of one of these gentlemen to step out, and buy some paper for him on the *Green;* but lest *Davis* should have a suspicion, and not allow access a second time; therefore the Prisoner contrived a message to *Wright's* wife at the *White-house,* and Mr. *Kelsey Bull* was so kind as to go to her, and at the same time to buy some paper for the Prisoner.

These gentlemen promised, at the Prisoner's request, to speak to a gentleman of the Lord Mayor's acquaintance in order to pave the way for an effectual application to take the Prisoner under his Lordship's protection, and deliver him from his horrid confinement, *but his salvation was evidently from God, and not from Man.* The Gentlemen told the Prisoner, that if their Mother's health had permitted, she had gladly seen him in a kindly manner before now.

Friday, May 19. The Prisoner being still chained night and day, in the afternoon was visited again by Mr. *Kelsey Bull,* and Mr. *Frederick Bull* with his young Lady, and Mr. *Thomas Fletcher* of *Ware.* His good Friend Mr. *Frederick Bull* set him up with a quire of Paper, a bottle of Ink, and a quarter of a hundred of Pens, which the Prisoner artfully hid under his bed. The Prisoner asked Mr. *Kelsey Bull,* whether the BLIND-BENCH had laid aside their design of sending him to *Bethlehem?* He answered that they had not, and that they had met last *Tuesday,* but soon broke up without doing much business. The Prisoner was evidently much concerned about the wicked contrivance of *Monro, Wightman,* and the BLIND-BENCH to send him to *Bethlehem:* Mr. *Kelsey Bull* said, that he did not believe that the Governors would receive the Prisoner, he not being a proper Patient for that place. The Prisoner had some reason to be afraid of the unjust influence of *Monro,* the mad Doctor of *Bethlehem,* who was *Wightman's* devoted Creature, and acted as if he had been determined to sign a blank to screen him from punishment. The Prisoner often asked, what business they had to do with him? But this Question can never be answered, neither by the BLIND-BENCH nor *Wightman.*

The Prisoner being still under disquieting fears of being carried to *Bethlehem,* this day wrote another Letter to the Governors, which Mr. *Frederick Bull* took care to get presented to them, while at board, next Day by his Uncle Mr. *William Bull.* One of the Governors asked him, if it related to the *Queen's Bookseller?* Mr. *Bull* said, it did. The Governor replied, I know him, and tell him to be easy, for he shall not be brought into this house; but the Prisoner knew nothing of this kind message till after he had made his Escape, and therefore continued under his racking fears. Mr. *Fletcher* greatly approved of this letter to the Governors, and hath declared that nothing could be writ more to the purpose. Mr. *Fletcher* desired a succinct Account of the Prisoner's Sufferings, and upon hearing them rehearsed, was much concerned to find he had been so unjustly and barbarously used. The Prisoner wrote also a Letter to *Wightman,* demanding by what Authority he, a mere Stranger, who had never been, except the week before his

Confinement, twelve hours in his company, had usurped a Power over him against Law and Equity, &c. which Letter Mr. *Frederick Bull* delivered next *Tuesday* to the BLIND-BENCH; and when read before them it influenced one of their new members Mr. *Thomas Morison*, to declare it was a well-penn'd Letter, and discovered nothing of madness in its Author; and therefore Mr. *Morison* never attended that *Bench* anymore. *Wightman* had that day cunningly invited Mr. *Morison* to dine with him, and asked him to be one of the sureties to the Governors of *Bethlehem*, in order to make way for the Prisoner's being transported to *Bethlehem*, but Mr. *Morison* wisely declined it.

Saturday, May 20. The Prisoner being still chained night and day, was visited by no body but *Hollowel* that shaved him. In the afternoon he wrote a Letter to the Lord Mayor and to two other Gentlemen, but they were intercepted and carried to *Wightman.*

The *Lord's Day, May* 21. The Prisoner being still chained night and day, spent the *Sabbath* religiously, and worshipped God alone.

Monday, May 22. The Prisoner being still chain'd night and day, had no visitors. He writ this day to the Lord Mayor and to others, but the Letters came into Pirate *Wightman's* hands.

Tuesday, May 23. The Prisoner being still chain'd night and day, Mr. *Crookshank*, a Member of the BLIND-BENCH, came in the Evening to *Bethnal Green*, and told him that this day those wise conspirators had read a letter of the Prisoner's to his Father, which had been intercepted by *Wightman*, and that the BLIND-BENCH had under their consideration the design of sending him to *Bethlehem.* It was their usual custom to read the Prisoner's Letters that were intercepted by *Wightman*, when he presented them to the *Bench.* The Prisoner asked Mr. *Crookshank*, what business had the BLIND-BENCH to meddle with him, upon the supposition he had been really mad? He answered, that they would meddle.

Wednesday, May 24. The Prisoner being still chained night and day, was visited by no body, but *Hollowel* that shaved him.

Thursday, May 25. The Prisoner being still chained night and day, wrote several Letters, particularly one to the Lord Mayor, and to some persons of distinction, but they were all intercepted.

Friday, May 26. The Prisoner being still chained night and day, spent his time as usual. *Anna Thomson* his keeper came into his room before he went to bed, and said that she had listned to hear his prayers, and that he prayed so hard that nothing could go against him.

Saturday, May 27. The Prisoner being still chained night and day to his bedstead in this hot season, and being alarmed with being sent to *Bethlehem*, happily projected to cut the bedstead thro' with a knife with which he eat his victuals. He made some progress in it this day. In the afternoon Mr. *Willock* the Bookseller came in *Wightman's* name, desiring to know the state of Mr. *Conon's* account with the Prisoner, for *Wightman* was ready to settle with him. The Prisoner answered that he had nothing to do with *Wightman*, and would settle no accounts in concert with him, who had no power to meddle in his Affairs, and that therefore he hoped that Mr. *Conon* would wait a little longer.

The *Lord's Day, May* 28. The Prisoner being still chained night and day, made his own bed himself very early to conceal his design, but used not his knife this day upon the bedstead. *Thomas Lindon* Apothecary, with a Friend, came to see him, who declared that he found him in the full exercise of his reason and judgment.

Monday, May 29. The Prisoner being still chained night and day, took Physick by *Monro*'s order in the morning; and in the afternoon he again used his knife upon the bedstead.

Tuesday, May 30. The Prisoner being still chained wrote a Letter to Serjeant *Cruden* to send him a hand-saw, doubting of the strength of the knife, but providentially did not deliver the Letter to his woman keeper; for if he had, it had certainly fallen into *Wright*'s Wife's hands, and been sent to *Wightman*, as other Letters were by that unfaithful woman's means, and so his Escape had been prevented, and he had been most severely used. Therefore he went to work again, prayed hard and wrought hard, till his Shirt was almost as wet as if dipt in water; and as if he had received more than common Vigour and Strength, he finished the great Operation about four o'clock in the afternoon: Upon which he kneeled down and returned God thanks. Then he sent for *Hollowel* to shave him, and began to prepare for his Escape. He prayed at night that he might awake seasonably for his Escape, and he slept some hours that night as sound as ever he did in his life, chearfully and believingly committing this affair to God *who had never left him nor forsaken him.*

Wednesday, May 31. The Prisoner's birthday, he awoke early, performed his Devotions, held his chain in his hand still fastened to his leg, and deliberately got out at the Window into the Garden, mounted the Garden-wall with much difficulty, lost one of his slippers, and jumped down into the back-way, just before the clock struck two. He went towards *Mile-End*, and his left-foot that wanted a slipper was sorely hurt by the gravel-stones, which greatly afflicted him, and obliged him to put the slipper on the left-foot. From thence he went towards *White-Chapel*, and in his way met with a kind Soldier, who, upon hearing his Case, endeavoured to get him a Coach, but in vain; therefore he and the Soldier walked undiscovered till they came to *Aldgate*, where the Watchmen perceiving a chain, and suspecting him to be a person broke out of Goal, several Watchmen and the Constable Mr. *Wardly* followed him to *Leadenhall-street*, and brought him back to *Aldgate* watch-house.[45] He acquainted the two Constables Mr. *Ward* and Mr. *Wardly* with his Case, which did much affect them. They allowed him some refreshment, and promised to carry him before my Lord Mayor, but sent a Watchman privately to *Bethnal-Green*, to know the certainty of the Account; upon which *Davis* and two more of their bull-dogs[46] came to the Watch-house with handcuffs to carry back the Prisoner; but the Constable perceiving his meek and sedate Conversation, would not allow it, and desired *Wright* their master to come before my Lord Mayor, at *Grocers Hall*,[47] about 11 o'clock, where he would see his Prisoner.

The Prisoner after five o'clock desired the Constable to carry him in a coach to *North's Coffee-House* near *Guild-Hall*,[48] where he was much refreshed and heartened about five hours. A Printer at *Aberdeen* in *Scotland* came this morning to the Coffee-house, and artfully insinuated to the Constable, that it would be the best way to deliver up the Prisoner to be confined some time longer. This Printer lodged at *Grant's* in *White's-Alley*, and it is supposed that he was sent thither by *Wightman* and *Oswald*, with whom he became suddenly much acquainted; and it's certain that he falsly said to the Prisoner, that he came to the Coffee-house accidentally without knowing of his being there. He was received kindly by the Prisoner he being lately come from *Scotland*; but this false man, as the Constable rightly judged, proved very treacherous in several respects; and particularly upon his going to *Scotland* he greatly injured the Prisoner by poisoning his relations with false reports; and his falshood is attended with great ingratitude, he being some years ago greatly obliged to the Prisoner, upon his first coming as a Journeyman to *London*, but now *Oswald* is become his Correspondent, and the Printer appears to be a selfish, ungrateful man.

The Prisoner went to *Grocers-hall* about eleven o'clock, with his chains on, for he would not have them taken off till the Lord Mayor should see them. Before he appeared, *Wightman* with some of his friends had been with his Lordship, in order to fill him with Prejudices against the Prisoner: And *Wightman* hearing the Constable speak very favourably of the Prisoner, and of his rational Behaviour, gave him half-a-crown, which the Constable looked upon as a bribe to be silent; and *Wightman* was so base as afterwards to charge it to the Prisoner. The Constable told his Lordship the situation of the Prisoner when he seiz'd him; and the Prisoner gave his Lordship a just and full account of his illegal and barbarous Imprisonment, and demanded that *Wightman* might be immediately sent to *Newgate*,[49] or held to bail. To which his Lordship made no reply.

The Prisoner was several hours in bed at *North's Coffee-house*, and had not time to send for his friends; but *Wightman* was surrounded both with friends and wretched Tools; for *London* the Apothecary, and *Grant* of *White's-Alley*, both took their oath before his Lordship that the Prisoner was *Lunatick*, tho' *Grant*, poor Creature, knows no more what is meant by *Lunatick*, than a Child of a year old, and had not seen the Prisoner for nine weeks and six days before. The Prisoner told his Lordship that, if he had complied with *Wightman's* earnest request to pardon him, he had long ago been out of that dismal place, but that he was always resolved to vindicate his own Character, and to have legal satisfaction. For proof of which the Prisoner shewed his Lordship the joint Letter of Dr. *Stukeley* and Dr. *Rogers*, which his Lordship read. His Lordship asked why he appeared before him with his Chain? To which the Prisoner replied, that this chain being put on by illegal power, he was resolved to have it taken off by legal authority ; and accordingly the Constable unlocked the chain in the presence of his Lordship. He also told his Lordship that base *Wightman* had intercepted all his Letters, and several to his Lordship, particularly one writ last week, which *Wightman*, like a cat who had lost her tail, sneakingly took out of his pocket, it being opened, and gave it to his Lordship. Vile *Wightman* said to his Lordship, that no body would receive the Prisoner as a lodger: To which the Prisoner answered that it was abominably false, and he named an honest family that would heartily receive him. Then the Lord Mayor said to the Prisoner, Will you submit to Dr. *Monro*'s Judgment? Which he refused to do with indignation, knowing him to be intirely *Wightman*'s Creature from his gross lies and calumnies against him. He offered to refer his Case to Dr. *Stukeley*, but no Physician came. It is supposed, that *Monro, Wightman*'s Tool, was at hand, ready to assert any thing, right or wrong, to screen guilty *Wightman*.

But when the Prisoner saw *Wightman* endeavouring to have him still under his care, he fell upon his knees before Sir *John Barnard*, and begged most earnestly not to be delivered into the hands of cruel *Wightman*, but rather into the hands of an honest Constable, or any body his Lordship pleased: And rising from his knees he pulled up his courage, and told his Lordship plainly, that he perceived *Wightman* had poisoned him too much, but that if his Lordship, or the greatest subject in *England* should send him to a Madhouse (when he was not mad) he would pursue him to the utmost. Then Providence soon gave a turn to the matter, and his Lordship recommended him to a lodging in *Downing-Street*.[50] And so Mr. *C.* glad to be delivered out of *Wightman*'s power, went in a Coach from *Grocers-hall*, to Mr. *Morgan*'s Joiner in *Downing-street* near *Hide-park-corner* this 31st of *May*, 1738; and there Mrs. *Morgan* his landlady took great care of him, particularly of his foot that had been greatly hurt this Morning, and was now much swelled. *Wightman* was much chagrined at the Prisoner's Escape, and refused at first to pay *Wright*, saying that he could not answer for his Escape.

Thursday, June 1, One *Butts* came to Mr. *C.* in the morning, and Mr. *C.* sent him to *Bethnal-Green*, with the Schedule of his things, and an order to *Wright* to deliver them to him, which order was despised by *Wright*, who sent Mr. *C.*'s account-books, paper, linen, and other things to *Wightman:* But whether *Butts* told that he went to *Bethnal-Green bona fide* or falsly by the instigation of *Wightman*, remains a question; for *Wightman* yet aimed to make Mr. *C.* his Prisoner, thinking it the way to escape punishment. Mr. *C.* was all day at home, and in the afternoon was visited by Mrs. *Galloway;* and afterwards by Serjeant *Cruden* and *William Simpson;* Mr. *C.* sent for a tankard of Beer to treat Mr. *Cruden* and Mr. *Simpson,* and drinking to them, *Butts,* a Tool of *Wightman's* interposed in a passion, saying, it was too strong drink for him, and would not allow him to drink any of it. What, quoth the Serjeant, have you only brought Mr. *C.* from one Prison to another? Or must he be still under the Tyranny of *Wightman* and his Tools? Hold, says Mr. *C.* be this as it will, I will drink no strong Beer, and I may give no Offence. Mr. *C.* was also visited this day by his good friend Mr. *Frederick Bull.*

In the evening Mr. *C.* was visited by the Rev. Mr. *Crookshank* and Mrs. *Gardner,* who spoke very civilly to him, and entertained him with some wishes and prophesies. They both said, *"That Mr. C. would be a great man, and make a great figure at court, and looked upon his Troubles to be designed by providence, to be an Introduction and Preparation to his future Advancement, and several things to this purpose;* and *particularly Mr.* Crookshank *said, that Mr. C. was* Joseph,[51] *meaning that God would be with him, bless him and make him a prosperous man after his Reproaches and Troubles."* Mr. *C.* said, *"That he was willing to be as humble or as exalted as God pleased."* But let the world judge if this Prophet hath acted a consistent part; for if Mr. *C.* be a *Joseph,* Mr. *Crookshank* hath consented to let *Joseph* down into the Pit, by being in the confederacy against him.

Friday, June 2. Mr. *C.* went up the River with an acquaintance for his amusement, and came home at night.

Saturday, June 3. Mr. *C.* visited several friends, and in the afternoon walked in *Hide-Park* and in St *James's -Park.*[52]

The *Lord's Day, June* 4. Mr. *C.* attended publick worship in *Swallow-street* all day.

Monday, June 5. Mr. *C.* took physick, which at his desire Mr. *Stone* brought to him, and was all day at home. Mr. *Duncombe* Bookbinder and Mr. *Oliver* Printer came to visit him in the evening, and declared him as sensible and well as ever they had seen him.

Tuesday, June 6. Mr. *C.* in order to convince the Lord Mayor of his sound mind, and of *Wightman's* unaccountable management, desired his landlord and landlady to give him a written Certificate, which was as follows;

"We hereby testify that Mr. A. C. our Lodger, is of a peaceable and agreeable Temper, and behaves every Way to so great Satisfaction, that we cannot desire a better Lodger. We discover nothing of Disorder about him, and think that there is not the least Occasion for any Person to look after Mr. C. for he is very capable to take care of himself. Given at Downing-Street *near* Hide-Park Corner, Picadilly, June 6, 1738.

Jacob Morgan.
Sarah Morgan.

But when Mr. *C.* waited of the Lord Mayor at *Grocers-Hall,* and wanted to give his Lordship a more full Account of the Injuries done him by

Wightman, his Lordship said that that Affair did not properly come before him, but was an Action at Law.

Mr. *C.* dined this day at Mr. *Frederick Bull's* in *Cornhill,* and in the afternoon went into the Country, and became acquainted with some Gentlemen. A Gentleman of *Richmond*[53] bespoke his *Concordance;* upon which he wrote for two or three Copies to his Servant *Scot,* who sent him some, but wrote him that *Wightman* expressly forbid it, and threatned to make him and the Bookbinder suffer if they should send any more.

June 11, *Oswald's* Maid came this evening to Serjeant *Cruden's* in *Dutchy-Lane,* tarried a considerable time, and most earnestly intreated Serjeant *Cruden* and his Wife to use their Interest with Mr. *C.* not to go to Law. They told her, that it was not in their power nor in any person's to alter his Resolution in that matter. Mrs. *Cruden* said to her, Don't you think that they have greatly injured Mr. *C.?* She replied, that she must own that they had injured him exceedingly, and that he was too wise for them all, but that she being only a Servant was afraid of losing her Place, and therefore must say little. The Maid also said, What shall we think of the religious Man now, who won't pardon those that sent him to *Bethnal-Green* ? It may appear not at all material to take notice of what is said by one in so low a station, but this Maid hath been often used as a Tool, and sent as a Spy by Mr. *C.*'s Adversaries, and *Wightman* even read to her some of Mr. *C.*'s intercepted Letters while he was his Prisoner at *Bethnal-Green.*

Monday, June 19. Mr. *C.* came to Town to his Lodging in *Downing-Street.* He went to his Shop, and ordered *Scot* not to regard any thing that *Wightman* said or threatned: This day he received a letter from Dr. *Rogers,* dated, *June* 17, wherein the Doctor says, "*I am favoured with yours, which I communicated to our Well-wisher Dr. Stukeley, who rejoices with me in your Providential Deliverance out of so sore a Confinement, as well as out of the hands of such Brutes. We wish a continuance of Health with all imaginable Happiness, and that you may have legal Justice done you.*"

June 22, Mr. *C.* writ the following Letter to *Wightman;*

Mr. *Robert Wightman,*

"I desire and require to know when you intend to deliver up to me my Money and Papers, and other Effects you seized at *White's-Alley,* and why you detain them. Pray acquaint me, by what Authority you meddled with my Money or any of my Affairs? By what Authority you sent me to the Madhouse at *Bethnal-Green?* By what Authority you intercepted and opened my Letters? And why you entred into that desperate and diabolical Connivance of sending me to *Bethlehem?* I have got many more Questions to propose to you, but at present pray give a particular Answer to those above-mentioned this Afternoon, and direct to me at Mr. *Frederick Bull's* in *Cornhill.* Written and signed at *London, June* 22, 1738.

A. C.

This day *Wightman* called at Mr. *Reynardson*'s in *Great-Ormond-Street*,[54] he having writ a letter at Mr. *C.*'s desire to him, to come and speak to him about Mr. *C.*'s Affairs. Mr. *Reynardson* expostulated with *Wightman* about his unaccountable Management; and asked him what business he a stranger had with Mr. *C.* even upon the supposition he had been in disorder? The poor unhappy Man most unaccountably said that he would not desist, but would run all risks, and endeavour to send Mr. *C.* to *Bethlehem, for he had a Friendship for him.* O *Wightman!* how unhappy is the Man that is your Friend! But *Wightman* acted like a vile Hypocrite, and intended the greatest Injuries to Mr. *C.* for the sake of that great *Idol Self.* The wickedness of *Wightman* and his Accomplices is greatly aggravated from their falsly covering it with the pretence of Friendship; which discovers them to have acted like the vilest of Men.

Friday, June 23. This day Mr. *C.* writ a second letter to *Wightman*, which was as follows;

Mr. *Robert Wightman,*

"I desire you may send me by Mr. *Scot* the Plate about Dr. *Rogers*'s Oils, a new Pair of Shoes of mine, my Account-Books, the Letters intercepted and scandalously opened by you, and all my Linen. I desire you may let me know when you are to deliver up my Papers and Effects seized by you. Your Man haunts my Shop: I desire you may call him home to mind your own Business; for I know no Business that *Wightman* or his Man have to do with my Affairs. Prepare to suffer the highest Punishments the Laws can inflict for your great and unaccountable Injuries done to me. Why don't you send me an Answer to the Letter and Questions in it sent you yesterday? Pray remember that I design not to allow one Six-pence of the Money you have pretended to pay for me. By what Authority did you do it? I trust in God that he will be with me, and guide me, and vindicate my Character. Written and signed in *Cornhill, London, June* 23, 1738.

A.C.

Mr. *C.* sent *Scot* this day to *Wightman* to demand all the Letters of his he had intercepted; but *Wightman* peremptorily refused to deliver one of them. Mr. *C.* let *Wightman* know by *Scot*, that, if he lost any of these letters, he should pay dear for it, and that he believed when the Judge had passed Sentence against him for his Crimes, he would not be worth a Groat[55] afterwards.

Saturday, June 24. *Wightman* thought fit to write a long conceited Epistle, dated *June* 23, which Mr. *C.* received this day, in which he gives not Mr. *C.* a categorical Answer. He acknowledges, "That a kind Providence evidently superintended Mr. *C.* who had been formerly called the meek Mr. *C.*," and concludes thus; "I have only to add, that, as this is the first Letter I have written you, in answer to several angry Letters, so it is the last I am to write you while your Disorder grows; And therefore I warn you to write me no more in any such manner, nor at all till you come out of *Bethlehem-Hospital*, for I will not read them: I will burn them unopened." *Wightman* must also add a most unaccountable Postscript. "I have just now received your Second Letter, and need only answer to it, that I look'd for Dr. *Rogers* Plate at his desire, but could not find it. Your prohibition to pay people what is due to them, goes for nothing with me. Is Mr. *C.* become so unjust as to refuse to pay what is justly due! and is he not disordered in his senses! How can that be? Among the Rest of your concepts, I hear you have talkt as if I wanted to be acquitted by you, I now tell you it is a Delireous Dream, I overlook your threats with Compassion, and will have no acquittance from you. You mistake your Man hugely."

Wightman's Nonsense appears in declaring Mr. *C.* mad for not allowing him to pay his just Debts, whereas *Wightman* seiz'd illegally his Money and Effects, and unreasonably pretended to pay his just Debts, for which he had no more concern than a *Turk* or an *Indian*. *Wightman* is not a Child for years, being an old Batchelor about sixty years, and ought to have understood *meum* and *tuum* better. *Wightman* seems to have acted in this affair, as if he had been in a delirious Dream, and writes as if nothing could rouse him out of his Lethargy, but *Newgate* and *Tyburn*.

This afternoon Mr. *C.* went to *Southgate* to visit his good old Friend Madam *Coltman*, to whose only Son he had been Tutor. He was kindly received at *Southgate*, and came to town about business on *Monday* afternoon.

Tuesday, June 27. This day *Wightman* assembled his BLIND-BENCH at *Oswald*'s namely, Dr. *John Monro* the Chairman, Dr. *John Guyse*, Mr. *William Crookshank*, *John Cooke* Apothecary, *Richard Horton* Pastry Cook: And Mr. *C.* went in among them where he found *Samuel Reynardson* Esq; who had been invited to come. *Monro* the Chairman teized Mr. *C.* with many impertinent Questions, such as, *Was you ever mad?* To which he replied, No. *Monro* asked, Whether he had not addressed a Widow-Lady, even after she had been married? To which Mr. *C.* replied, that he had indeed formerly courted that Lady, but never since he knew that she was married. *Monro* asked, if he had not acted as a Madman at *Bethnal-Green?* To which Mr. *C.* replied, that tho' that place and the barbarous usage thereof might have made any body mad, yet he defied all his Enemies to prove him mad; and as for their Slanders and Lies he disregarded them, having strongly proved himself, blessed be God, to be in the full use of his Reason to many persons who came to see him. Mr. *C.* expostulated with *Monro*, about ordering physick for him before he visited him. Mr. *Reynardson* said, that he had often conversed with Mr. *C.* since he came from *Bethnal-Green*, and that he behaved very well, and that he found no signs of madness in his Conversation: Mr. *C.* told *Monro*, that an eminent Physician had told him, "That Dr. *Monro* had been always on the severe side of the Question, with respect to the poor Patients, and that he had always observed it to be so;" and that therefore, on that and some other accounts, if he wanted a Physician, *Monro* should be the last man he would choose. Mr. *C.* bid *Monro* mind his own Business, for that with him he had no Concern; which *Monro* forthwith obeyed, and said he would so; and then left the room.

Mr. *C.* demanded of *Wightman* his Money, Effects, Papers, and Accounts, but was absolutely refused before them all.

Dr. *Guyse* shew'd much dislike at Mr.*C.*'s Courage and Bravery. *Cooke* looked as if he had been self-condemned. *Crookshank* was entirely led by the Nose. *Horton* looked audacious; and *Wightman* like a condemned Malefactor. Mr. *C.* indeed throughly despis'd this Combination of foolish meddling Men, especially that they had no business with him; and that he plainly saw that their grand Plot was only to screen the Criminals *Wightman* and *Oswald*, and themselves, who were also become Criminals by their aiming to send Mr. *C.* to *Bethlehem*: And at last, at the desire of Mr. *Reynardson*, Mr. *C.* retired.

After he was gone they passed their solemn Decree, like unaccountable Men, "That Mr. *C.* ought to be sent to *Bethlehem*; and that proper means should be used for sending him thither as soon as possible." But Mr. *Reynardson* interposed, saying that he had often seen Mr. *C.* since he came from *Bethnal-Green*, and that he always behaved very sensibly, and that in his opinion their Resolution was ill-grounded; that he had influence enough with Mr. *C.* to give an evident demonstration of his being of a sound mind, even by ordering him to keep in his Lodgings for a week together, which no man fit for *Bethlehem* could have such a Command of himself as to do. Some of them replied, they were sure he would not stay so long within doors: But Mr. *Reynardson* assured them that he would; upon which they seemed to acquiesce in that proposal as a Trial of Skill, but did not reverse their black and unjustifiable Decree.

Wednesday, June 28. Mr. *C.* waiting of Mr. *Reynardson*, kindly received his Commands to stay in his Lodging for a week, and not so much as to go out on the *Lord's Day* to publick Worship, which Mr. *C.* religiously obeyed.

June 29. *Wightman* having formerly declared to Mr. *Reynardson*, that he would run all risks to have Mr. *C.* sent to *Bethlehem*, did this day write to Mr. *Fletcher* Master of a Boarding-School at *Ware*, (with whom Mr. *C.* had formerly been Usher)[56] and fully told him of *the Decree* of the BLIND-BENCH at their Meeting on *June 27*, to send Mr. *C.* on *Saturday* se'nnight to *Bethlehem*, but that in order thereunto he desired Mr. *Fletcher* to get the Church-Warden of that Parish to sign a Certificate, signifying that he belonged to their Parish; because in *Bethlehem* the Governors receive none who don't belong to some Parish, and that two of his Associates were ready to be bound to *Bethlehem*-Hospital, according to their usual Form. To which Mr. *Fletcher* replied in a very short Letter, *That he was wholly averse to be concerned in any such Transactions*. Wightman *had been at great pains to find Suereties, and promised to indemnify them.*

Notwithstanding Mr. *Fletcher*'s refusal, yet *Wightman* found means to continue his Application to the People of *Ware*, who scorned him as an impertinent meddling Fellow, and thought him more fit for *Bethlehem* than Mr. *C.* In the Postscript of his Letter to *Ware*, *Wightman* says, "*I have done my utmost to obtain a Certificate from the Parish where he lodged in* London, *and where his Shop is, but in vain; because a Man's being a Lodger or Shopkeeper, entitles him not to be a Parishioner.*"

Friday, June 30. Mr. *Reynardson* did Mr. *C.* the honour to come in his Chariot, and to visit him in his Lodgings in *Downing-street*, when he shewed him a Letter he had received from *Wightman*, signifying that he design'd as soon as possible to send Mr. *C.* to *Bethlehem*. Mr. *Reynardson* desired Mr. *C.* to commit to his custody some of *Wightman*'s particular Letters, lest he and his Associates should come and spoil him of them, and to commit his other Papers to the care of his Landlady, which were carefully and securely hid. Mr. *C.* said, that he thought *Wightman* and his Associates could not be so foolish as to attack and seize him a second time: To which Mr. *Reynardson* replied, that considering what they had done, he did not know what they might do, and desired his Landlord and Landlady to call a Constable, and send for him, in case they should make another Attack upon him. Mr. *C.* being pensive upon what had passed, desired his Landlord to secure his Windows and the Door, that none might come in upon him without leave; and he prayed earnestly that God might frustrate their Devices against him, and deliver him from unreasonable and wicked Men.

Saturday, July 1. Mr. *C.* after the Alarm and Disturbance sent for Mr. *Stone*, the Surgeon, who opened a Vein, and took from him nine ounces of blood, and said, he was always ready to declare that he had never seen Mr. *C.* in a mad Condition, but ever regular and reasonable.

The *Lord's Day, July* 2. Mr. *C.* stayed closely in his Lodgings as formerly, and spent the *Sabbath* religiously.

Monday, July 3. Mr. *C.* was visited by some Friends, who were of opinion that *Wightman* and his Accomplices designed to kidnap him, as soon as they found him abroad, and to carry him into a place where he should never be heard of.

Tuesday, July 4. Mr. *C.* hearing that *Wightman* was to go off the Premises in a few days, sent a Letter to a Gentleman of Distinction, who advised him to employ an able Attorney: And in the afternoon he writ to Mr. *Reynardson*, who returned by the Bearer a very kind answer.

Wednesday, July 5. Mr. *C.* wrote this day to *Wightman*, requiring his Money,

Effects, Account-Books, Papers and Letters he had intercepted, but got no answer. The Letter was as follows;

Mr. *Robert Wightman,*

"It is a great Inconvenience and Disadvantage to me that you are so unreasonable as to refuse to deliver me up my Money, Papers and Effects, and make an Account to me about my Affairs you have most unaccountably and foolishly meddled with. I desire you may send me word by the Bearer, when you intend to deliver up every thing relating to me. Pray remember you have no Authority to pay a Six-pence for me, and don't expect I will allow it. I think my self more capable to manage my own Affairs than you are to manage them for me. I desire not to entertain a revengeful Temper against any Man, but to wait on God for Direction to take such methods as may vindicate my Character, and make you suffer according to the Demerits of your uncommon Crimes. Perhaps you have been left to fall into such gross and unaccountable Actions to humble you for your Pride and Self-conceit. You began the Week you sent me to *Bethnal-Green* in a very bad way, by having a Shoemaker in your Room fitting you with Shoes on the *Sabbath-morning.* Dated in *Downing-street, July* 5, 1738.

A. C.

Thursday, July 6. This day Mr. *C.* finishing his voluntary Confinement in his Lodgings, and fearing lest his Enemies should again make him their Prisoner, went abroad with two Friends to Justice *De Veil,* desiring his Protection; but the Justice said, he was already under the Protection of the Law.

Mr. *C.* thought it prudent to have a trusty and stout Friend to guard him this day when he went abroad, whom he sent to *Oswald*'s for an Answer to his last Letter to *Wightman*; but *Oswald*'s Wife haughtily replied, *"That Mr.* Wightman *regarded none of his Letters, and that he would trounce all Persons that came to trouble him about the Affairs of Mr.* C. *"*

Mr. *C.* dined this day at Mr. *Charles*'s Master of St *Paul*'s School,[57] who had lately seen his Friend Mr. *Newcome* of *Hackney,* and said that Mr. *Newcome* had told him, *"That he thought Mr.* C. *was very well when he saw him at* Bethnal-Green, *and that he was very ill used."*

Friday, July 7. The following Attestation was signed by the famous Dr. *Alexander Stuart,* and Dr. *William Stukeley* two of the College of Physicians;[58] and afterwards *July* 26 by Dr. *Robert Innes* a Physician in *London* of long Practice.

"We whose Names are underwritten have seen and conversed with Mr. A. C. Bookseller to her late most Excellent Majesty, and do think him in good Health and Order, and that it is a most injurious and unaccountable thing, to propose to send him to Bethlehem. *Given at* London *the seventh day of July in the Year of our Lord God* 1738.

Alexr. Stuart, *M.D.*
William Stukeley, *M.D.*
Robert Innes, *M.D.*

Saturday, July 8. Mr. *C.* advised with some Friends about arresting of *Wightman* for the Money that he had seized of his.

Friday, July 14. Mr. *Reynardson* finding that Mr. *C.* had difficulty to get *Wightman* arrested, went with him in his Chariot into the City this day, and got *Wightman* to give in Bail for Mr. *C.*'s money he had seized. His Bail were *John Cooke* Apothecary and *Richard Horton* Pastry-Cook, two members of the BLIND-BENCH.

Tuesday, July 25. Mr. *C.*'s Case had been several times mentioned in the News-papers, and this day in the St. *James's Evening-Post*[59] there was an Account, "That lately there had been in *Lincoln's-Inn-Fields*[60] a publick Disputation about his Case, and that it was ended with great and distinguishing Success, on the part of Mr. *C. Wightman*'s Servant pleaded for him, but it was evidently concluded that Mr. *C.* had been exceedingly Injured, and that *Wightman* was a great Criminal by Law, and every way. A Letter writ by *Wightman* was produced, which he wanted Mr. *C.* to sign, it being a full Pardon for him, and then he would directly release him; but Mr. *C.* for many Reasons had absolutely refused to sign it. The Discourse before Disputation was from that remarkable Text, St. *Mark* iii. 21. *And when his Friends heard of it, they went out to lay hold of him, for they said, He is beside himself.*"[61]

Saturday, August 5. Mr. *C.* with *Oliver Roberts* appeared before Lord Chief Baron *Comyns*[62] and being sworn, they made their respective Affidavits: The Substance whereof follows:

"*Oliver Roberts* Chairman, made oath that *Robert Wightman*, in *March* last, gave orders to him to carry Mr. *C.* to a *Madhouse* at *Bethnal-Green*, and directed him to take *John Anderson* Coachman for his assistance; and to induce Mr. *C.* to come out of his Lodging, the said *Wightman* directed *Roberts* to inform the said Mr. *C.* that *Wightman* desired to speak with him at his lodging in *Spring-Gardens*; and the said *Roberts* and *Anderson* went to Mr. *C.*'s lodging in *White's-Alley*, and told him as above, and thereby prevailed with him to go into a Hackney-Coach provided by the said *Roberts*; and the said *Roberts* and *Anderson* went into the said Coach, and immediately drew up the windows to prevent Mr. *C.*'s seeing where he was carried; and *Roberts* delivered Mr. *C.* to a servant belonging to the master of the said Madhouse: And the said *Roberts* further declared, that Mr. *C.* for all the time that the said *Roberts* was with him in the said coach behaved himself very sensibly, and without any signs of Madness."

"Mr. *C.* made oath of his being imposed upon by *Oliver Roberts*, and thereby being prevailed upon to go into a Hackney-Coach, was carried to *Wright's Madhouse* at *Bethnal-Green* on the 23d of *March* last, and confined there for nine weeks and six days; and that on the *Saturday* after his Confinement *Davis* the Under-keeper did put upon Mr. *C.*'s body a *Strait-Wastecoat* with long sleeves, which intirely deprived him of the use of his hands, and greatly hindred him from sleep; with which said *Wastecoat* Mr. *C.* was made very uneasy for four to five days; and during the first five weeks of

Mr. *C.*'s Imprisonment he was chained to his bedstead every night, except one, by *Davis* or some other of *Wright*'s servants; and for the first three or four weeks Mr. *C.* was frequently handcuff'd by *Davis*: And *Wright* came to Mr. *C.*'s chamber in the said *Madhouse* on *April* 26, and laid hold of all Mr. *C*'s papers, pen and ink, and account-books, which he could then find: Upon which Mr. *C.* commanded *Wright* to lay them down; but the said *Wright* delivered the said Account-books to *Davis*, who then locked them up from Mr. *C.* And the rest of the said things *Wright* carried out of the said room; and the said *Wright* then ordered *John Davis, Richard Turner* and *William Caesar* his servants to pull off Mr. *C.*'s shoes, and to chain him to the bedstead in his chamber, and to lock the door thereof, which orders were then immediately executed: And the said *Wright* the next day told Mr. *C.* that he had received a Letter from *Wightman*, giving him authority for what he had done the day before: And Mr. *C.* farther declared, that the lock and chain were not for one moment off his leg from *April* 26 to the 31st of *May*, on which day Mr. *C.* made his Escape out of the *Madhouse* by means of sawing his bedstead, and loosening the chain from the said bedstead."

This day Mr. *C.*'s Attorney applied to the *Lord Chief Baron* for an order to hold *Wightman* to bail, upon the above Affidavit; and at last only desired bail for the sum of 500*l.* His Lordship said it was a very uncommon and unprecedented Case, but that if the Plaintiff could prove his allegations, he could get much more damages than five hundred Pounds; and so his Lordship suspended the consideration of this Affair, who was then the only Judge in Town. If bail could have been then applied for before a Bench of Judges, it might have been done with success.

Thursday, August 10. Mr. *C.* not being able to hold *Wightman* to bail, ordered his Attorney to take a Writ out of the *King*'s *Bench-Court*, which was personally executed this day upon *Wightman*.

Tuesday, August 22. Mr. *C.* after visiting some friends went this afternoon to Madam *Coltman*'s at *Southgate*, and was kindly entertained at her house for two months. This judicious Lady hath declared that she found Mr. *C.* always rational. About a week or a fortnight after Mr. *C.*'s going to *Southgate*, Mr. *Reynardson* came to visit his Aunt Madam *Coltman*, and told Mr. *C.* that he had received a letter from *Wightman*, dated *August* 23, wherein he most unaccountably proposed that Mr. *C.* should have his settlement fixed in the Parish to which *Southgate* belongs, to make way for his going to *Bethlehem.* Mr. *Reynardson* observed, that the thoughts of *Bethlehem* made Mr. *C.* pensive, and told him that he had no need to be troubled about *Wightman*'s behaviour, for it was to be hoped that he should suffer for it in due time. Mr. *C.* has great reason to be thankful to God all his life for frustrating the unjust and wicked Devices of his adversaries; and it may evidently appear to the reader, that they richly deserve to be brought to shame and punishment in an exemplary manner.

It would be too tedious to continue this Narrative any farther, for blessed be God Mr. *C.* can, with Courage and Integrity, dare his bold enemies to prove any thing against his regular and good Behaviour; but it is not in any man's power to put a stop to deceitful and lying lips, for the best of men have been unjustly and falsly abused in this manner. The reader may by this time be convinced that Mr. *C.* has acted more reasonably than his Adversaries, and that there was no foundation to send him to *Bethnal-Green*; for if all Lovers were to be sent thither, there would be a necessity to erect *Bethlemetical* Cities instead of Hospitals. The adversaries of Mr. *C.* were guilty of a wrong step, and, like proud and infatuated men, seemed to be determined to be guilty of many more wrong steps, rather than humbly to acknowledge the first. A few Observations on the management of Mr. *C.*'s adversaries, seem not unnecessary to be added to this Narrative.

Mr. *William Crookshank* and *John Oswald* Bookseller were the first that raised a false report of Mr. *C.* and being once guilty of slander and falshood, they have been so foolish and wicked as to go on in it for above these ten months; for about the end of *January* they both told to a particular friend of Mr. *C*'s that he was still mad. This gentleman said to Mr. *Crookshank*, that he had been often in Mr. *C*'s company, and found him very sedate and serene, and without any signs of madness. Mr. *Crookshank* was so bold as to answer, "Are you become *mad* also?" It is plain that these two men had no other ground for their false report, but a piece of Love-gallantry on *Saturday* the 18th of *March*, 1737–8, when he came to have the final Resolution of Mrs. *Payne*.

These two imprudent men told their ill-grounded sentiments to Mr. *C*'s foolish and ignorant landlord and landlady, *James Grant* and his wife in *White's-Alley*, which occasion'd them to behave so disobligingly and strangely towards him, as in the Narrative. 'Tis certain that *Oswald*'s wife took the lodging at *Bethnal-Green*, and *Wightman* and *Oswald* were first joint actors in the Affair; but afterwards *Oswald* endeavoured to slip his neck out of the collar, and *Wightman* managed the whole barbarous Affair; and *Oswald* and others were his assistants and accomplices. Dr. *Monro* soon told *Wightman* that he had acted precipitantly and illegally, which made him use all means fair and foul to screen himself; and *Monro* was willing to run all risks to assist him.

Wightman is a known projector,[63] a busy-body, a meddler in other peoples concerns without leave, as appears from many parts of his conduct in life at *Edinburgh*; but he was a very slender acquaintance of Mr. *C.*'s, no relation to him, no creditor of his, had no wordly concerns with him; nor did Mr. *C.* give him any power or authority to meddle with his Person, Money or Effects, and he was therefore the more astonished at his insolent and officious undertaking. What authority had *Wightman* to countenance the maletreatment Mr. *C.* met with at *White's-Alley*? To kidnap him into a Hackney-Coach by his *Myrmidons*,[64] and send him to the *Madhouse* at *Bethnal-Green*, to seize his Money and Effects, to receive his Money and pay his

Debts, to order him to be treated in the *Madhouse* worse than any in a *Spanish Inquisition*, to debar him the use of pen, ink, and paper? And when he got these privately, to intercept his letters, to deprive him of the comfortable visits of his friends? And all to extort from him a full pardon for all his wicked conduct, which Mr. *C.* would never grant upon any consideration; trusting in God, and depending upon the Justice of his Cause, and the Equity of the Laws of *England.*

This projector *Wightman* was so bold and unmannerly as to break open several things sealed up by Mr. *C.* to examine his papers, to settle his accounts, and to act as if Mr. *C.* had been dead, and *Wightman* had been his heir and executor. But how *Wightman* can account for his management is not easy to imagine, he doing it without authority, and even contrary to Mr. *C.*'s express orders. *Oswald* and his family were Tools to serve him upon all Occasions. 'Tis said that *Wightman* their lodger spent a great deal of money in their house, and entertained them often with suppers, yea he was so bold as to send to Mr. *C.*'s lodging in *White's-Alley* for a handsom present of Bacon, that was sent to Mr. *C.* from the country, and treated his landlord and landlady with it; and in all respects he acted most unaccountably. A Gentleman of uncommon worth who knows *Wightman*, asked Mr. *C.* "How *Wightman* came to do it at first?" Mr. *C.* said, "That he did not know how to answer that Question, but that he knew that *Wightman* was a man full of conceit." The Gentleman replied, "That he knew that very well."

Wightman being soon convinced that Mr. *C.* was not fit for a *Madhouse,* and finding he could not procure his pardon, continued him still in prison by his arbitary power; and *Wightman* and *Wright* are to answer for all the deplorable cruel Usage Mr. *C.* met with during his Confinement there; yet *Wightman* willing still to screen himself found means to assemble his Associates, in a strict combination (called in the Narrative, The BLIND-BENCH) that they might act in concert with him in his barbarous designs.

His after-conduct needs not be rehearsed, it being in the Narrative; which plainly shews that he designed to cover one crime by another more heinous, and to justify his sending Mr. *C.* to a *Madhouse* by fixing him in *Bethlehem,* whereby he thought all his former crimes would be covered: *But,* blessed be God, *who disappointed the counsel of this* Ahithophel,[65] *and turned it into foolishness.*

'Tis hoped no considering person will disapprove of Mr. *C.*'s prosecuting of *Wightman* in the *King's-Bench,* and his trying to recover damages for his loss of Reputation and Credit, his long cruel Sufferings, even to the danger of his Life, his loss of Money, Goods and Effects, the alienating of the hearts of many of his friends by horrid lies and falshoods, the intercepting of his Letters, and many other Damages that can be proved in law before the Judge and Jury: And most rational Men will readily judge, that if such barbarous Treatment in *Wightman* goes unpunished, no man can be secure from being carried to *Bethnal-Green* upon the least groundless surmise.

Matthew Wright that keeps the *Madhouse* on *Bethnal-Green,* has been often punished for unjustly receiving, detaining and maletreating many innocent persons in his abominable *Madhouse.* He is an old offender, and 'tis great pity that those in authority should not order a due inspection and examination of the conduct of his house, where may be seen some scores of miserable wretches treated worse than Galley-slaves by his sovereign arbitary pleasure, like a *Turkish Bashaw,*[66] without being allowed the kind visits of their friends, or of any persons to hear their Case; which is a violent breach upon the liberties of the subject, and a great disgrace upon a Christian Country. His wife is as bad as himself, tho' more cunning: His servants are all his obsequious Cannibals. *Wright* said of his man *Davis,* "That he neither feared God nor the Devil, Heaven nor Hell!" Sure none can blame Mr. *C.* for prosecuting those vile people for the barbarous Treatment he met with at *Bethnal-Green,* and the great Damages he thereby received.

As for the people that assisted *Grant* and his wife in *White's -Alley,* they can tell, when they appear in Court, by whose order they acted as they did, and who misrepresented Mr. *C.'s* Case, and made the first false alarm to them.

As for Dr. *Monro,* he soon became intirely *Wightman's* Creature, and afterwards Chairman of the pretended Court of the BLIND-BENCH; and used all possible means to screen *Wightman,* tho' in vain. It is to be wished that the Doctor's conduct in his office was narrowly inspected for the good of many poor Patients; and that his authority in declaring men mad might be impaired; and that he might be severly punished, if he deserves it, seeing he is always on the severe side with his poor Patients. *Monro* hath raised several gross Calumnies against Mr. *C.* to screen *Wightman,* and hath been his great Confederate.

As for the members of *Wightman's* BLIND-BENCH, the Question is, whether they may not be properly termed Conspirators, along with *Wightman,* against the Honour, Credit, Life, Liberty and Property of Mr. *C.* to screen *Wightman's* horrid Conduct; for by what authority could they meet in Judgment from time to time, from the 14th of *April* when they commenced to the 27th of *June,* having had a Being during ten weeks and five days? Their infatuation in meeting about a month after Mr. *C's* amazing Escape greatly exposes them, and lays open their wicked designs.

Sure Mr. *C.* gave them no authority, nor can they pretend to be Commissioners of Lunacy under the great Seal. Did the Lord Chancellor, or any of the twelve Judges, or the Lord Mayor of *London,* or any other competent authority empower them to meet, to consider of a man with whom they had nothing to do?[67] Nor can they justly pretend, that it was out of kindness to Mr. *C.* for they met to make insolent and barbarous decrees, particularly about sending him to *Bethlehem,* the sorest Evil that could befal him, and which he dreaded more than Death. If such illegal Combinations should not be discountenanced, what man in *England* can be safe? But the consideration of this point is left to the Judge and Jury.

But their own Reflexions will chastise them somewhat; for *Wightman*, who came to town only the week before, would have done better to have minded his own affairs, than to have undertaken a Trust, without leave, of managing a person as a madman who was not a madman.

Monro had better have minded his Patients in the several *Madhouses*, (which perhaps are too many to be well minded by one man) than to be Chairman of this BLIND-BENCH, and at the head of the Combination to carry Mr. *C.* to *Bethlehem*. What reward he received from *Wightman* is best known to himself.

Oswald, who with *Crookshank* began the Hue and Cry without cause, was so bold as to stop Mr. *C.*'s messages when at *Bethnal-Green*, and to usurp a power over him by giving a written order to those he had a mind should visit Mr. *C.* *Oswald* was *Wightman*'s Tool in assembling the BLIND-BENCH, and a member of the BENCH; but let the world judge whether this BENCH had a very learned member when they had him, and whether any man can be more skilled in the *Res Medica*[68] than he, or can know better the Laws of *England* with respect to *Lunaticks* and *Madmen*, except his audacious Wife who governs him: It is supposed that *Oswald* and his Wife will be brought to Shame (if they have any) for their horrid Lies, Aspersions, Calumnies and Injuries against Mr. *C.*

Dr. *John Guyse* an excellent Divine, but not a great Politician, was certainly too sanguine in favouring his Bookseller *Oswald*, for whose sake he first earnestly pressed Mr. *C.* at *Bethnal-Green* to grant *Wightman* a full Pardon: He thought his Authority over Mr. *C.* greatly slighted by Mr. *C.*'s refusal to comply, and the more readily joined the BLIND-BENCH, dishonourably assisted *Cooke* and *Oswald* in opening Mr. *C*'s Letter to his Father, and vigorously adhered to the insolent and illegal Decrees of that BENCH for lodging Mr. *C.* in *Bethlehem*, whereas he might have been better employed.

Mr. *William Crookshank*, who with *Oswald* began the Hue and Cry, in his profound Penetration joined the BLIND-BENCH even to the last, and tho' he had declared to several people that he believed Mr. *C.* not to be mad when he saw him at *Bethnal-Green*, yet he adhered to the dreadful Decree of sending Mr. *C.* to *Bethlehem*, no doubt to screen himself for his former illegal Conduct, as thinking it below him to make a deep and humble Submission for his former Crimes. If all this Gentleman's Conduct was narrowly canvassed, it would appear to be full of Blunders and Mistakes, and that he hath often acted inconsistently with himself.

John Cooke the Apothecary in *Grace-Church-Street*[69] had, it seems, little business to mind when he meddled with one that never employed him, and never would thank him; but after he had the honour of a Seat on the BENCH, and had once opened Mr. *C.*'s Letter to his Father, which he had promised to forward to the Post-Office, (for opening of which Mr. *C.* had threatned him) he became a vigorous Adherer to the Decree of the BLIND-BENCH for sending Mr. *C.* to *Bethlehem*.

Richard Horton the Pastry-Cook at the *Peacock* in *Cornhill*, in order to serve Dr. *Guyse* and *Oswald*, used all means to get a Parish-Certificate for transporting Mr. *C.* to *Bethlehem*, tho' in vain; and to the last he adhered to the foolish and illegal Decree of the BLIND-BENCH.

As for *London* and *Grant* who swore before the Lord Mayor that Mr. *C.* was Lunatick; *London* had often declared him to be in his right Senses at *Bethnal-Green*, had not see him for above eight days before he stood before my Lord Mayor, and so could not *bona fide* take that unlawful Oath.

Grant poor Creature, a silly timorous old Taylor, understood no more of *Lunacy* than he does of *Astronomy*, and not having seen Mr. *C.* for nine weeks and six days before, seems therefore to be guilty of corrupt and wilful Perjury. *Grant* several years ago made oath before the *King's Bench* in *Westminster-hall*[70] that a Tallow-Chandler,[71] who was sent by his Wife to *Wright's* Madhouse, was mad and fit to be confined, yet the Jury saw cause to bring in their Verdict to the contrary.

John Scot Mr. *C's* unfaithful Servant, became wholly obedient to *Wightman's* Orders to the great detriment of his much injured Master, and sign'd the above-mentioned Letter of *Wightman's* composing to Serjeant *Cruden*, full of horrid Lies and impudent Threatnings, discharging the Serjeant to meddle with Mr. *C.'s* Concerns, tho' he had Authority from Mr. *C.* himself. *Scot* spoke at first much against *Wightman* as being a strange unaccountable Man, but it seems he was either wheedled or threatned into a very criminal Compliance.

The following Accounts of Mr. *C.* by Mr. *Simpson* and Mr. *Robinson*, the Originals of which can be produced, are a full Evidence of Mr. *C.'s* being of a sound Mind at *Bethnal-Green*.

At the particular Desire of a Gentleman I give the following account of Mr. *A.C.* who was confined Prisoner at *Bethnal-Green*.

"Mr. *A.C.* is a Gentleman with whom I have had the happiness to be acquainted upwards of seventeen Years; and I must do him the Justice to say that in the place of his Nativity where our Acquaintance commenced, his strict Piety and Christian Deportment endeared him to the highest and best Inhabitants of the place; and the friendly Correspondence they have kept up with him since he left his native place, shews their Regard to have been real and sincere. The Winter before he came into *England* he was Candidate for being a Regent or Professor in the University where he had his Education, but his Friends were not successful in that Design.[72] In *April* 1724 he came to *London*, and in *June* following, by the Recommendation of his constant Friend the great Dr. *Calamy*, he became Tutor to the only Son of the valuable *Henry Coltman* Esq; at 31 *Elms* at *Southgate*. The young Gentleman his agreeable Pupil died much lamented in *June* 1736. Providence hath always favoured Mr. *C.* in providing creditable Business for him, and also honoured him to be the Author of a very useful Book that will perpetuate his Memory.

Since I came into *England* in *May* 1731, I have had an opportunity of knowing Mr. *C.* as much as many, and have particularly observed that Persons of the best Character were always his Companions, and he was precise in his choice this way. Knowing this to be the Gentleman's Character, I was greatly surpriz'd to hear in *March* last of his being sent to a Private Madhouse. This News was very shocking, and I had several Reasons to give him a visit; accordingly on *Friday, March* 24, which was the Day after he was confined, I went to *Bethnal-Green*, supposing from the Accounts I had heard of him to have found him in great Disorder; but when I was admitted to his Room, where he was chained to his bed, he accepted of my visit in his usual civil manner; and after asking me how I did, began to relate the particular Steps taken by his Enemies towards having him imprisoned, which he did in a very distinct composed manner, and appealed to me if they had done him Justice in those unaccountable Steps they had taken. We talked on several other Subjects, and I was in his Company that day about three hours, in all which time I could observe nothing of Disorder in Mr. *A.C.* only the Blows and Wounds he had received made his Face somewhat disfigured; and I may venture to say, that the Usage he met with would have put any person in greater disorder than it did him. At parting he delivered me some few Commissions to different Persons, and desired I would be so good as to return next day with an Answer to these Commissions. Accordingly, *Saturday March* 25, I went to *Bethnal-Green* along with two Friends of Mr. *A.C.*'s, whom he had sent for; but upon calling at the Madhouse we were told by the Servants, that no person could see Mr. *C.* without an Order from Mr. *Wightman*, Mr. *Oswald*, or Dr. *Monro*; so we were obliged to return without seeing him.

Finding there was no Access to him, I delayed offering him a visit for some time, till I was told by a Gentleman that I could be admitted, and that Mr. *A.C.* wanted to see me; so next day, being *April* 23, I went to *Bethnal-Green*, and found that Mr. *C.* was at his liberty to walk in the Garden. We walked for some considerable time in the Garden, when he gave me a very affecting History of the barbarous Treatment he had met with since I was last with him; to have heard which would have drawn Compassion and Sympathy from any Heart but one of Stone.

It being the *Lord's Day*, he spoke with greater mildness than the Subject required, wondering at the folly of his Adversaries; yet telling that they had done him so great Injustice, in taking away his Character and Reputation, and injuring him in his civil Concerns, that he thought it his duty to bring them to publick Justice. I advised him to apply to the Lord Mayor, telling him that I thought his Lordship was in honour obliged to protect a *London-Citizen:* The Proposal he readily complied with but complained greatly of his being kept from the use of Pen, Ink and Paper, which hindred him much in his Enterprises. Afterwards he made me dine with him, which time he spent in serious Discourse according to his ordinary way, especially he pitied *Sabbath-Breakers*; which Subject he was led to from some observations he had taken of the Conduct of a Man whose Care he was unhappily then under. Dinner being over he read in his Bible, and then went to Prayer, which he set about with the greatest Composure, Distinctness, and Fervency; and I could not observe the least mistake in his Performance, nor could another of no mean Capacity, who happened to join him in that Performance. A Gentleman with his Son visited him that afternoon, and had a long Conversation with him, and we were all unanimous that he had no business in that Place, nor any need of such babarous Keepers; for none of us could observe the least signs of Disorder during the whole Conversation of the day. At parting he desired I would visit him next day, because he had some things of Importance to acquaint me with, which he did not think proper to communicate on the *Lord's Day*; and in compliance with his Desire I called next day *April* 24, but was refused access; nor was I allowed to see him any more, till I saw him in his Lodgings in *Downing-Street*, after his wonderful Escape.

I could not but in Justice give this Account of Mr. *A.C.* which I sign this 12th Day of *January* 1738–9.

William Simpson.

"Sir, I think my self bound in Justice to give the following Account of Mr. *A.C.*.

After receiving a Letter dated *April* 11, at *Bethnal-Green* from Mr. *A.C.* Bookseller to her late Majesty the Great Queen *Caroline*, then Prisoner in *Wright*'s Madhouse, I came according to Direction and visited the said Mr. *C.* in the Garden, when to my great Surprise on the one hand and ineffable Satisfaction on the other, he discoursed rationally and accurately, giving me a long Narration of the mad Proceedings of his self conceited, proud and foolish Adversaries, in all which Narration he expressed his Submission to divine Sovereignty, believing that infinite Wisdom and Goodness would bring Meat out of that Devourer, and Sweetness out of that most bitter Potion.[73]

Then he read a part of the Scripture, and prayed accurately and fervently according to his usual manner. A few minutes after he desired me to pray, desiring me to remember his Case at the Throne of Grace. I din'd with him, and he gave Thanks to God distinctly, and had the air of a lively and undaunted Christian; and if I may be allowed to speak what I think, that Place was more suitable for his Adversaries.

About the middle of *April*, being the *Lord's Day*, I came to visit him and stayed about six hours, and after his usual manner he sanctified that sacred Time according to the Scriptures. He desired me to go over the way to the Meeting-house and bring him an Account of the Sermon; which I did. Several People of Fashion came to see him, and I went into the Garden. I heard not their Conversation, but he parted with them after his usual sedate, complaisant, rational and Christian manner. After I came into his Room he conversed of revealed Religion[74] suitable to the Day: He prayed most rationally and fervently as at other times. At Parting being eight o'clock, he desired me to call at the Minister's House, being desirous of a Visit from him.

About three Days after I came to visit him and saw him in great distress of Body, he having taken a Vomit. In the Intervals of his excessive Straining and Reaching he discoursed faintly, but most rationally, telling me he was sure God would make all tend to his Good. He never dropt a Word tinctur'd with Fretfulness, Passion, or private and personal Revenge.

At another time, being the *Lord's Day*, I stayed, I think six or seven hours; and all his Discourse was worthy of a Man of Reason, Learning, and Religion. I visited him in all five times; and all his Conversation would have sustain'd the Trial of an exact Printer, an accurate Corrector, and a censorious, if candid, Reader.

I came four or five times more, but was denied access, the Under-keeper telling me that he was strictly forbid to let any Person have access to Mr. *C.* without a written Order from *Wightman.* I never saw him till after his amazing and almost miraculous Deliverance; but when Judgment returns to Righteousness a *Nigrum Theta*[75] will be printed on the Foreheads of such wretched Creatures: Tho' I'm sure he bears them no private Hatred, yet I should rejoice to hear that they were made sensible of their Wickedness, his Character restored, and Losses repaired.

Written and subscribed this 24th of *January* 1738–9, by me.

John Robertson.

It is humbly hoped that Mr. *C.*'s mis-informed Friends, who had conceived wrong Impressions and disagreeable Ideas of him, by the malicious Industry of his unjust Adversaries, will again receive him into their good Graces, and the rather that he has been so exceedingly injured.

It is hoped every *London-Citizen* and every free-born Subject will take the just Alarm by this dreadful Case of Mr. *C.* their *Fellow-Citizen*, a *Livery-man* of the *Stationers* Company,[76] and take care of any Combinations against their Lives and Liberties, their Credit and Substance; or else Farewel good old *British* Liberty.

The best way for the *London-Citizens* and all his MAJESTY'S Subjects to have true Conceptions of the great Injuries done to Mr. *C.* is to suppose the Case to have been their own; What Satisfaction and Reparation would they have expected from *Wightman, Monro, Oswald, Wright* and the other Accomplices? It is plain that those Men at first acted rashly and without consideration, unjustly and without cause, pragmatically and without authority; and when they afterwards perceived that Mr. *C.* firmly resolved to demand legal Satisfaction, their corrupt guilty Hearts prompted them *to endeavour to conceal,* as it were, *Adultery with Murder,* or *to cover one heinous Crime with another more heinous:* And they have by their stubborn and impenitent Behaviour rendred themselves greatly deserving of the strictest Justice, by endeavouring to colour over their Management by propagating Lies and Calumnies against Mr. *C.*

Mr. *C.* being at *Southgate, Wightman* went for *Scotland Sept.* 15 with Dr. *Monro*'s Son:[77] Whether he may be called a Fugitive from Justice or not, time will discover; for two Actions were commenced against him before that time; the first for seizing Mr. *C.*'s Money, the second for Personal Injuries. The Declaration for the second Action before the *King's-Bench* is to the Damage of Ten Thousand Pounds. The false Imprisonment, *for nine Weeks and six Days,* at five Pounds an Hour being 8280 *l.* and the Assault and other Damages at 1720 *l.* The first Action for the Money seiz'd began in the *Sheriffs-Court*[78] at *Guildhall;* and it appears that Mr. *C*'s Adversaries are much hardned, and have given a great deal of trouble to him in this Action: They have moved it to the *Lord-Mayor's-Court,* and it has been brought back to the *Sheriffs-Court;* where they supposing Judgment would be signed against them, moved it to the *Common-Pleas,* as if they were very fond to breathe a little before they expire.

Many valuable ends may be answered by bringing *Wightman,* the BLIND-BENCH, &c. to Justice, namely, the recovering of Mr. *C.*'s Character, a full Reparation and Satisfaction for Damages, the making of them Examples to deter others from committing the like crimes for the time to come. And it is humbly hoped that the LEGISLATURE will see the Necessity of bringing in a Bill to regulate *Private Madhouses.*

Mr. *C.* is far from being of a revengeful Spirit, and desires not to say, *That he will recompense Evil, but trusts in God who delivers him out of all his Troubles, that he will save his Character and every thing relating to him: And that his Integrity shall shine as the Light, and his Innocence as the Noon-day:* Prov. xx. 22. Psal. xxx. 6.[79] His former great Deliverances, by the Goodness of a kind Providence, encourage him, to wait on God for Salvation, in every Respect, thro' *Jesus Christ* our I ord. *Amen.*

FINIS

ONE MORE

PROOF

OF THE

INIQUITOUS ABUSE

OF

PRIVATE MADHOUSES.

BY

SAMUEL BRUCKSHAW,
Late of STAMFORD,
LINCOLNSHIRE.

Provoco ad Populum.[1]

LONDON:
Printed for the AUTHOR, and to be had of him,
at No. 28, Poultry. 1774.

To The Right Honourable Frederic Bull, Esq. Lord Mayor of the City of London.[2]

It is with singular propriety these sheets are addressed to YOUR LORDSHIP, As they contain a faithful account of the consequences of

AN ILLEGAL EXERTION OF AUTHORITY.

From the support of those who interest themselves in the cause of GENERAL LIBERTY, and readily stretch forth a helping hand to such as labour under the arbitrary Fangs of Despotic Violence; from such support alone (*my whole property dissipated*) I can now hope for Redress:– And to whom can a Sufferer so properly complain of *the illegal acts of arbitrary magistrates*, as to HIM, whose WHOLE CONDUCT hath done him honour as a MAGISTRATE, and marked him singularly a DEFENDER OF THE RIGHTS OF HIS FELLOW CITIZENS.

The contrast between your Lordship and my Destroyers, is striking and compleat.

I am

YOUR LORDSHIP'S

Most obedient servant,
S. Bruckshaw.

Introduction.

When an obscure Individual presumes to appeal to the Public, and to state to them his private grievance, two things ought to be a part of his case; First, that those grievances are of importance to the public at large; Secondly, that Legal Redress hath been sought in vain. When matters are thus situated, the complaint is no longer a private one; the oppression which crushes me to-day, may fall on my neighbour to-morrow, nor can any one assure himself He shall be able to escape.

It is on this ground the attention of the Reader is requested to the following melancholy narrative. He will find a series of transactions, oppressive and cruel beyond belief, were they not supported by the most authentic Documents, and an administration of justice that would disgrace the records of a Divan.[3] Magistrates shamefully interfering in a private dispute, and prostituting their authority to gratify the malevolence of their Pot-companions: Afraid of the consequence of this illegal prostitution of their Office, they plunge yet deeper into iniquity, and under a charge of insanity, (*a charge since acknowledged by the* PRINCIPAL CULPRIT *to be utterly without foundation,*) they drag the wretched victim of their despotic violence from his business, confine him in a gaol, load him with irons, and are not ashamed to call in the aid of a Keeper of a Private Mad-house: in which, (having artfully deceived his friends, residing at a considerable distance) they prolong his confinement for near a year, to the total ruin of his fortune and of his character.

Justly irritated at such treatment, and irreparably injured in substance and good name, his property dispersed, his business annihilated, the unhappy man seeks redress from the laws of his country, and commences an action in the Court of King's Bench.[4]

After being led through the various mazes of the law's delay, the venue changed from London to Lincoln, a nonsuit[5] obtained in March 1773, but leave at a considerable expense graciously obtained, "to begin again," the cause was a second time brought on before Mr. Baron Perrot,[6] at Lincoln, in August last, when the Jury's Verdict is again refused, and

HOC VOLO, SIC JUBEO,[7]

the Plaintiff is again nonsuited without being heard: For,

Unfortunately for him, the defendants are MAGISTRATES, and that, which adds to their guilt in every other eye, secures them the favour of congenial spirits. Men do not readily condemn their own vices in other men.

The ground of these nonsuits is, that the action is brought out of time, that the Defendants are sheltered from prosecution by the 24th Geo. IId. Chap. 44;[8] *not a circumstance of the complaint is DENIED, or even EXTENUATED.*

Are then indeed magistrates so screened? and is it thus in the power of an ignorant or venal attorney* to trifle away the day of reckoning for his injured trusting Client? if so, surely the personal liberty of the subject is slenderly protected, and his property very insecure. Of what advantage is it

---

* *Immediately* after his release, Bruckshaw applied to an eminent attorney in Manchester, who declined his cause, under the pretence that the above act cleared the offender, as the commitment was made nine months before.

that the Supreme Magistrate is restrained, if every ignorant officer of every paltry borough, elate with insolence, or intoxicated with authority, may thus with impunity trample on the dearest rights of his fellow subjects? By one Arbitrary Prince, a few (comparatively a few) individuals might be cruelly injured, but *"Procul á Jove"*,[9] the body of the people would be safe: By this determination every corner of the kingdom is over-run with tyrants; and we hold our boasted liberty and property at the will and pleasure of every arbitrary Upstart who hath interest to procure a Dedimus.[10]

It may not be unworthy notice to remark, how much doctors differ. – In a trial* before Sir William de Grey, at Guildhall London, in June 1771,[11] the learned Judge was of opinion, that if the Plaintiff insisted on it, no power was delegated to him, to prevent a matter going to the jury. In the present case, on the motion to set aside the Nonsuit in May 1773, (in London also) Lord Mansfield[12] declared, had the cause come before him, he would have subjected the Defendants to the verdict of the jury. Such was the determination of two Lawyers, confessedly the first in ability as they are in rank: but at Lincoln, in August 1773, Mr. Baron Perrot declares – Boo – he will judge for himself – it shall again be a Nonsuit.

In a late popular cause, the Prosecutor silenced a very able judge, who refused to receive the jury's verdict, by observing, "If their solemn determination was to be rejected by the judge, he did not see that juries were of any use." How much more reason has this much-injured man to echo that observation? May he not well add, except to load with additional expence the party who has least interest with the ——? Twice has this man been at the expence of a *Special* Jury,[13] and twice been refused their verdict. Such it seems is the practice in some of our courts of justice.

Wonder not, ingenuous Reader, that these things are so! you will find in the course of the following narrative, the majority of a respectable Corporation combine to support their Magistrates in the illegal destruction of an unoffending individual. No wonder, from the temptation such an union could tender to law, that *"some of the corps were a disgrace to it."*

Throw not from you, O indignant humanity, these sheets with detestation. Providence, for wise and good purposes no doubt, suffered a Jefferies and a Ryder[14] to stain the Annals of our Courts – Sigh however for such beings – a day of retribution must come.

For the rest: This tale of woe is set before the Public in the very words of the unlearned sufferer. Indulgence is therefore requested for inelegance of style, to which its Author, bred to business, has no pretensions. *Even though*

---

* Common Pleas, Mayer against Hunter, June, 1771, the Judge proposed a Nonsuit, but the Plaintiff demurring, the Judge made the above declaration, on which it was left to the jury, who gave a verdict for the Plaintiff.

he should not be enabled by this means further to pursue legal redress, he still hopes this appeal to the public will not be wholly useless, since if, in consequence of its publication, others may escape so fatal a shipwreck of fame and fortune, and such unmerited severeties; if by that general detestation which must follow this narrative, other Magistrates are withheld from such shameful and flagrant oppression; or, being hardy enough to commit such acts, should not be able to escape condign[15] punishment by Chicanery or Venality, this unhappy man will at least enjoy the melancholy satisfaction of not having wholly suffered in vain.

S.B.

One More Proof, &c.

At Bourn, near Stamford,[16] in the county of Lincoln, I pursued my business of woolstapler,[17] &c. in such a manner as made a considerable addition to my paternal fortune; improved my business and established my credit with people of the first reputation in the woollen manufactories in most parts of this kingdom.

After many years experience, I found that Bourn was not so good a situation for Buyers calling for my articles in trade as several other towns in the said county, particularly upon the North road; therefore, as my paternal estate lay in Cheshire, where I was never likely to reside, in the year 1768 I disposed of it, and resolved to fix myself properly for my business in Stamford. Accordingly, I made enquiries, and laid wait for a roomy situation there, suitable for my purpose. At length, in April 1769, my friend, Mr. John Trueman, enclosed to me the description and conditions of sale of the remainder of the late Hon. Mr. Justice Noel's estate in Stamford. On the 18th Mr. Trueman went with me to survey the premises, and I fixed upon such as we thought best suited my business: I returned to Bourn, and informed Mr. William Dyer, attorney at law, what my friend, Mr. Trueman, and I had concluded on; that it would be a considerable purchase, and that my money lay out in trade, which I should not like to curtail; that I purposed taking a part of my intended purchase-money up upon interest, therefore if he could furnish me on those terms, I would take him with me the next day, to be my purchaser, &c. To these terms he agreed, went with me, and we purchased something under the price we had fixed on, owing, as it afterwards appeared, to a concerted plan, that the said premises should either fall to the friends of a certain family in the neighbourhood, whose son was the proprietor's Sollicitor in this sale, or into the owner's hands again. Immediately after the sale we were apprised of this, and the Auctioneer having omitted to bring down with him the necessary credentials, to assure us he could make a good title, we thought proper to postpone paying the deposit, till he got them down from London, which he did upon the 22d, and they being satisfactory, I paid him a deposit of 20 per cent. and took his covenant for further time than the conditions of sale specified; and then the Auctioneer offered me a small adjoining house, which had fallen into the proprietor's hands, at a price which I thought worth my notice, therefore agreed to give him my answer in two days time; took my friend with me to make a re-survey of these premises, when we concluded to close that bargain upon the same terms, as it was a very convenient situation for the residence of a partner in trade, and the next day I paid him a deposit of 20 per cent. upon these premises, when Mr. Thomas Banister, deceased, the said Auctioneer, declared to me, "that he never was so abused by his employer about any business before, that he was afraid some mischief was in premeditation against me in my said purchase, but that, for his own part, he would lose his right hand before he would forfeit his Integrity," and desired me "to be aware, and take care of myself." The keys were left with Mr. John Dixon in Stamford, with orders "to let no person see the said premises without an order from me." In a few days after this John Mayer, Gent. of Gray's-Inn,[18] Mr. Dyer's agent, called upon him at Bourn, and Mr. Dyer advised me to let Mr. Mayer make my conveyances, and gave me such reasons why he was more proper than himself, that I consented to it, and then Mr. Mayer advised me, by all means, to take immediate possession of the said premises, and met me at Stamford on the 27th instant, to direct the mode and to be witness thereto; where he informed me, "he found several persons in the town much dissatisfied that I was the purchaser; that the premises were very cheap, and that if he had been down at the sale, he would have given more for them; wished me joy of my bargain;" and said, "he would compleat my conveyances as soon as possible, and pay the remainder of the purchase-money himself, for which he should only require a private mortgage, 'till I could fix that matter more agreeably, as it could not be supposed that a person situated as I was could have his money at command at such short notice." I immediately gave notice to the said Mr. Dyer, that he might furnish me with what money he pleased upon personal security; that I had fixed with Mr. Mayer to provide the remainder, at which Mr. Dyer took umbrage. Upon the 29th I came to reside upon the said premises, for two reasons; first, to secure possession; and, secondly, to prepare them for reception of my business; when I found several other persons in the town my enemies, merely because they could not endure me as their rival in trade, so advantageously situated, these joined in trumping up false reports, which injured me much in the good opinion of my friends. The corporation summonsed me to take up my freedom, and several of them intreated me to come into the body; to which I answered that, unless it was a free one, I should be much happier out of it, and that my business was called an art or mystery, and not one of the trades mentioned in the statute; therefore I was under no necessity of taking up my freedom.[19]

About this time Mr. Joseph Hargraves, of Wakefield in Yorkshire, (a gentleman very conversant with business, particularly the woolstapling branch) on his return from London called on me at Stamford, surveyed the said premises, and offered me one thousand pounds for my bargain. Mr. Mayer, my sollicitor, after perusing the Vender's title-deeds, wrote me from London a very satisfactory account of the title I was to have of these premises, and that Mr. Hill and Mrs. Noel were to levy a fine to me;[20] but concluded with, "*burn this letter,*" which very much surprized me.

My sollicitor, notwithstanding his aforesaid engagement, wrote pressingly to me to have my money ready in ten days time, in the interim to send him a small bill, to enable him to go on with my conveyance, which increased my suspicion that all was not right with him; I therefore wrote to Mr. William Trollope, Chancery-Office, the late proprietor's sollicitor, that I should be obliged to change my conveyancer, but would pay interest for any delay that arose on my part; he immediately shewed by his answer, that he was very unwilling I should change Mr. Mayer for another: first he tells me, "that He is not aware of any ill treatment I have met with from Mr. Mayer; next that the conveyances are ready, and nothing but the money wanting, and that it is most adviseable to let Mr. Mayer compleat the business;" and to enforce me to it, tells me, "he will not allow of any delay, but resell the estate, whereby I shall lose my deposit, and a very beneficial bargain, which he pretends he shall be very sorry for." Instantly after this, I found every engine at work to destroy my credit, throwing by this means several of my creditors suddenly upon me, which embarrassed my affairs in such a manner, that I judged it prudent to make an assignment of my effects[21] for the satisfaction of the rest. It was propagated at Stamford, with great diligence, that I was first doubted by the principal trades-people in Manchester, whither I immediately went, and called them together to chuse trustees. On the 31st of August, 1769, I executed a general deed of assignment to four of my creditors, in trust for the payment of such others as executed the said deed any time within three months, the overplus returnable to me, *in which the aforesaid premises were not included,* yet they compleated the said purchase on my account: only two of the trustees acted, and very few of my creditors gave themselves any trouble about executing the deed; my stock in trade, which was considerable and well laid in, was pushed off by my factors,[22] much under the market price, which at that time was greatly below the average; hereby I lost a great part of my property, and was deprived also of a very beneficial advantage in trade, with a prosperous established business, which in its infancy had produced me a considerable increase to my paternal fortune, over and above maintaining me genteelly: my acting trustees took upon them to resell my said purchases at Stamford, at the same time they disposed of my other effects at Bourn, and elsewhere, and for this purpose sent an advertisement up to London to be inserted in the St. James's Chronicle,[23] with a distinct description of three separate lots, to be sold upon the premises at Stamford, on the 15th of November, 1769; by some means or other it was erroneously inserted, viz. The late possessors name falsely spelled, and two of the lotts run into one, specifying them to be held on lease, under the corporation of Stamford, at the yearly rent of forty shillings. The close is so held; the house &c. jumbled with it in the advertisement, is freehold, and cost me five hundred and thirty pounds. The sale nevertheless went on, and there were scarce any bidders; those there were, had planned their own interest so closely, that they made purchases at their own price, and got contracts from these acting trustees, (*in which I did not join with them*), "to make them as good a title as they could," upon "their paying such purchase money, on or before the 25th of March, 1770;" which was about four hundred pounds less than the said premises cost me only the April before. Mature reflection upon the iniquitous manner in which I was thus deprived of every thing that was dear to me, in the very flower of my life, brought on an aguish disorder,[24] which was near baffling the skill of my physician, and which held me several months so low, that I never expected to recover, but it pleased God to restore me to my health; when I found that these said purchasers had failed to make good their aforesaid contract with my trustees, and that these had received nearly as much of my money as would satisfy the creditors who came into the said assignment; and thereupon I told the acting trustees, that I would make up the deficiency, and take my affairs back into my own hands, which they objected to, alledging that they lay under promises to many others of my creditors, who had not executed the said deed of assignment; the true reason, I believe was, they were unwilling the world should know that they had sold the premises, to which they could not make a title. I was also very desirous of re-establishing myself amongst my former acquaintances, and for that purpose, I looked out for people in trade, who were inclined to contract with me, to transact their business for them by commission, upon two compleat journeys in the year, from Manchester to London, through the manufacturing parts of Yorkshire, the counties of Lincoln, Norfolk, Suffolk and Essex; counties where I was conversant and well acquainted; and where I could easily sollicit the woollen manufacturers to give me commissions to buy up wools for them in my spare time, which I intended to spend in Lincolnshire for that purpose. At Stockport, in May 1770, I met with Mr. James Barnard, Hatter in London, who chearfully complied with my proposals at a certain price per cent. commission; at Manchester, I made no general contracts, but had several promised me they would consider on my proposals and write to me, if I would leave them my address, which I did, to the Bull Inn in Stamford.[25] At Halifax, Mr. Thomas Chambers executed a contract with me, upon the same terms as the said Mr. Barnard, for the disposal of his partnership's articles in trade, with his son, comb-makers, and another for the buying wools or yarns for his own trade, as a shalloon maker,[26] depending upon his orders from time to time; he observed that my proposals were such as he could not avoid complying with, all his fear was that I should have more "business than I could possibly look after myself." Many of the manufacturers promised to consider of my proposals betwixt then and the sheep-shearing, and to write to me at the Bull Inn, in Stamford; a certain family, who had used me very ungenteely the year before, interrupted me in getting commissions at Halifax, where I saw the principal, and expostulated with him upon this repetition of their unjustifiable behaviour; who seeming at a loss for an answer, at length said, "did not Mr. Prescott* inform my wife, that you some time ago spoke very disrespectfully of her?" to which I answered True; and I at that time told you, that what Mr. Prescott had informed her, I said was false; to which you answered, "Take no notice of it. I don't think it worth my while, so let no more be said about it." Then he said, but Mr. Prescott says a great deal more, was rather enraged, which created a quarrel, in which they made use of threatening expressions; but as they were considerable consumers of wool, I was very desirous we should part reconciled to each other, and staid a few days longer at Halifax than I intended, for that purpose. On the 10th of said June I paid them a visit; when I found that the Principal was not at home, I desired to speak with his wife, and when I saw her she was in a great rage, whereupon I immediately withdrew without hopes of a reconciliation, and the next day sent to my friends in Norwich and London, acquainting them with my plan of business, and that I should be glad to contract with them upon the same terms which I had done with the said Messrs. Chambers and Barnard, and that if I did not give them a call in the course of this said month of June, their answer to me directed to the Bull Inn, in Stamford, would come safe to hand, and be duly attended to: and on Tuesday the 12th of the said June, 1770, I left Halifax, and that night stopped to lay at Tuxford,[27] where Mr. Sellers, the landlord of the Red Lyon Inn, spent the evening with me, when I shewed him my contracts, to which he answered, as Mr. Chambers, "that I must certainly have more business upon those terms than I could possibly execute myself,"† and the next day,

---

* Mr. Prescott is a very considerable buyer of wool in Lincolnshire; connected with a capital house in Halifax.

† Excuse, Reader, the uninteresting detail. To palliate actions in their nature, incapable of extenuation, it has been affected, among many matters equally false and equally frivolous, that Mr. B—— was from the time of making his assignment wholly without employ. With what truth the above account, in which several reputable traders are mentioned, will best shew.

Those who know Mr. Barnard, and Mr. Bullock, of Manchester, Mr. Chambers, &c. are desired to consider whether such opulent and intelligent gentlemen, conversant as they are in trade, would enter into contract with a mad-man. In May the two former, on the 9th of June the latter, signed articles with B——; on the 14th of the same June, the upright Mayor of Stamford cancelled these and all other contracts by his commitment.

viz the 13th inst. I arrived at Stamford, which happened to be at the time of the races; I paid a visit to Mr. Fothergill, who contracted for the leasehold close with my acting trustees as aforesaid, for one pound more than they put it up at, when I told Mr. Fothergill I would not join in making out titles to the premises my trustees sold, for the reasons aforesaid, and as I did not want my money to go into business with. After I got to my inn, Henry Cumbery, Esq; came there and gave me an invitation to a bed at his house, which I accepted; he also was one of the purchasers of my trustees. The next morning at breakfast I informed him I would not join in making a title to any of the premises my acting trustees sold in Stamford, for the reasons aforesaid; to which he answered "that he had laid out money in repairs:" I answered him, "that as to the repairs, he should enjoy them as my tenant, in preference to any other person, if he chose it, as I did not want to reside on the premises myself at present." I then waited upon Mr. John Bowis, attorney at law, the person who contracted with my trustees for the capital messuage[28] where I intended fixing my business, at the said re-sale. At the time of the sale he desired of my trustees, he might have the keys to now and then make fire to keep the house aired; by this means he crept into possession and re-sold the said premises to one —— Langton, Esq; as I am informed, at the price* I intended to have given before I would have left it; and Mr. Bowis had put the said Langton into possession, who was making alterations, under an expectation that Mr. Bowis would make him a good title; therefore I desired Mr. Bowis would walk with me to him, to let him know what he had to depend upon; Mr. Bowis refused to go with me, but I thought it my duty to let Mr. Langton also know my resolution, as it might prevent him laying out any more unnecessary money in alterations, and went; when a servant boy came to the gates, to appearance a stable boy, whom I asked, "if Mr. Langton was within?" he answered, "no." I then asked "if Mrs. Langton was within?" to which he answered, "no." I then told him I would take an opportunity of calling again, and went to Mr. Cumbery's, and sat down to write a letter, and soon after saw Mr. Langton go into the yard gates; I immediately went to the gates, which the same boy opened and gave me the same answer as before, viz. "that his master was not within." I asked him what he meant "by denying his master, when I knew he was at home?" Seeing another servant down in the yard, to whom I went and asked the same question, he gave me the like answer: I told him "I knew he was, and if he did not chuse to let him know one wanted to speak with him I would step as far as the lobby myself, and see if I could not meet with him; as I had been once before to no purpose, I did not chuse to come a third time when

---

* Bruckshaw bought these premises for 1470*l* the trustees sold it to Bowis for 1130*l* Bowis sold it to Langton for 1600*l* – about 50*l* had been expended by Bruckshaw in repairs; by Bowis not one shilling.

there was no occasion for it:" still he would not move; in the passage I met a servant-maid, to whom I put the same question: she answered, "her master was at home," but came past me to the man, then called out "no, Sir, he's gone out again," which I did not believe, so went into the lobby and knocked at the door, where I heard men in conversation; then Mr. Langton presented himself with a supercilious air of consequential importance, and demanded "what business I had there," which vexed me, and I believe I might answer him short, with "as much business as you have, Sir, and that I came here to inform you, that you have got in here without any knowledge or consent of mine, either as a purchaser or even a tenant, therefore you might have behaved like a gentleman, especially upon these premises, where you ought to consider yourself as only an intruder; however, as you are in possession, if you propose any equitable terms for quitting these premises at some certain time, I have not the least inclination of behaving to you ungenteelly: Mr. Bowis, who has let you into possession here, has failed to make good his contract with my acting trustees, and has not, even to this day, paid any part of the said purchase-money, therefore my whole business with you is to inform you, that I shall not join in any conveyance of these premises to the said Mr. Bowis: as this is the case, all I want further with you is, to know your resolution respecting your present situation with these premises;" at this he seemed a great deal confused, civilly desired me to walk into the room he came out of, where were only his two friends which I saw go in at the gates with him; he sent for Mr. Bowis; I apprehending these gentlemen might be come in upon business, made that apology for withdrawing into the garden till Mr. Bowis came; as I returned into the house, he arrived at the same instant, when Mr. Langton eagerly addressed him with "Mr. Bowis here's a fellow comes and tells me I'm an intruder;" which vexed me, and some few words of altercation passed between us, which immediately subsided; Mr. Bowis went into the parlour, and Mr. Langton walked out with me into the court-yard, when Mr. John Arnall, and Mr. William Raunsley, woolstapler, my successor, at Bourn, aforesaid, came up to the gates; I told Mr. Langton "they were two of my friends, with his leave I would admit them;" to which he gave consent; they came in, and I repeated to them the insolent behaviour I had just met with from Langton as aforesaid, which concluded by telling him, that we three would take a little walk in the garden, if he chused to have any consultation about his answer, with Mr. Bowis. When we returned, Mr. Langton was withdrawn from Mr. Bowis, who I asked if he had left any answer? he said, "none at all." I told him I would wait no longer then, if he chused to send it me in writing, any time betwixt that time and the next day afternoon it would do quite as well, if not, I should then have the trouble to call again, so went to the Bull inn with my friends to dine, with Mr. Arnall at the ordinary.[29] Soon after we got there, the town serjeant[30] came to me, and informed me that the Mayor desired I would not call at Mr. Langton's any more, to which I answered, "that Mr. Mayor's officiousness very much surprised me, and that I thought he interfered officially very prematurely, but as he was a civil messenger, and I acquainted with Mr. Hopkins, he might give my compliments to him, and tell him, that I would not, till I had spoke with him."

After dining at the ordinary, I went to the Mayor's who put into my hand a card, containing these words: "Mr. Langton's compliments wait upon Mr. Mayor, to inform him, that notwithstanding Mr. Bruckshaw's promise to the town serjeant, that he would not call again before he had spoke to you; he has been again, and frighted Mrs. Langton so, that she is like to miscarry;" whereupon I told Mr. Mayor, "Mrs. Langton had certainly been imposed upon, I had not been there, therefore if he would walk with me to her, we would ease her of her fears, which were entirely groundless." At first he agreed to go, but immediately declined it: I thought it my duty to go, and instantly went, and found two constables[31] placed with their staffs within the yard gates, whom I asked "if Mrs. Langton was within," they answered with a disappointed confusion, "no," waiting Langton's word of command, who without making any enquiry, instantly called out, "seize him, and take him before the Mayor." Whereupon, Ely Buswell, seized me by the collar: in return, I seized Buswell by his, demanding his authority, who up with his staff to knock me down, which I catched in my other hand; then Needham, the other constable, collared me, and they dragged me through the public streets just as the company were going to the race, to the Mayor's, who was upon the watch, and come out at the door as we arrived thus before his house, when I addressed myself to him, with, "Mr. Mayor, do you permit your constables to act the part of ruffians? they have seized me and dragged me through the streets before you thus, meerly by the order of Langton; you know the errand I went upon; I have demanded their warrant, and they do not so much as pretend that they have one."

Whereupon, without asking the constables a single question, he ordered them to let me go, and they instantly quitted their holds; all this happened in the public street, before the Mayor's door; I have no doubt, but that the aforesaid card was written with a design to send me irritated against Langton, to the said premises, as the constables were placed there ready for seizing me.

I went to my inn, and as I was ordering my horse out to go meet my friends at the race, the aforesaid Mr. Arnall and the Mayor were in close conference together in my inn yard, Mr. Arnall leaning out at a window, presently the Mayor turned about, and called to some men about St. Mary's church, "seize him and take him down to the goal;" whereupon four or five men came into the yard, seized me and instantly dragged me to the goal, without either warrant, hearing, or mittimus;[32] when we got to the goal, these ruffians were at a loss how to dispose of me: the dungeon door being open, I told them, that was the proper place for prisoners, and they were going to put me in there, which when the mayor saw, he came running to us, and said, "no no, he must not go in there; take him into the house;" so they dragged me into

William Clarke's, the goaler's house, which is a public one, facing the goal, where they fixt me in his parlour, these men remaining as my guard; the mayor went immediately to the race, where he was much blamed for what he had done, by the recorder[33] and his friends; soon after I was fixed in the goaler's parlour, one of the gentlemen that was at Mr. Langton's, when we had the altercation in the morning, came to me, whom I told, "that I had rather have been put into the dungeon, than be a prisoner where I was; as Mr. Hopkins, would endeavour to give it the air of favour," who answered, "that makes no manner of difference, as you are deprived of your liberty, you are in every sense of the word as much in goal here, as you would have been in the dungeon, I will maintain it." He soon after left me, and proves to be Edward Read Thong, gentleman, attorney at law, in Huntington. I being then of opinion that the same conspirators were concerned in this imprisonment, that so iniquitously wrought my ruin the year before, and that providence had permitted them to fall into this unjustifiable predicament; for their immediate punishment, and my re-establishment; reason dictating to me that I had an undoubted right to fix my own price upon my time, and that my restrainers would say in answer to such a charge, "it is very hard that we should be made liable to the payment of a sum of money which are thus made debtors for without our knowledge or consent." I thought it adviseable to get pen, ink, and paper, and make out a regular charge per time against them, publickly declaring my price to these ruffians, and lay it open to the inspection of any person who came to see me; and further declared, that I would double it if I was not released before the half hour expired, and desired the ruffians to let their employers know it. This method I pursued during the whole of my imprisonment at Stamford, being convinced, that this opportunity was thrown in my way to make them sensible of their last year's crimes. When Clarke came from the race, he seemed much dissatisfied that I was his prisoner upon these terms, and that we deprived him of the use of his parlour, as a publican. That evening he set the table for five to sup together. At that instant Thickbroom,[34] the town-serjeant, came in, and made enquiry of Clarke who were going to supper in the parlour; and being answered, said, "Why, Clarke, do you think it decent to set Mr. Bruckshaw down to supper with the constables?" which irritated Clarke, and a warm altercation immediately arose between these two Corporation Officers.

In the morning, ruminating how I could come at some intelligence why I was thus imprisoned before we went to the Mayor's, I at length determined to send for Doctor Jackson as a physician, and Apothecary Judd,[35] an Alderman, meerly to see if I could learn any thing to my purpose from them. When I arose I wrote to each of them a card, desiring their immediate attendance at the goal, each in his respective profession.

Doctor Jackson attended, but was remarkably reserved. To enforce conversation, I told him my spirits were rather languid and flat, owing to the treatment I had met with, and sleeping little in my last night's confinement; therefore desired he would order me some comfortable, cordial-like medicine. When he sat down to write the prescription, I clearly perceived him involved in the utmost perplexity; when he seemed to have finished it, he put it into his pocket, refusing to leave it with me for the apothecary; saying as he went out of the room, "I will send you something that shall do you some good." This raised my suspicion, that it was more than probable, that he might be the person who had engaged the mayor to make the said imprisonment, engaged thereto at the instance of his brother-in-law, Mr. John Prescott of Halifax. In a short time after his visit, three bottles of physick were brought to me by Sarah Burton, the goaler's maid, labelled, "Take one every three hours." She said they were given to her by a girl, who she understood came from apothecary Judd's; therefore as he had not attended, I put the said physick into my pocket, with a design to have it examined by the college of physicians. Soon after the goaler took me before the mayor, who appeared much confused; and at length confessed, "That he made the said imprisonment, at the request of the aforesaid John Arnall," who had large connections in trade with the said John Prescott. I asked him, "how he could think of making an imprisonment, meerly at the request of any person whatever?" and told him my suspicion of, and intentions with, the said physick; he immediately answered, I will send for Dr. Jackson, and Mr. Judd, and make each of them take a bottle of it, before your face, for your satisfaction."

I then laid before him my charge for false imprisonment; adding with that, "I always desired the men whom you thought proper to place as my guard, to advise you of this charge, prior to my making the respective advances in it." He took it in his hand and said, "Sure! We can tax this bill;[36] I was not convinced that it was a false imprisonment, till as I now find Mr. Langton refuses to attend: But I have him secure, in a good hundred thousand pounds, and you may have the Rev. Mr. Thomas Hurst, as security for Mr. Langton's future good behaviour." To which I answered, "it was a considerable sum, and very extraordinary that he, as a magistrate, should require such a security, and that, if that was the case, I do not see how that security could be liable to answer your own commitment, from the Bull Inn, which you acknowledge you made at the request of Mr. Arnall, therefore I am not surprised, that Mr. Langton refuses to attend; and as to your taxing my Bill, you have not the smallest shadow of ground for it; I am inclined to believe that my Lord Chancellor would not tax it under these circumstances of the case." Here Mr. Daniel Ding of Bourn, one of my silent trustees, called upon me, and gave me a letter he had received from Mr. William Hardy of Stockport, one of the acting ones, which inclosed his draft upon Mr. John Dixon in Stamford for thirty-eight pounds on my account, drawn in favour of Mr. Ding, who asked me if I wanted any money; to which I answered, "I do not, but am much obliged to you for the offer." Thickbroom, the town-serjeant, was in and out all the morning as a messenger, and the mayor informed me thus; "I have sent for Mr. Judd, and he refuses to come; Dr. Jackson has sent for answer, that the faculty are at breakfast with him, so he cannot leave home till they are gone." Soon after, the mayor came into the room and informed me thus; "Mr. Langton has just now sent word, that he will meet us in the town hall at eleven o'clock, and repeated that he had him safe in the aforesaid security," and ordered me thither; I went through the hall into a room adjoining, and waited there till past eleven, when James White, the jailor's servant, came through the room where I was, went into the town-hall, and secured the door upon me, and I immediately found myself a prisoner there; I called to White "to open the door," who refused to give any answer; I then told him, "If he would not open it, I would force it open;" saying, "You have no right to shut me out of a public court of justice where I am ordered to attend by your chief magistrate:" he disregarded this; I forced the door open, and waited in the hall about an hour, when John Walker and Robert Whittle, two porters, came into the hall; I asked them what they wanted; they, with downcast looks, answered, "We are come to attend upon you," and were as perversely contradictory as possible. No Langton attended, neither did the Mayor come into the hall to execute the duties of his office.

In the afternoon, meeting with a Freeman's oath, I wrote under it my compliments to the mayor, desiring "he would maturely consider whether he was forsworn or not," and ordered the goaler's people to carry it to him, and desired them to tell him from me, "that the corporation were forfeiting their charter, which could only be legally prevented by a release and discharge of my demand for false imprisonment, which was now grown so high by his own delay, that it accumulated fast; therefore desired he would put a stop to it by a release. In the dusk of the evening a male voice, seemingly desirous to be unknown, in passing under the town-hall, called out, "Continue to behave like a man, you will have some desperate work presently." Soon after, William Clarke the goaler, and White his servant, came into the hall; they and the said two porters all assaulted me at once: I made all the resistance I was able, whereupon Clarke clasped his arm upon my throat several times, each time thus strangling me till my life was just gone; at length they all fastened upon me, in such a manner, that they were enabled to drag me through Clarke's house up into an obscure garret, and there they threw me upon my back on the bed, and three of them, to wit, Clarke, Walker, and Whittle, held me down while White picked my pocket of the aforesaid physic; Clarke's servant-maid, Sarah Burton, and his daughter, held their aprons to receive it; then White picked all my pockets of every thing they contained, except my watch, one sixpence, and a few halfpence; amongst my papers was the aforesaid letter from Mr. Hardy to Ding. I demanded an inventory of what they had taken from me; they answered, "You shall have no inventory; every thing shall be carried to the Mayor." I then threw open the window, and called out, as loud as I was able, "Murder! murder! murder!" in hopes that some humane person or Peace Officer would come to me and enquire into the reason of my cries, but I was answered from the bridge, "You may call out, but they will let nobody come to your relief." The next day, viz the 16th, Walker and Whittle threw me upon my back on the bed, and Walker clapped his elbow upon my mouth, and burst my lips against my teeth; they bled into my mouth, and I was held down in such a manner that I was near being suffocated with the blood, at the same time I was otherwise savagely treated by Whittle; then they took out their bludgeons[37] from under their pillow, and came brandishing them over me, and said, "We'll make use of these if ye don't behave as we like." The next day, immediately after dinner, they two and White threw me on my back upon the bed, and bound me down hand and foot to the bed; in that situation they kept me close bound till the next morning, without any subsistence: some time after, the said ruffians were severally called down below stairs to receive further instructions, and urged to prosecute their cruelties; but they returned into the said garret dissatisfied, declaring to each other, "that they had strictly observed their engagement, and solemnly vowed that they were determined to proceed no further; their Employers were all a parcel of fools, and were as much at a loss how to get me out of the garret as they were to get me into it." They said they wished they had never been concerned, begging that I would deal mercifully with them, "as they were poor men* seduced by the hopes of a large reward, which was secured to them BY A BOND EXECUTED BY THE WHOLE CORPORATION, and such of their friends as they could influence who were at the race." At my request they informed me of as many of their names as they could recollect; of which I made out a regular list, then called up William Clarke the goaler, and read to him the said list of names, who stood like a statue, never attempting to disavow a single name or circumstance of the said confession, but instantly withdrew.

I omit the publication of the said list, as it would lay a foundation for an infamous reproach to their families. Walker, Whittle, and White, further informed me of many persons who refused to execute this bond, among which was George Denshire in Stamford, Samuel Reynardson *a justice of peace of the quorum*,[38] and one of the six clerks in chancery, and Roger Parker of Peterborough, Esquires; and of some who expostulated with the corporation, *shewing them the iniquitous conspiracy of such an instrument,* of which *they would certainly repent.* Among those who opposed it were *the Lord Lieutenant of the county*,[39] his Grace the Duke of Ancaster, Lord Carberry, and the Rev. Richard Wright deceased, *a magistrate,* and his Grace's chaplain;

---

* They added, that several of their fellow porters had said to them, "I would not have had your employment for all the world."

and that this was at a general meeting after the race was over, when, it was concluded *to write to my relations in Cheshire that I was insane*, in confinement, *and taken proper care of.* Strong opposition was made to this determination by many gentlemen present, *but to no purpose.*

On the 20th Mr. John Collings, common-councilman, deceased, and his friend, visited me in the said garret, and voluntarily confessed, "*that he was one of those who executed the said bond,* looked over the list and charge, then begged *that I would excuse him.*" I could not procure my bags from my inn till the 21st, as Mr. John Terrewest, my landlord, never once came to see how I did, *know what I wanted,* or how I chused to have my mare taken care of; and when my bags were brought to me, *the sewing on of the strap* which makes them up *evidently appeared to be entirely new,* my papers had been rifled, as I apprehend, to see my connection *in Norwich and London;* then I also got my journal, where I made a minute of every letter I had been permitted to write *to my friends in this garret,* which I'm informed were carried to the mayor, *and there stopped, broke open, and read.* And upon settling my cash account, I found that the said ruffians *had picked my pockets,* as aforesaid, of upwards of *twelve pounds,* consisting of pieces of gold, one 3 l. 12s. piece, one moidore,[40] six guineas, and some silver; *no physician attended to the care of my health,* notwithstanding the malady which they pretended *I laboured under* in the said garret, which would have been *naturally inflamed* by such treatment, the heat of the season, *and drinking wine,* which was never denied me.*

Mr. Ding visited me in the said garret the 8th day of the Imprisonment; John Wych, town-clerk, visited me several times, and looking over the aforesaid list of names and charge for false imprisonment, said, "*We may thank Will Trollope for this.* What do you intend doing with us? *Do you imagine the bond able to pay your demand?*"

Just before my dinner was brought up, on the 26th of June 1770, two strangers came abruptly into the said garret, and with an air of great familiarity addressed themselves to me thus; "Well, Mr. Bruckshaw, *how doone you,* Com yoo'sen go with us, t' see yoor friends i' Yorshire." I asked their names; they answered, Wilson. I replied, "I came from thence only a fortnight ago. My business lies in London, requires my immediate attendance, *and I will be there as soon as possible.*" They still importuned me to go with them, to which I answered, *If your business here is to insult me,* I desire you will immediately quit the room, which will save me the trouble of shewing you the way out. If you choose to behave civilly, sit down, and

---

* The gaoler's maid and the aforesaid ruffians importuned me "*to let them convince me of the innocency of the aforesaid physic,* by any one of them taking a bottle of it," which they pretended had never been out of the next room. *This I refused; as the bottles had been several days out of my possession, of course I would not be satisfied the contents were the same.*

welcome, *my dinner is coming in.*" Upon which they sat down, and after some time said, "Well, Maister, if yoo winnow goo with us ween be getting towards hoom, han-you any messuage that yoo chus'en to send by us to your friends." I thanked them and said, "You may tell them the situation I'm in; *that I have been most barbarously treated*: but these men who are placed in the next room as my guard have repented of what they have done, *and that they were hired to it* by the mayor and his friends; and since that they have behaved to me with some civility. *I expect to be released every minute*, and then they shall hear from me, and *that I am very well*." To which they answered, "We win, *so fare yoo weell*, they'll be glad to hear fro' yoo;" and immediately withdrew.

In the evening, *to my great surprize*, the aforesaid Wilsons returned into the said garret, and with the assistance of Clarke the goaler, Walker, Whittle, and White, seized me, threw me upon the bed, *clapped irons on my hands and legs*, and dragged me into a chaise.[41] In the first stage, Wilson senior said, "*The mayor wanted us tak yoo with us without his warrant*, but I knew better; I have one i' me pocket, *signed by the mayor and one alderman Exton*; the mayor seemed to sit on thorns when he had ge'en me the warrant." Walker, who went with us the first stage, informed me of two other Persons *who executed the aforesaid bond*.

A fresh chaise was taken at the Bull Inn upon Witham Common,[42] and I enquired of the landlord, John Brandon, if he saw or knew of any bond or deed being handed about by the mayor and town-clerk of Stamford, on the 14th or 15th instant, soliciting hands, to engage William Clarke the goaler, James White his servant, John Walker and Robert Whittle, two porters, to take and treat me as aforesaid? who answered, "*I did see such an instrument*, with a number of names to it." He acknowledged with much concern *that he had himself signed it*. On my asking his reason, he made me no answer, but immediately withdrew from the chaise door *exceedingly affected*.

We stopped at the Angel Inn in Grantham to take chaise; here I desired Mr Crabtree's waiter to step for me to the mayor, and acquaint him with my situation, *and that I requested to be brought before him*; whereupon the Wilsons immediately ordered the chaise out, and in their hurry forgot to tell the boy to drive for Nottingham, so he took us to Newark,[43] and we stopped all night at the Kingston's Arms, where the Rev. Richard Barnard of Cortlingstock, in the said county of Nottinghamshire, was attending the visitation,[44] and came into the room where I was, *and took me by the hand*, in a very friendly manner, expressing himself in these words; "*Sir, you are as well as I am*, but let me intreat you, *to be as patient and still as possible*, till you get to London; *you will have no justice till then*: there, you may depend upon it, you will be properly redressed, with exemplary damages." He has since informed me thus; "when I first heard the irons, I supposed some of Sir J. Fielding's men *had apprehended a felon*,[45] and sent my Pallator[46] out to make enquiry, who brought me for answer, that it was a person of a respectable appearance, whom they were conveying to some place of confinement, *under a pretence that he was disordered in his senses.* So was I led into the room to you, by the *irresistable feelings of humanity, tho' prejudiced with that idea.*"

The next morning, the 27th, we stopped to breakfast at the Red Lyon Inn in Tuxford, where I was in full expectation of procuring a hearing before a magistrate, as I was personally known by Mr. Sellers, the landlord, with whom I spent my evening, and lay at his house on the 12*th inst.* and shewed him my contracts by commission; when he observed in answer, "Your terms and acquaintance in the specified counties will induce the most respectable people in trade to contract with you, *even to any quantity of business you chused to undertake,* it clearly appears to me a very beneficial plan to you, *and equally eligible to your employers.*"

I requested of Mr. Sellers to be carried before a magistrate, whereupon he sent for Mr. Edward Thornton a constable, who I desired to demand Wilsons authority for conveying me through the country in that manner; *they seemed frighted,* and produced him the order of *John Hopkins, Mayor, and John Exton, Alderman,* two magistrates of Stamford, dated the day before, viz. the 26th, which the said Thornton read aloud, and found that it was directed to "John Wilson, and J. Wilson his son, *Surgeons,* to take me *at the request of my friends* to Scout Mill in the parish of Ashton, in the county of Lancaster, *and take care of me as a person insane,*"[47] without shewing *either information or complaint.* I then desired the said constable to carry me before a magistrate, who answered, "*there is none near.*" By my desire he took the handcuffs off for me to breakfast, then loosed one of the irons off my leg, and went with me into the garden; when we returned, Wilson put the irons on again, ordered a chaise out and carried me through Worksop Park to the town, there took chaise to Sheffield, where we arrived at the George Inn, about noon; I desired Mr. Thomas Watson the landlord, to get me carried before a magistrate, and he sent for one John Morley, a constable, whom I desired to demand Wilsons authority for treating me in this manner: they immediately produced him *the aforesaid order,* which he also read aloud. I then desired him to carry me before a magistrate, to which he answered, as Thornton, "that there is none near." My legs being swelled by the weight and tightness of the irons, I desired Morley would direct them to be taken off, which he did, but Wilsons insisted upon keeping the handcuffs on. Morley stayed most of the afternoon with me, and desired to be paid for his attendance; as I had not a sixpenny piece, I desired Wilsons to pay him; they answered, *We did not want his company,* nor send for him, *we winow pay him.* When I went to bed, they took me into a two-bedded garret, and Wilsons chained me by the leg to the bed-post all night, and lay in the other bed.

The next morning the 28th inst. Wilsons ordered out a chaise and four, to run by the way of Woodhead, to Scout Mill: I observed to them, that that was a very improper road for a chaise, and desired to go the turnpike-road to Stockport, which was full as near,[48] and there I should see my friends; but I could not prevail. Wilson sen. declared at Sheffield in my hearing thus: "he is as weel as I am," and said to me, yo'or Brother will be at our house as soon as he knows yo'or there, which was not till near five o'clock in the afternoon.

On our arrival at Scout Mill, I told Wilson, that the words of the warrant which they had with me from Stamford were, *that they should take me to Scout Mill,* which they now had literally obeyed, and that their further orders by it were, "*and there take care of him,*" which were too vague for them to keep me a prisoner upon; therefore I advised them to consider well what they were about, for unless they (*Wilsons*) declared to me, that I was at liberty to go about my business, *I should consider myself as their prisoner,* to which they gave me no answer. When Wilson shewed me to bed, he carried me up into a dark and dirty garret, *there stripped me,* and carried my cloaths out of the room, which I saw no more, *for upwards of a month,* but lay chained to this bad bed, *all that time;* this appears to be their breaking in garret; under the ridgetree[49] is a box for the harbour of pigeons, which they disturb in the night time, to affright their prisoner when he should rest. For this purpose some of Wilson's family are up all night long, sometimes they throw pails of water down under the window, now and then brushing across, with a few small rods, or rubbing with a stone or brick upon the wall, sometimes put a light up to the window, and every now and then make a disagreeable noise, to awake you in a fright. In the day-time the window is darkened, and common necessaries denied; they gave me bad victuals, short allowance, with sour beer, oftener water, and sometimes not that; no attendance, but what was as contradictory and provoking as they could possibly invent, and frequently the most barbarous stripes; and to keep these inquisition-like transactions a secret from the world, Wilson's wife does the office of a barber, but I refused to come under her hands; and by that means got a Barber, who is a very respectable evidence.

At the expiration of about a month, I was permitted to have my cloaths *for a day,* and to walk about the house in irons; when any person was in conversation with me, Wilson made it a rule to interrupt us with "Why maister, yo'r weel us'd, *yoo getten plenty of good victuals and drink,* and rest in your bones, *yoon be fitt for any thing* when yoo gone from here; I'm liken to be the best friend *yoo han'*;" which generally had the intended effect of enraging me.

This Wilson never failed to observe to the person who I had been conversing with, adding, "*that I was very subject to rave in this manner,* and that I behaved very audaciously at Stamford; *or the mayor (who is a very good kind of mon)* would not *have imprisoned him.*"

In this manner I was treated, (*now and then a day below stairs,*) in the said garret, till the beginning of November, when I was reduced to a skeleton; I really thought I must have died with pining, cold, and severity of treatment; Wilson had the like apprehensions, allowed me a fire, but refused me a doctor and nurse, permitted me to come down into the family as soon as I was able to stir about, where Wilson's wife threatened me thus: "*I'll lay yoo o' the head with the poker, if yoo doo make complaint to any body that comes into th' house."*

While I enjoyed this privilege, there came a servant maid out of a respectable family in Manchester, and wanted Wilson to cure her complaint in one week, which he undertook to do; Wilson's family gave it out, *"that her disorder was a dropsey, and lowness of spirits,* which made her incapable of doing her business." – I being of opinion that this woman might have got superior advice in Manchester, and that real dropsies were not to be cured in a week, happened to say, that this woman's disorder must certainly, from her applying to Wilson, be of a nature that required secrecy and the assistance of a rogue,[50] and the next day I was chained up in this second garret, which was exceedingly smoaky; sometimes allowed no fire at all. Here I was confined EIGHTY-TWO DAYS.*

I was at at length permitted to write letters to my friends, which Wilson promised to send as directed, yet stopped, broke open, and read them; one of which was found by a fellow prisoner and brought to me.

My journal was taken from me, when they perceived I took minutes of their transactions, along with a ten pound bank note, my charge for false imprisonment, and the list of names which I took from the mouths of the ruffians at Stamford, who they confessed executed to them the aforesaid Bond.

On the eighty second day of the close confinement in this garret, Wilson came up and addressed me thus: *"weel maister, as this chimney smooks so,* if yoon behave mannerly, *yoos' cn go down into' ith house;"* and took the irons off my leg. I immediately found that it was through the persuasion of a respectable gentleman, well acquainted with maladies of the nature Wilsons and the magistrates of Stamford publicly reported that I laboured under. When I thanked him for my release from the irons, &c. he told me he prevailed upon Wilsons, by reasoning with them in these words: "I have spent more than once, some hours with Mr. Bruckshaw, and I find him *no more disordered in his senses,* than any one of your own family, or any person *in this parish;* you are destroying his health, which I find he has been as careful in preserving *as if directed by a physician and called in for that purpose,* you cannot mean any good by such treatment. He is naturally of a strong, healthy constitution, *which requires exercise,* why don't you let him come down into the family, *and*

---

* "He was sitting upon the ground upon a little straw in the furthest corner of his dungeon, which was alternately his chair and bed: a little calendar of small sticks were laid at the head, notched all over with the dismal days and nights he had passed there – He had one of these little sticks in his hand, and with a rusty nail he was etching another day of misery to add to the heap. As I darkened the little light he had, he lifted his hopeless eye towards the door – shook his head, and went on with his work of affliction. I heard his chains upon his legs as he turned his body to lay his little stick upon the bundle. – He gave a deep sigh – I saw the iron enter into his soul – I burst into tears." SENT. JOUR, V.II. P. 31. [51]

take a little air? I am moreover informed that he never was otherwise than he now is, and that it is unanimously allowed by a number of your own neighbours who saw him get out of the chaise at Lusley,[52] upwards of six months ago, that he was no more disordered in his senses at that time than any person there present, which is well confirmed to me, by what I have seen myself, and been informed by the Barber who has shaved him all the time he has been confined here, and the same is avouched by your neighbours all round you." This gentleman is a surgeon and physician of eminence.[53]

I being thus released, out of the said garret; my friend and I walked out together, and called upon several of the neighbours, who informed me, that my confinement would soon be at an end; for the neighbours took such notice, that Wilsons were very uneasy that they had any concern in the matter, notwithstanding all the money they got from the people of Stamford; which they had reason to believe was a considerable sum, and that they might have had more, if they had asked it, and that they were very poor before they fell into this way, scarce able to keep themselves off the parish." That they had seen my brother come and go several times, seemingly in great trouble, and that Wilson's landlord had taken him to task respecting my confinement, and that Wilson answered him, "I want to know how I'm to be paid before I let him goo'a."

They advised me not to think of running away, as my enemies would gratify their malignaty with observing, that I run away from a madhouse. I answered them, that I would not, and told them of the young woman from Manchester, as aforesaid, to which they answered, that they had heard Wilson accused of the like before, but were always willing to hope it was not true.

When I returned back, I made some enquiry of my fellow prisoners, if they had seen my Brother, to which they answered they had, *he had been several times*, and was very importunate to see me; but that Wilson always put him off, with saying, "it'll be better for him, that yoo don't, he's so bad, that he'll be ready to tear you too pieces; I hardly dar go ney him sometimes mysel, and it all as makes him worse." And that Wilsons had denied many others in the same manner, yet they durst not contradict them, for fear of their cruel resentment; they threatened me with close confinement again, if I dared to call in at any of their neighbours houses. I gave them no answer, but walked out, and importuned the neighbours to make a complaint in my behalf, before a magistrate; some of them promised they would, if I was not released soon; they would speak to Wilson first; as he was a desperate fellow, and their neighbour, they had rather not incur his resentment. On my return, I again demanded their authority for detaining me, whereupon they brought me the aforesaid order of John Hopkins, and John Exton, and after reading it, I put it into my pocket, and Wilson's wife immediately called her husband and son, and gave them orders to take it from me by force, which they obeyed, at the same time promising me thus: "yoo'son hav a copy on't when yoo gune fro here." I also presumed to to arraign their judgment, in the management of pretended Lunatics; to which they answered, "Yoo'en been used just as twas fixt on before we touch't yoo." The neighbours importuned them so closely to release me, that they at length let my Brother know I was recovered, and might be at liberty as soon as he pleased: my brother came over on the 25th of March, 1771, and I was released from the aforesaid imprisonment of *Two hundred and Eight-four days*, by order of John Hopkins, and John Exton, Magistrates of Stamford, under their aforesaid charge of insanity.

SUCH, READER, are the actions of men vested with power, and unrestrained by Principle.

Accustomed to venerate the Laws of your country, and to consider them as equal – as the Protectors of every man who pays them due respect, as particularly averse to oppression, and denouncing the severest vengeance against those who dare to encroach on the freedom of their fellow subjects, you will be ready to exclaim with a generous eagerness – Let this man, now at last released, apply to the Laws of his country, which will inflict suitable punishment on these evil-doers; and amply, most amply, recompence his losses and his sufferings.

Alas, my Good Friend, you know nothing of the matter. – God forbid you should know it experimentally. – You are yet to be told, That where Wealth and Influence are opposed to an obscure individual with a moderate fortune, you may as well hope to

"Drink up Eisel, eat a crocodile,"[54]

as to obtain redress, even for such injuries as these.

"Fabrigas against Mostyn." – True, my Good Friend – but Fabrigas was supported by a Noble Duke,* of princely spirit, and of princely fortune; and happy it was for him that he gained that protection.[55]

In the following pages you will see what chance an *unprotected* Individual stands, who seeks redress at law against powerful opposers, and you will be ready to agree that the Sabre of a Dey[56] would be *tender mercy*, and *equal justice*.

UPON my enlargement, I went amongst my acquaintance, and found many of them irremoveably prejudiced, with a belief that insanity was the cause of my imprisonment at Stamford; which filled my mind with much anxiety and displeasure against my unjust oppressors, for having so infamously and irreparably injured me.

I immediately drew up a declaration of my sanity, and went with it amongst Wilsons neighbours, and not one of them refused to sign it,

---

* His Grace of Richmond.

although I was an intire stranger to them only nine months before, and Wilsons abused them for that proof of their impartiality, refusing, with much abuse, to give me a copy of the order as they had promised. When I came to settle my trustees accounts, I found myself debtored with the expences of the aforesaid imprisonment, and mentioned them as unjust; to which they answered, "We have paid these sums, apprehending them to be necessary for the restoration of your health.* However, it being a great hardship upon you, we will make you a present of our trouble as it turns out that we have been unwarily imposed upon, by artful designing people.

I then applied to the trade in Stockport and Manchester, for commission employment, as in May 1770, to which they refused to pay any attention: in June 1771, I applied again at Halifax, and in general met with the like refusal.

After a few days stay there, I proceeded on a journey to add evidence to what I had collected at Scout Mill, at Sheffield, and Tuxford: I was successful, and hoping to find the aforesaid Rev. Richard Barnard, a resident of Newark, I came up as far as there, and then turned back to my friends in Cheshire, not daring to come within the reach of these enemies at Stamford, nor prepared with a character, &c. sufficient for my purpose, in London, in the predicament I then stood.

From Stockport, I then wrote to Mr. Hopkins, the said Mayor, "demanding a reasonable satisfaction;" and not doubting that he would be glad to procure an acquittance upon equitable terms, and apprehending that he would chuse to consult his aforesaid friends, I waited a considerable time for his answer; but this offer he chose to treat with contempt. My friends discouraged me from rushing into law, against such powerful opponents, *whose principles I knew by fatal experience.*

I then was inclined to come up to London, but my friends were unwilling I should leave them without a more favourable prospect was to offer. I staid with them till December, 1771, much dissatisfied with such losses, treatment, and present situation. At length I resolved to try if I could not remedy some of these grievances in town; so got a character drawn, and executed by the principal trades people in Stockport, and came up to London, applied for commission employment, from those houses I wrote to from Halifax, on the 11th of June 1770, who all declined to enter into any connection with me.

I then mentioned my situation, with all its circumstances, to an acquaintance; and that I was inclined to seek redress from the laws of my country: who answered, "You are certainly richly intitled to it in this case, and if you will give me leave to recommend you to my attorney, I will speak to him about it. He is a man of integrity, and you may depend upon it from me, he will take no bribe, which in my humble opinion is the only thing you have

---

* Wilsons bill does not so much as intimate any insanity, cure, or physick.

to fear." I left with him the necessary papers, and the next day, viz. the 10th of January 1772, I received his note, containing these words; "I have left such of your papers as were necessary with Mr. Raincock, No. 11, Bearbinder-lane,[57] who will immediately go upon the affair in question. Mr. Bruckshaw must call as above, about nine o'clock to-morrow morning, in order to give Mr. Raincock a farther explanation of some necessary relative particulars. I will endeavour to meet you there at the time appointed as above."

Whereupon I waited upon Mr. Raincock accordingly; when he informed me the same, saying, "I only wish to have a few affidavits[58] of your sanity from persons who saw you at the identical time of your confinement." I gave him instructions for drawing up affidavits for Messieurs Gee, Ding, and Raunsly, which he did, and they were duly executed and returned to him.

The next time I saw my friend who put us together, he said, "I have just been with Mr. Raincock, and he is now fully satisfied about the truth of your case, and declared to me that he would go through it, if he never goes through another case as long as he lives."

Soon after I saw Mr. Raincock when he said, "Your case is a serious and very consequential concern; you shall go with me to a counsel, without whose advice I never pursue things of such consequence as yours." We went to – Kitchen Esq; of Staples Inn,[59] who, after perusing our papers, and making the proper enquiries, said, "If this case was my own, I would bring a common action of trespass in the court of King's Bench against some one or two delinquents, declare specially, and lay my venue in London; as a special jury of merchants, conversant with the value of trade, are the most proper persons to try this cause; I have not a doubt but in this case they would give a verdict, with very heavy, exemplary damages; under all its circumstances, they *will not know how to give enough*. I think it is more than probable, whoever you make defendants, they will endeavour to carry the cause to Lincoln; and if they do attempt it, you should have Mr. Dunning, properly instructed, to oppose their motion, and then 'tis two to one in your favour, that the court will refuse them leave." We proposed making John Hopkins, mayor, and John Exton, alderman, the two magistrates who presumed to give, as aforesaid, colour to the imprisonment, the defendants; both Mr. Raincock and Mr. Kitchen agreeing, that proceeding under colour of office wilfully wrong, the courts have ever held as an established rule, *that such delinquents are not intitled to any protection by the act* of the 24th Geo. II. cap. 44, which was originally *only* intended "to render magistrates and the other judicial officers more safe, with regard to *small and involuntary errors* in their proceedings in the execution of their office, neither of which is the case here;" then it was finally concluded on, to make these two officious magistrates the defendants, merely as individuals; as they were not intitled to notice, it was not necessary to honour them with any stile or title of Magistrate." At this time I was in treaty with three capital houses in the city, who were inclined to contract with me by commission; but before I could get their contracts closed, some evil-minded persons made it their business to give information that I had not been long out of a private madhouse, where I had been confined for insanity nine months; so when I went to close with them, they all three declined to fulfil our agreements, one of them giving the reported insanity as his reason. It happened so, that I got information of the aforesaid John Hopkins, Mayor of Stamford in 1770, (the acting magistrate who made the aforesaid imprisonment originally) being then at the Half-moon tavern in Grace church Street,[60] of which I immediately informed Mr. Raincock, who gave me this advice; "Take some friend with you, and call upon him; see how he will behave to you after these injuries which he has done you in the officiousness of his office as Mayor, expostulate with him upon them, and desire your friend to be very attentive to his answers." Accordingly I went and engaged Mr. James Bradock of Lawrence-lane[61] to step with me in the evening. We went and met with him; he received us with some civility, but more surprize; we had not seen each other since the aforesaid imprisonment at Stamford. "I told him I was seeking for employment, and wanted a character from Lincolnshire, where I had been accustomed to business many years; shewed him the character which was given me by the trade at Stockport, and asked him if he had any reason to doubt its truth? He answered, No. I then said, I hope you can have no objection to favouring me with your name to it; at which he was exceedingly alarmed, and wanted to put me off to a future day; I urged, that I was making enquiry every day, and should be obliged to him for his name *then*; adding, "that as you have acknowledged it to be a true one, what can be your objection?" At length he signed it; and then I expostulated with him more fully upon the iniquity of the aforesaid imprisonment, and charge of insanity; and asked him if he received my aforesaid proposals for equitable damages in May or June last? to which he answered, "I did receive some such letter." I then asked him his reason why he did not answer it? he declined to reply. At length, being still pushed upon that subject, in a public room, he addressed himself to Mr. Braddock in these words; "I did imprison Mr. Bruckshaw, being Mayor at that time, *but I never did consider him as insane.*" I immediately asked, "Then what did you imprison me for?" To which he replied, "*It was done in a hurry*, I beg I may hear no more of it." He seemed much dissatisfied with our company, and we soon after withdrew. The next day I met with Mr. Henry Ward of Stamford, of whom I requested the same favour to my character, who chearfully obliged me with his name, and told me Mr. Bellars was in town, and lodged, as well as himself, at the Bread-street coffee-house,[62] where I called and also got his name.

I furnished Mr. Raincock with all these additional materials for my said action, and then I wrote to the said Mr. Hopkins at Stamford, informing him that he might expect to be called upon along with his colleague, to legally answer the aforesaid imprisonment and charge of insanity; but he still persisted in refusing to propose any equitable terms to prevent it; and, on the 12th of February 1772, the last day of Hilary Term, Mr. Raincock took out of the Honourable Court of King's Bench, a common Latitat Writ,[63] against the aforesaid John Hopkins, and John Exton, agreeable to our final determination, to pursue the action according to the advice of his Council, the said Mr. Kitchen, which was returnable on Wednesday next, after fifteen days, from the day of Easter, and he retained Council, Messrs. Dunning, and Wallace, for Guildhall, and Mr Wheler, for Lincoln, in case the Defendants should succeed in a motion, for leave to try the cause there; on or about the 26th, Mr. Raincock sent the Writ down to Mr. Torkington, Attorney at Law, in Stamford, with orders to serve the Defendants with copies, and said, "before I have done with them, I will convince them, that they have no jurisdiction over any persons, even if insane, except in such cases where his Majesty's subjects are in actual danger of their lives from the lunatic." Mr. Torkington thought proper to demur to this piece of agency business, and a correspondence arose betwixt him and his employer, who thought proper to keep me out of the secret, of which I made some complaint to Mr. William Bolton, (now Mr. Raincock's partner,) who answered, "you may make yourself easy, the Writ will be served in proper time. I cannot see how they can set up any defence; I think they will let judgment go against them by default: if they do, I will immediately execute a Writ of enquiry,[64] try it by a special jury in Guildhall, and in that case, I will insure you a verdict, with twenty thousand pounds damages."

I continued my enquiries after employment, and sollicited my acquaintance to do the same, none of which was attended with any success; on the 10th of April, the Writ still lay in the hands of Mr. Raincock's agent, Mr. Torkington, unserved, when I insisted upon that business being executed, or turned over to Mr. William Dyer, Attorney at Law, in Bourn, at that time in town; whereupon the said Mr. Bolton furnished me with proper authorities for that purpose, and Mr Dyer got the business executed on the 14th of April, 1772, and sent Mr. Raincock an affidavit of the service.

About this time the Manchester creditors to a person who had withdrawn himself from thence with his books, and most of his effects, employed me to make enquiry after him at his attorney's, Messrs. Exley and Crispin, in Chancery Lane,[65] from whom I could learn nothing to the satisfaction of my employers; but was struck with their remarkable fidelity *to this Client*. My attorney, Mr. Raincock, now began to demur in my action, but was exceedingly lost in shewing his reasons, delaying to declare till the eve of *Easter Term*, and at length entirely declared off from proceeding any further with my action; when I pressed him for his reason, he answered, "I cannot go to trial, with a nonsuit full in my face, upon the act of the 24th of Geo. II. Chap. 44." whereupon Mr. Bolton looked into the said act, and said, "I cannot see that this act has any thing to do, in this case." I replied, "that both Mr. Raincock, and his counsellor Mr. Kitchen, declared themselves fully satisfied it had not, before he commenced this action; therefore this could only be a pretended reason for declining:" And then I took my papers and the cause out of his hands.

In the beginning of June, 1772, I acquainted the said Mr. Crispin with the situation I was in with my action, and the cause of the imprisonment, as aforesaid; to which he answered with some surprise, "will any man presume to say, that these are the actions of a man disordered in his senses? I am of opinion your action is maintainable; but if you chuse to come to us, I shall recommend to you to take counsel's opinion with respect to that act, as Mr. Raincock has stated it as his objection to going on; I should chuse Serjeant Walker[66] to draw the declaration, and the same instructions will serve for him to give his opinion upon." "I told him Mr. Raincock had retained Messrs. Dunning and Wallace for town, and Mr. Wheler for Lincoln, in case we were obliged to try the cause there." To which he replied, "*that cannot be*, your's is a transitory action, therefore if you cannot hold it in London, you may try it in any of the counties you chuse, *where you was at all a prisoner*. But what could be Mr. Raincock's reason for returning Mr. Wallace along with Mr. Dunning who I would always have for my first counsel, which cannot be the case where Mr. Wallace is concerned?" I replied, "I did not know Mr. Raincock's reason, that I would put the cause into their hands," which I did upon the 10th of June, 1772.

They employed Serjeant Walker to draw the declaration, and to give his opinion relating to the aforesaid act; telling them, I should chuse the venue in Nottinghamshire, if it would not lie in London. When I saw Mr. Crispin again, he said, "Serjeant Walker says the action will lie, and in London, that there is no occasion to draw the declaration special, as he says he is well convinced that the defendants sent you to Scout Mill, meerly to gain an elapse of six months, with a design to avail themselves of the aforesaid act, which is such an aggravation of their crime, as will totally destroy their intentions." So he drew the declaration as in common cases of assault, and false imprisonment, and laid the Venue in St. Mary le Bow, in the ward of Cheap;[67] that it might come on to be tried agreeable to Mr. Kitchen's advice in Guildhall, before Mr. Raincock commenced the said action, Mr. Crispin delivered the declaration to the defendants agents, Messrs. Burton, and Peart, in Lincoln's Inn, who he said made light of the matter; telling him thus: "We have a cloud of witnesses ready to prove the Plaintiff's insanity."

He now began to demur in the action, and suffered the Defendant, Hopkins, to come with his affidavit before the Honourable Court of King's Bench; swearing, "that the whole cause of action, if any he has, arose in Lincolnshire, and not in London, nor any where else but in the county of Lincoln, praying for leave to have the cause tried at Lincoln assizes, which was granted of course: Mr. Crispin refused to attempt holding my action in London. Then the Defendants ventured to plead the general issue, "not guilty," and threw themselves upon their country; Mr. Crispin declined joining the issue, alledging, as Mr. Raincock, that he was afraid of a nonsuit upon the aforesaid act, observing thus; "I cannot think of throwing your money away in such a manner, as you have suffered so much already. I should like to have Mr. Wallace's opinion respecting the said act."

Whereupon he drew a case, and got it answered by Mr. Wallace, just upon the eve of the Summer Assizes, in 1772, in this manner: "I conceive that the Mayor acted under a supposed authority, vested in him as a magistrate, and under colour of that character will claim the protection of the act of the 24th of Geo. II. Chap. 44.

Then Mr. Crispin took this opportunity of declining prosecuting my action any further; after thus trifling with me till it was out of my power to get properly fixed with another, time enough to try the cause at these assizes, where in all probability it would have been fully and fairly tried, before that learned and upright judge, Lord Chief Justice de Grey. All this he did under a pretence of friendship; therefore I took my affairs out of his hands, well convinced of the truth of Gay's sentiments, that

"An open foe may prove a curse;
But a pretended friend was worse."[68]

At length a friend of mine informed me, that he knew a Mr. Jenkenson, Attorney at Law, in Hoxton Square,[69] who had in several instances gone through business in his profession with great integrity, after others of reputed abilities, &c. had thrown cold water upon the matter; whereupon I laid my business and papers before him, who was dissatisfied with Mr. Wallace's aforesaid opinion, and laid it before Serjeant Walker; and upon the 30th of October, we went together to take his opinion, upon Mr. Wallace's opinion and case; when he informed us thus: "I have looked over this case very carefully, but will read it over again." then said, "I am clearly of opinion, this action will lie." Mr. Jenkenson then asked him, if he would advise him to go on with it; to which the Serjeant answered, that is no part of my business, that belongs to Mr. Bruckshaw. I have only to say, as I said before; "that the action will lie." We withdrew and parted in Fleet Street,[70] when Mr. Jenkenson said, "I will give the Defendants notice of trial, as soon as you please." A few days after, I saw him, and the aforesaid Mr. William Bolton, walking arm in arm, along St. Paul's Church Yard,[71] and the next time I called upon him in his office, he began to raise objections, which I interpreted into some desire he had to decline; therefore I told him, if he chose to give me my papers, we would part, which he immediately did.

A friend of mine having informed me that Mr. Charles Funter, Attorney at Law, in King's Street,[72] to whom he had intimated my case, had expressed a wish, that the cause had fallen into his hands, as a clearer and more substantial case could not be. I immediately laid my papers before him; to which he said, "I see Mr. Raincock commenced this action: I can give you no answer, till I have spoke with him; he is my very good friend, and I must know what he says respecting this matter;" here the business hung some days, and when I pressed him for an answer, he said, "Mr. Bolton tells me, it will be as much as my life is worth to go to Lincoln and try this cause. Besides, I am afraid that I shall be liable to an action, if I was to carry it on, as it is against magistrates." Then I got my papers out of his hands as soon as I could. He is an Attorney of the Sheriffs Court, and Messrs. Raincock and Bolton, Secondaries of Wood Street and Poultry Compters.[73]

Soon after this, the said Mr. Funter made me an offer of a wager of one hundred pounds that my cause never would be tried.

A Client of Mr. George Theakston's, Attorney at Law, in the Temple,[74] being informed how I had been drove about, from one attorney to another, expressed a wish that he had the opportunity of taking me to his Attorney, the said Mr. Theakston, and I being informed of it, waited upon him, and told him my papers were then in my own hands, and disengaged, therefore if he chused, I would go with him to his Attorney in the Temple, and know of him what service he could do me in it. We went, and on the 26th of November, 1772, I laid the action before him; all this while, neither I nor my friends were able to procure me any employ.

About this time, Mr. Mark Huish, of Nottingham, was in town, to whom I related my aforesaid case, and the situation of this action, who replied, "the principal matter you want with Counsel is a good examiner, that can work unwilling witnesses about, till they give full evidence of the truth: I take Mr. Newnham to be infinitely the best that goes the Middle-land Circuitt.

When I next saw Mr. Theakston, he desired me to draw up my instructions for the briefs in writing, which I did in the manner of an affidavit, and delivered them to him in December, when he declared they were to his satisfaction. I consulted him upon retaining Messrs. Newnham and Wheler for our Counsel; he approved of them, and left them retainers, and made out the Briefs,* and other necessaries for bringing the action to trial: (on the 22nd of December, I saw with him in Lincoln's Inn Hall,[75] the aforesaid Messrs. Jenkenson and Bolton), and he took out subpoenas[76] for twenty witnesses,† in

---

* On this occasion my Brother inclosed to me an order signed by the Defendants, John Hopkins, Mayor, and John Exton, Alderman, declaring me insane; without either information from Dr. Jackson, or the complaint of Mr. Langton, as the order to Wilsons, and dated the 15th, the day after the imprisonment was made, directed to the parish officers, of All Saints, in the said borough, &c. Please to observe, the alderman never saw me at all upon that occasion; my Brother in his letters says he received it from Mr. Hopkins, along with the papers that were taken out of my pocket by the ruffians, in the garret aforesaid, on the said 15th of June. Why not made out to warrant William Clarke, John Walker, Robert White, and James White?

† When we called upon the aforesaid Mr. Barnard to know what evidence he would give respecting my consequential damages; he answered, "that I expected him in town, in June 1770, to take my accounts, and instructions according to our agreement at Stockport, in May, and a letter which I received from him, dated Halifax, June the 11th, 1770. I cannot say what improvements he might have made to my establishment in those counties we fixed upon, as I then stood in them, his business for me would have produced to him a good hundred per year; I could not think of renewing a contract of such trust with him, after what was so publickly reported of his insanity." I applied to other houses, and found the same report had done me irreparable mischief.

the different counties aforesaid, and we sent a special messenger to serve those in and near Stamford, and he got the rest served by agents in the usual way.

We went down together to Lincoln, and on the 6th of March, we called upon Mr. Wyche, the town clerk of Stamford, in our way, of whom Mr. Theakston demanded to see the records of my said imprisonment, &c. To which he answered, "We never record any such transactions." That evening we arrived at Lincoln, and I attended a private consultation with him upon our counsel, Messrs. Newnham and Wheler; when we were informed the Defendants were in great hopes of nonsuit, upon the act of the 24th of Geo. II. as they had not had notice, as magistrates, agreeable to the aforesaid act. To which Mr. Theakston observed, "It cannot be known whether they are intitled to such notice or not, without going into the merits of the case, and then it will be seen how they have acted as Magistrates;" and said, that Mr. Newnham recommended it, to have another councel, as there were twenty of our own witnesses to examine, and a special jury. To this I consented, and Mr. Theakston retained Mr. Balguy, and took down his private examination of our witnesses in writing, all of which answered our expectation, except a few from Stamford, and the aforesaid Mr. Thong of Huntingdon. The cause came on in the forenoon on the 10th of March 1773, before

Mr. JUSTICE BLACKSTONE,

When only eight Special Jurors appeared and were sworn; then I prayed a talis[77] for four more, to make up My Jury, which was granted, and they were accordingly called and sworn.

After Mr. BALGUY had gone through the Declaration in the usual manner,

Mr. NEWNHAM rose and expatiated a little upon the Special Matter, and observed, That the Defendants had been guilty of a very heinous crime, if his client's case, "contained in these sheets in my hand (says he) are true;" and without going over the contents, or putting in the defendants order, called the third witness in his brief; neither did he put in the letter purporting to be Mr. Ding's answer to Mr. Hardy.

Edward Read Thong sworn. The evidence taken down; by Mr. Balguy he says, "I never saw the Plaintiff, till the 14th of June, 1770, was in his company that day, once at Langton's, once at the Bull. The Plaintiff sat in the same room at the Bull, and was in a violent passion, in respect of an estate which Langton had got. – Hopkins was also at the Bull, and recommended to the Plaintiff not to go to the race, unless he went with him, and on the Plaintiff's ordering his horse to go, Hopkins insisted he should not, and on persisting afterwards, ordered him into custody of the common Serjeant, who carried him to goal; saw Plaintiff in prison same day, and he was very angry; never saw Plaintiff afterwards till Trinity Term, 1772, in London."

Cross Examined.

"Plaintiff made a great noise at Langton's house. – Langton said he was mad. – Mrs. Langton took her children up stairs. – It was about 12. – They dined at the Bull at 2. – That he advised him not to go to the races, lest he should go to Langton's. – Plaintiff talked sensibly, though he was furious. – Hopkins talked of sending for his officers, and he believes they came. – He thinks he remembers Langton's complaining of Plaintiff at the Bull."

In his private examination by Mr. Theakston, he says, "that Hopkins ordered four or five men, to seize Plaintiff in the Bull Inn yard, and take him to the goal; that he saw no Process;[78] that Hopkins followed Plaintiff to goal, and that two magistrates are obliged to commit.

James Gee sworn; but not permitted to go on in his evidence: no notice is taken of the little he did say, by my counsel.

Serjeant Hill, for the Defendants, then proved the Defendant Hopkins Mayor, and that he had not had notice conformable to the act of the 24th of George the second; observing that the Mayor only took proper care of the Plaintiff, till his friends who lived at some distance, could be informed by a special messenger, which he sent to know how the Plaintiff was, and that in a few days his uncle and brother came and took him away, therefore as my client only acted in the execution of his office, we are entitled to a nonsuit upon this act, as the action is brought without notice," his lordship was not so clear in that point; so permitted us to call the constable who first seized me at Langton's, and released me in the street, by the Mayor's order.

Elias Buswell, sworn. His evidence is not noticed by my three counsel. I remember he contradicted himself several times; said he was sent to Langton's by the Defendant Hopkins, with no warrant but his staff; that Joseph Needham assisted him in taking me from Langton's to the Mayor's, and made confused work about that release; but was very confident that Thickbroom, the town Serjeant assisted him in seizing me in the Bull Inn yard, and taking me from thence to the goal by the order of Defendant Hopkins. – Thickbroom himself says in his examination by Mr. Theakston, that he saw and spoke with me in the Bull Inn yard, before dinner, on the said 14th of June, 1770, and again at Clarke the goaler's in the evening, at Defendant Hopkin's next morning, and that he never saw any Process for committing Plaintiff, &c. When we came out of court, he positively declared he saw no part of the seizure in the Bull Inn yard; that he believes he was at the race at that time.

The Defendants were not even called upon to produce Langton's complaint, nor any of the other requisites to a commitment.

Serjeant Hill again pushed for the nonsuit: Mr. Wheler replied, "there are a number of instances solemnly determined where magistrates and other judicial officers have not been intitled to notice or any protection, under the said act, and quoted Money and Leech,[79] Smith a constable in Chancery Lane, an action tried at Norwich, and many others: And has noted upon his Brief, "*Sane or not Sane gives the jurisdiction.*"

His lordship, with the said act before him, said, "I think the Plaintiff had better be nonsuited than have a verdict against him. I'll not certify; and then he may move the Court of King's Bench to set the nonsuit aside, which the courts have made an established rule occasionally to do, and by that means he will get the opinion of the four judges.

My Counsel made no reply, and his lordship ordered the Plaintiff to be called, and a nonsuit declared. He was straitened for time to go through the business of the Assize.

As we came out of court, some of my jury expressed their surprize to several of my witnesses, that the action, with all its circumstances, did not come fully before them for their verdict; adding, "which would have been for every halfpenny laid in the declaration, as we are fully satisfied of the injustice: Mr. Crispin ordered the declaration to be drawn for no more than 5000 *l.* damages against the Defendants.

Mr. Thong came to my quarters, and contended for genteel payment as a witness, alledging that he was an Attorney; he was paid accordingly, and immediately afterwards went to Mr. Hopkins quarters, to give him joy of this nonsuit, which he did in the presence of many witnesses.

I was immediately advised to set this nonsuit aside, and my Attorney was asked the mode and expence by several of my witnesses; to which he answered, "about 12 or 14 *l.* will set it aside, it will only require a few more affidavits to those three we have, to support Mr. Bruckshaw's own." I now find by the Defendant's bill of costs, which I have paid,[80] that they had for witnesses at these assizes, the three aforesaid ruffians, Walker, Whittle, and White, the said Mr. Langton, and five respectable persons more, who never saw me during the said imprisonment. I staid a few days amongst my acquaintance in Lincolnshire, when I was informed by *one of the Common Council* of Stamford, that THE CORPORATION HELD A COMMON-HALL,[81] PRIOR TO THIS TRIAL COMING ON, AND MADE AN ORDER THAT THE EXPENCES SHOULD BE PAID OUT OF THE CORPORATION-STOCK: and that they had my Stamford witnesses up at the Crown Inn, and Buswell at the town clerk's, the morning he came off to me at Lincoln.

When I came up to town my Attorney got the necessary affidavits to those three Mr. Raincock drew, retained Mr. Dunning for the motion to set aside the nonsuit, and prepared him a Brief as I understood of the affidavits abstracted, and the Defendants order of the 15th of June, 1770; and on the 28th of April, in Westminster-Hall,[82] we had a consultation with Mr. Dunning, when he declared himself exactly to the same purport as Mr. Kitchen; viz. "That the courts did not permit judicial officers, to shelter themselves under the aforesaid act, when they have proceeded wilfully wrong;" and the next day he obtained a rule for the Defendants to shew cause why the said nonsuit should not be set aside: the business hung in court till the 14th of May, it was then called on, when

Lord MANSFIELD said,

"I can see no cause for the imprisonment at all. If this cause had come on before me, I would have subjected the Defendants to the jury's verdict. Have any proposals been made to the Plaintiff?" I was called upon to answer that question, and said, "none my lord, they have even rejected my offer to accept of any equitable proposals." Then his lordship set the nonsuit aside, "*without prejudice to the question,*" as none of my affidavits had been read, nor the order: Then Serjeant Hill said, "but my Lord we are intitled to costs:" his lordship said, "how can that be in this case?" "it is the condition of the rule, my lord:" "how so? Mr. Dunning, is the rule drawn with payment of costs?" Mr. Dunning answered, "the rule is so drawn my lord, I did not mention it, because I thought it unreasonable;" to which all the judges said, "*certainly.*" – Serjeant Hill said, "but, my lord, it is the express condition of the rule:" they answered, "*then be it so.*"

I met Mr. Cooper, Attorney at Law, in Quality Court, Chancery Lane, a few days after this in Westminster, who had said "he knew I should be nonsuited at Lincoln," when I addressed him thus: "well, Mr. Cooper, what do you think of my action, now the nonsuit is set aside? he answered, "I think you will have a jury's verdict, with exemplary damages," and mentioned the cause of Mayer against Hunter, himself Attorney for the Defendant, confident of a nonsuit for his client; "but I find by this experience there is no such thing without the Plaintiff's consent". I also asked Mr. Theakston's opinion; he answered "you may depend upon it we shall now go fully into the case, and have a decision by a Jury's verdict; neither judge nor counsel will chuse to let it come nonsuited again before my Lord Mansfield." All this time I could not, even with the assistance of my friends, get into any employ. When I saw Mr. Theakston again, he said, "I saw Mr. Newnham to day, and he desired I would let you know that he has been offered a retainer by the Defendants, but will not accept it till he hears from you." I replied, "you could have given him his answer; you must join in the opinion of my friends, that it would be very imprudent in me to trust my cause in his hands a second time: if you approve of it, you may retain Messrs. Wheler and Balguy:" he answered, "I will, and you are to consider that Mr. Newnham is acquainted with the secrets of our case:" "true, but does he know of a weak part in it?" "no, I don't believe he does:" "then don't retain him." A few days after I saw Mr. Theakston again, when he said, "I have given Mr. Newnham his answer, to which he replied, I did not intend taking any fee with Mr. Bruckshaw's Brief, but now I would not take his Brief if he was ever so desirous that I should."* He taxed and paid the Defendant's costs; made some amendments to his Briefs; subpoened nineteen

---

* About this time I met the aforesaid Mr. Raincock, and Mr. Crispin, and told them that I was informed Mr. Newnham was retained against me: they both replied, "nothing more likely, but you may be assured Mr. Newnham will not risk his own reputation so much as to plead in a cause against you, in which he has been concerned, and which never has been opened."

witnesses; drew a fresh record meerly as a new action, without taking the least notice that it had been once nonsuited upon the aforesaid act, and that nonsuit set aside by the court of King's Bench; gave notice of trial and other requisites for bringing the cause before the court of assize at Lincoln, to be held at the castle of Lincoln on the 14th of August, 1773.

About this time we were apprised that Serjeant Glynn was going down to Newcastle to plead the cause of the freemen of that borough, at the assizes which opened there on the 7th inst. and my friends being apprehensive that the Defendants had a great superiority of counsel, advised me to try if the Serjeant would take my Brief, with a fee of twenty or thirty guineas upon his return from Newcastle, as it would be about his time, and not above twenty miles out of his way: they were of opinion he would give me his assistance on those terms, under all the circumstances of the case; accordingly on the 2d inst. we waited upon the Serjeant at his own house, and acquainted him with our desire as aforesaid, and that we would give him thirty guineas with the Brief: he replied, "I should have thought FIFTY sufficient, but if you call at my chambers, whatever my clerk does will be right." We immediately withdrew and called accordingly, and informed his clerk with our business, who replied, "this is a business out of the common way; I can say nothing to it, till I have spoke to the Serjeant; if you'll call to-morrow, I'll give you your answer," therefore as I was to leave town the next morning, Mr. Theakston was to call, and inform me of the answer at Norwich, which he did, "that the Serjeant declined giving us his assistance, alledging he was afraid it would be too great a fatigue for him."

I then went amongst my friends in Lincolnshire, who informed me, "that the Defendants were more confident of a second nonsuit, than they were of the first, and that their Attorney was in London making preparations for it, that they were afraid of no expence, as they had made an order of common-hall that all the expences should be paid out of the corporation stock." On the 16th Mr. Theakston met me at Lincoln; we entered our record, and I informed him as aforesaid; he answered, "I have been informed the same, but you need not be afraid, though I don't like our Stamford witnesses so well as I did in March, but I myself will insist upon our jury's verdict, and the counsel are determined they will not be nonsuited: this is the last place in this circuit, therefore the judges are not straitened for time, and I find we are likely to have a very good jury:" our witnesses all attended, and Mr. Theakston went to a private consultation with our counsel by himself.*

On the 18th, when his lordship had been in court about 10 hours, my action was called on before

---

* At Lincoln my witnesses from Scout Mill informed me thus, "Wilsons are afraid that you will be upon them next, and has made their property over in trust to their friends."

Mr. BARON PERROTT,

and eight or nine of my special jurors appearing they were duly sworn. I prayed a talis to make them up twelve, which was granted me, and they were also sworn. Then

Mr. Balguy, read the declaration, as at the Lent nonsuit.

Mr. Wheler rose up, and without looking into his Brief, made an opening as near as I can recollect in these words: "my lord, and you gentlemen on the jury, my client, the Plaintiff, was a woolstapler at Bourn, a business of considerable consequence in this county, made a purchase in Stamford which embarrassed his affairs, he made an assignment and was imprisoned at Stamford several days," and then called the same unwilling witness as at the Lent nonsuit, (which he did not so much as notice in the slightest degree:) this witness stands the third in his Brief, the Attorney of Huntingdon Mr. Langton's friend.

Edward Read Thong, sworn, his evidence taken down by Mr. Wheeler; "was at Langton's on the 14th of June, when Mr. Bruckshaw was there, can't recollect the particular conversation, only that in general they talked about the house.

"Hopkins was in company after with witness at the Bull – Hopkins desired overheard Bruckshaw about being at Langton's and behaving in an outrageous manner at the Bull – Hopkins sent him to goal, as witness conceives on the complaint of Langton – Bruckshaw came in custody of the constables into the Bull.

"Heard Hopkins order him into custody prison; Langton was there – Hopkins a Justice of Peace – Bruckshaw was brought to him."

Cross-Examination taken down by Mr. Balguy.

Edward Read Thong. "Before the order of Defendant's commitment, rather thinks Langton came there – rather thinks he was in custody of a peace-officer."

For the Defendant.

Mr. Newnham rose up and said, "Produce your Notice; you shall proceed no further 'till you have produced your Notice:" and put the said statute of the 24th of G. II. into his Lordship's hand. – Then my counsel called

Daniel Ding, sworn; but no part of his evidence is noticed upon my counsel's brief. He said, "Mr. Bruckshaw and I have lived in the same house many years; I heard he was at the Mayor's on Friday the 15th of June, 1770, and called in there to see him, and gave him a letter which I had received from Mr. Hardy, on his account; and I saw him again the Friday following, in a garret, in Clarke the goaler's house: and at both these times he was as much in his senses as I ever saw him, and as capable of managing his business." I handed out to him a letter which Mr. Hardy gave me, saying, "it came to him as Mr. Ding's. Mr. Ding looked at it, and gave in evidence, "I never wrote a syllable or letter of it, nor ordered such letter to be wrote: I know nothing of it." – The Cryer of the Court[83] was ordered to take it from him, which he instantly did, and he was not permitted to proceed in his evidence. Then Mr. Newnham, for the Defendants, called one

Halford Allam*, sworn. Says "he was servant to Langton;" and my counsel have taken his evidence down in these words: "Plaintiff forced his way into Langton's house, and was near knocking the witness down. Langton sent him to the Mayor Hopkins, to lay a complaint that Plaintiff was a madman, had broke into his premises, desiring him to send his peace-officers – peace-officers came immediately."

His Cross-Examination taken by Mr. Balguy – *thus.*

"Don't say Plaintiff touched him – no writing at the time of his applying to the Justice Defendant."

Defendant's second Witness taken by my Counsel in these Words.

Elias Buswell, sworn. "Was a constable at Stamford; June 1770, he had orders from the Town-serjeant by Thickbroom's orders – Plaintiff came in and behaved ill, struck him, and threw him against the wall – witness caught him by the collar first, when Needham came, took him before the Mayor at the Bull."

Cross-Examination taken down by Mr. Wheler.

"Had his staff in his hand, but produced no authority;" whereupon Mr. Newnham moved again for a nonsuit under the aforesaid act of parliament, without producing any of the requisites to a commitment: whereupon his Lordship said,[†] "Call the Plaintiff." I immediately rose up and said, "This action was non-suited here at the last assizes upon the same account, and that nonsuit has been set aside by the Court of King's Bench, when Lord Mansfield declared, that he could see no cause for an imprisonment at all; and that if the cause had come on before him, he would have subjected the Defendants to the Jury's verdict: The Defendants have been indulged in having the venue changed hither: They cannot apprehend any injustice from the verdict of a Special Jury of their own county; and as they are here for the second time impanelled and sworn at my expence, I chuse that my cause shall be finally decided by their verdict." To which his Lordship answered, "I do not regard either what was determined or said in the Court of King's Bench: I will judge for myself. I am determined to protect

---

* This witness has not the least resemblance of the boy who opened the gate to me twice at Langton's, both times in the forenoon. The Defendant's bill of costs, which I have also paid, shews that he was procured from Highgate,[84] and scholar sufficient to examine the original Rule of Court for setting the Lent nonsuit aside, and appeared as if he had not been used to a livery.

† It may be necessary to inform those readers who are lucky enough to know nothing of law, that a nonsuit is always obtained by the supposed default of the Plaintiff, who is said not to pursue his cause (*non sequitur*) to the hearing of the court. Hence it is always a form *to call the Plaintiff,* who not answering, the nonsuit takes place. This is so necessary, that it is always so asserted in the Postea Endorsement on the back of the Record;[85] how truly, in this case, facts will be best declare. – "A nonsuit, says Judge Blackstone in his Commentaries,[86] is a DEFAULT and NEGLECT of the Plaintiff."

Magistrates. If my Brother Blackstone had not omitted to take notes of the evidence given before him at the last Assizes, that nonsuit would not have been set aside; I have taken notes, and will make a different report; call the Plaintiff." My counsel were quite mute, but my Attorney rose up and said, "My lord, if you call the Plaintiff he will answer, we will not be nonsuited." To which his Lordship sternly replied: "who are you? – you shall learn to behave decently in court, or I will commit you," and abruptly retired from his seat of Justice, which threw the whole court into the utmost confusion: neither I, nor several of my witnesses heard this nonsuit publickly declared.

I soon after arrived in London, where my friends considered it as an impossibility that I could be again nonsuited upon the same act, and several gentlemen learned in the Law and of the Legislative Body, expressed their astonishment, but unanimously agreed that the Defendants had now waded so deep that if I was to carry the cause to trial again at the Assizes at Lincoln, they would find out means to defeat justice in this case there, and therefore that it is now most adviseable to bring this action special in the Court of Common Pleas, lay the Venue in London and try it by a special jury of Merchants in Guild-Hall.[87]

Whereupon as my whole property is now become dissipated, my character ruined, even with seeking legal redress, and my friends discouraged from lending me a helping hand, I was advised by some to draw up a petition to his Majesty,[88] as short as I could possibly convey these grievances with propriety, and I being very desirous of procuring legal redress, I readily attended to these hopes and set about abstracting the whole of my case, and drew them into a petition which I presented to his Majesty at St James's, on the 8th of December last, which he was graciously pleased to receive, and upon Christmas Day, I learnt it was lodged in Lord Suffolk's office, in Cleveland Row,[89] where I soon after called to know the success of my hopes, when I was answered, "that his lordship has been, and now is confined with the gout, but Mr. Fraser, bids me to inform you, that if you will call again in three or four days, your petition shall by that time be looked over, and then you shall have an answer what can be done in it." I withdrew very well satisfied with my answer, which seemed to promise some hopes of success. After my aforesaid abstracted case the petition concluded thus:

"Your Petitioner humbly begs to make this observation upon a cause which was lately tried in Guildhall, in your Majesty's Court of Common Pleas, where the learned judge took the evidence and sumed it up to the jury, (with that patient, impartial candour, which clearly shews his lordship's integrity in executing the duties of his important office,) who brought in their verdict for the Plaintiff: the action was brought by one Mr. Fabrigas, against Governor Mostyn, for a wilful abuse of his judicial-office, in inflicting upon him a false and cruel imprisonment, fundamentally similar to the aforesaid, inflicted by the said Defendants, John Hopkins and John Exton upon your Petitioner; the Governor being dissatisfied with the jury's verdict, presumed to dispute the competency of your Majesty's Court of Common Pleas to try the said cause, and when that would not avail him, he moved the said court for a new trial, which motion the learned judges of the said court have unanimously thought proper to over-rule, thereby confirming the legality and justice of the said verdict: that learned and upright Judge, Lord Chief Justice de Grey, in giving his reasons why the said Court judged it right to discharge the rule for a new trial, observed, "that all imprisonments ought to be inflicted with humanity, and that on account of the different feelings of men, particularly in personal wrongs, the Law very wisely instituted twelve honest men as the properest judges to apportion those damages, as the evidence and the particulars of the case may point out to their judgment and feelings." THEREFORE, as your petitioner has twice been denied the verdict of a jury, he is inclined to believe, that some collusion must have been practised against him, which greatly aggravates the oppression of your petitioner, as he is thus not only a second time subjected to the payment of the Defendants costs, but also totally ruined in both his property and character, besides laid open to the prejudiced censure of the public, and the personal insults of his malignant opponents and their adherents; circumstances which every feeling man of principle must wish to see legally rectified by a jury's verdict, and sacredly preserved inviolate to posterity; under such accumulated oppression, it is impossible for your Majesty's subject to re-establish or even support himself, without the humane interposition of superior assistance, which is the sole cause why your Petitioner humbly presumes to trouble your Majesty with this address, case, and petition, and as your humble petitioner, has been thus inhumanly treated, twice denied an appeal to a jury, subjected to his own and the Defendants costs, deprived of his property, with every other hope and prospect of relief, begs to throw himself at the foot of the THRONE, in hopes your Majesty will be most graciously pleased to consider his case, and to do therein as shall appear most equitable:

And your humble Petitioner, as in duty bound, shall ever Pray.

LONDON, *December* 1773,

No 28, *in the Poultry.*"

On the 31st in the said office, I met with three of the clerks, one of whom gave me back my Petition with this answer, "nothing can be done in it." I asked who's answer it was? the reply was, "Mr. Fraser ordered me to give that answer." I asked him if he apprehended Lord Suffolk was acquainted with the Petition? he answered, "I cannot say: his Lordship has not been able to come to the office for some time, and is now confined to his room." I immediately withdrew without any hope of my Case being properly known, either to his Majesty, or Lord Suffolk.

Therefore, I resolved to publish the whole of my Case in this Pamphlet, for the good of my Fellow-Subjects, and with hopes of its procuring me necessary assistance to come at a full litigation with a decision of my accumulated grievances by a jury's verdict.

S. BRUCKSHAW.

Conclusion.

To the humane feelings of those who suffer at others woe, to those liberal spirits who have been accustomed to rejoice in the idea of the security of British Subjects, this narrative is addressed.

Spurn it not, good reader, because the language is artless, and perhaps tedious: nor wonder if in every circumstance the unhappy sufferer may not have acted wisely. "Unhacknied in the ways of men," and irritated by such accumulated wrongs, perhaps he may not have known how to tread such a thorny path with the propriety which apathy may point out. As to the manner of laying this tale before you, it would perhaps have been unjust for any other pen to have undertaken the task.

If proceedings, such as have been the subject of these sheets, may pass with impunity; say, ye Idolizers of the British Constitution, in what do you excel the subjects of the most despotic states?

Able calculators assert, that nine tenths of every community consist of people of or under the rank of this man; does then our laws enable the other tenth to oppress these at their pleasure?

I have nothing to say on the proceedings of his various Lawyers; they speak for themselves; only just suffer me to remark, *en passant*, that it fully verifies the wisdom of that Christian Precept, "if any man sue thee at Law and take away thy Coat, let him have thy Cloak also."[90] I defy the most able of our Divines, with the aid of First, Secondly, Thirdly, and Lastly, to illustrate this text more fully.[91]

Upwards of Five hundred and twenty pounds has it cost this man in paying his own law expences and the costs of those who have thus destroyed him.*

"To hope every thing even against hope."[92] –

There is I think somewhere such a sentence, and the case is not imaginary; for this much injured man is yet willing to believe that by the aid of such of his fellow subjects as may think his case deserving their assistance, he may yet drag to the altars of the offended law, victims the most worthy ever sacrificed on them.

---

* It is justice due to Mess s. Raincock and Jenkenson to add, that neither of them made any charge for what they did.

Appendix

Numb. I.

The Town or Borough   To the Constables,
of Stamford, in the   Church wardens, and Overseers of
County of Lincoln.   the Poor of the Parish of All
                             Saints in the said Borough, and
                             to every of them.[93]

WHEREAS Samuel Bruckshaw, of the said parish of All Saints, Yeoman,* is so far disordered in his senses, that it is dangerous for him the said Samuel Bruckshaw to be permitted to go abroad; THESE are therefore to order and command you the said Constables, Churchwardens, and Overseers of the Poor, or some or one of you, to keep, or cause to be kept, the said Samuel Bruckshaw, safely locked up in some secure room at the house of William Clarke in the Borough aforesaid, so that the said Samuel Bruckshaw shall not have it in his power to do or commit any injury or violence upon his own person, or the person or persons of any of his Majesty's subjects, and for your so doing, this shall be to you, and every of you the said Constables, Churchwardens, and Overseers, your sufficient Warrant and Authority. Given under our Hands and Seals the Fifteenth day of June, in the tenth year of the reign of our Sovereign Lord, George the Third, by the Grace of God, of Great Britain, France, and Ireland, King, Defender of the Faith, and in the year of our Lord One thousand, Seven hundred, and Seventy.

John Hopkins, Mayor.
John Exton, Alderman.

[I apprehend this order was not manufactured before that to Wilsons on the 26th inst. which stiles me "Woolcomber,"[94] and commands the "aid and assistance of all Constables, Peace-Officers, &c. in case I was refractory." Some time afterwards this was given by Defendant Hopkins to my unsuspecting Brother, as I conceived to shew him the judiciousness of their proceedings in the execution of their office as magistrates. – Yet it is dated a day after the said imprisonment was made, and was never exhibited at any of the aforesaid litigations.

The Alderman did not even see me, upon this occasion]

* Woolstapler is interlined with a paler ink, and Yeoman erased.

Numb. II.

WE whose names are hereunto set and subscribed, being inhabitants of the Parish of Bourn in the County of Lincoln, do hereby certify, that during the time that Mr. Samuel Bruckshaw resided in the said Parish, which was about ten years, he exercised and followed the trade or business of a Woolstapler; and in all his dealings conducted himself (to the best of our knowledge) with Honesty, Sobriety, and Punctuality. Witness our Hands this Sixth day of January, 1772.

> *Humfrey Hyde*, Vicar.
> *John Hyde*, Apothecary.
> *J. Hardwich*, Tanner.
> *Robert Osborn*, Ironmonger.
> *John Dove*, Church-warden.
> *E. Musson*, Grocer.
> *W. Dyer*, Attorney at Law.
> *Daniel Ding*, (with whom

Mr. Bruckshaw boarded all the time of his residing in Bourn)

Numb. III.

Stockport, Nov. 27th, 1771.

WE who have here subscribed, can recommend the bearer Mr. Samuel Bruckshaw as a very honest, sober man, and qualified for any business that he will undertake.

John Prescot.	*John Hopkins.*
Tim. Hainsworth.	*Henry Ward,* Jun.
Richard Crafton.	*James Bellaers.*
Robert Godby.	*John Langworth.*
Thomas Hall.	*Samuel Daniel.*
William Mariot.	*William Hardy.*
William Fowden.	*James Gee.*

Numb. IV.

Between S. Bruckshaw, Plaintiff,

In the King's Bench. and

John Hopkins and John Exton, Defendants.

JAMES BRADDOCK, of the Parish of St. Lawrence in the City of London,[95] warehouse-man, maketh oath, and saith, that one evening (he believes in January, 1772,) he accompanied the said Samuel Bruckshaw, the Plaintiff, to the

Half-moon Tavern in Gracechurch-Street, where they spent the evening with the Defendant John Hopkins, whom the said Plaintiff sollicited to sign a written character that might enable the said Plaintiff to get into employment, which, after much hesitation, the said Deft. J. Hopkins, did; and this deponent further saith, that in the course of the evening the said Plaintiff interrogated the said John Hopkins, the Defendant, as to an imprisonment of the said Plaintiff, by the said Defendant John Hopkins in 1770, as a person insane, (which charge of imprisonment, the said John Hopkins admitted to be true, but said *it was done in a hurry, and begged of the said Plaintiff not to think of or name it any more,*) or the said John Hopkins then made use of words to that effect, and this Deponent saith that the said Defendant, John Hopkins, then declared *that he never looked upon the said Plaintiff as a man out of his senses,* and this Deponent further saith that he has known the said Plaintiff ever since December 1771, and since that time has had many conferences with him upon business, and that he always appeared to him this Deponent, a quiet, peaceable, and orderly man, perfectly in his senses.

James Bradock.

Sworn this 26th day of April, 1773,
at my house in Bloomsbury-square,[96]
before me, MANSFIELD.

Numb. V.

In the King's Bench.

WILLIAM RAWNSLEY – of Bourn, in the County of Lincoln, Woolstapler, maketh oath and saith, that he hath known Samuel Bruckshaw, late of Bourn, aforesaid, Woolstapler, for several years last past, and that during the whole time of this Deponent's knowledge of him, he appeared to be a Quiet, Peaceable, and Orderly Man, perfectly in his senses; and this Deponent further saith, that on or about the 7th day of June, 1770, this Deponent was in company with the said Samuel Bruckshaw at Bradford in the County of York, and on the 13th and 14th* of the same month at Stamford, in the County of Lincoln aforesaid, and at all the said times, the said Samuel Bruckshaw appeared as he had usually done, perfectly in his senses.

William Rawnsley.

The above named Willliam Rawnsley came voluntarily this
First day of February, 1772, before me at Bourn, aforesaid, and was duly sworn to this Affidavit, by me,

WILLIAM DYER.
One of the Commissioners, &c.

* The very day of the imprisonment.

Numb. VI.

In the King's Bench.

DANIEL DING, of Bourn, in the County of Lincoln, Baker, maketh oath, and saith, that he hath known Samuel Bruckshaw, late of Bourn, aforesaid, Woolstapler, for twelve years last past and upwards, and that during ten of the said years, the said Samuel Bruckshaw lodged in the house of this Deponent, and behaved himself in a quiet, peaceable, and orderly manner, and in no transaction whatever during the whole of the said time, which this Deponent was privy to, shewed the least mark of Insanity; and this Deponent further saith, that having been informed that the said Samuel Bruckshaw had been committed to the goal at Stamford, by the Mayor of that Corporation, under some colour or pretence of Insanity, this Deponent went twice to see the said Samuel Bruckshaw, when he was under such confinement, and at both the said times, the said Samuel Bruckshaw appeared, and this deponent verily believes, was in his perfect senses.

Daniel Ding.

The above named Daniel Ding, came
voluntarily this First day of January,
1772, before me at Bourn aforesaid,
and was duly sworn to this affidavit,
by me,

WILLIAM DYER.
One of the Commissioners, &c.
(Examined.)
J. DODGSON.

Numb. VII.

Upon Serjeant Walker's drawing the declaration, and giving his opinion to Mr. Crispin as aforesaid, I wrote to my acting trustees with whom I let the remainder of my property lie at interest, for a remittance, which my Brother inclosed to me in his letter dated Bredbury[97] within the Parish of Stockport, 14th July, 1772. Concluding with, "I heartily wish you success in your affair with Hopkins and Exton, and that it may be legally settled to your satisfaction."

Other extracts from my Brother's Letters.

July 17th, 1772.

"I immediately went over to Wilsons as you desired for the order, but to little purpose. – He said, he received my letter, but was advised not to part with the order, nor a copy, therefore did not chuse to let me have either. I used all the arguments I could to prevail with him, but could not: when I was coming away, he promised to send me a copy to Mr. Daniel's," which he never did.

After the Lent Nonsuit, I informed him what Serjeant Hill said in the defence of his Clients, the Defendants as aforesaid, to which he answered on

May 14th, 1773.

"As to what Serjeant Hill says, – I hope you're not so weak as to believe it to be truth. How can it be that the Defendants should be desired to take care of you only a few days, by your Brother and Uncle, when neither of us knew any thing of your confinement till they sent a messenger over to inform us, that you was in that unhappy situation? indeed after we had information, I cannot tell what was wrote to them, as it is so long since, and no copies of the letters took: We believing you to be in the state represented, was not at all upon our guard, never expecting any thing of this kind happening: the information came from such persons as we thought would not deceive us. I should be glad that you and every other injured person might have justice done them. This is truth, whether you believe it or not. I desire I may hear no more of this disagreeable subject."

I remain,
Your affectionate Brother,
JOSHUA BRUCKSHAW."

To Mr. Samuel Bruckshaw,
Lawrence-Lane, LONDON.

Numb. VIII.

To Mr. William Hardy, *in Stockport.*

Bourn, June 15th, 1770.

SIR,

I received your letter yesterday, with a draft on Mr. Dixon, value 38*l.* which he will pay; I am very sorry to acquaint you of Mr. Bruckshaw, he is now in Stamford goal, very mad, I hope you will send somebody over with the bearer to take care of him, for he will not be set at liberty till Mr. Bruckshaw, or somebody comes, my compliments to you all, and am

Your humble servant,

D. Ding.

Mr. Ding declared on oath it was not his writing, nor did he know any thing of it. Its effects on Bruckshaw's relations may be seen in the next Number.

Numb. IX.

Extracts from my Uncle's Letters.

Stockport, June 22nd, 1772.

"SIR,

Your Brother has told me, that Mr. Ding has made affidavit that the letter sent to us in his name, was without his knowledge and direction. If so, it was exceedingly base and villainous in those that sent it, and I am afraid the black author of it has took care to conceal himself: – for that letter, and one from Mr. Fothergill, removed from us all doubt and suspicion of their veracity.

It would give me pleasure for you to obtain satisfaction: – yet I cannot say I could wish you to enter into a state of law, as the expences are so great and the event so uncertain.

I am sorry that any person should be so vile as to endeavour to injure you in the opinion of your friends; it shews a base, malicious disposition, the more so as you would not willingly injure any person. – As to your Brother and I being concerned in the seizure of you at Stamford, you know that to be false, being both of us ignorant of it till their messenger came here, but* the above letters led us to consent to the imprisonment, and think it necessary.

I will omit no opportunity of serving you, and that it will give me pleasure to convince you of, &c."

August 2d, 1773.

"I received yours of the 29th, and still think that if you had a full hearing you would have a verdict, but if it must only be a partial one, for the jury to judge whether the Defendants acted in a judicial capacity, I would recommend it for you to drop it; I don't wish to give you any uneasiness, I only wish you to go on good ground, and not to throw your money away to no purpose, for how can you expect any benefit, unless the merits of your case must be argued?

I am, Sir,
Your humble servant,
Samuel Daniel."

---

* It is necessary to remind the reader, that the magistrates of Stamford and their auxiliaries, the keepers of the madhouse, agreed in representing Bruckshaw as raving mad, and that the sight of his friends would make him worse.

Numb. X.

JAMES GEE of Stockport, in the county of Chester, manufacturer of checks,[98] maketh oath and saith, That he hath for several years last past known and been well acquainted, and had several connexions in trade with Samuel Bruckshaw, late of Bourn, in the county of Lincoln, woolstapler; and that particularly in the months of April and May, 1770, this deponent had frequent conversations with the said Samuel Bruckshaw, and during all the time of this deponent's knowledge of him he appeared, and, as this deponent believes, was, in his right senses. And this deponent further saith, that having been informed that in the month of June following the said Samuel Bruckshaw, under some pretence of insanity, had been sent to a private mad-house at Scout-mill, in the parish of Ashton in the county of Lancaster, this deponent did, on or about the 27th day of September 1770 following, go to the said mad-house, and then saw and conversed with the said Samuel Bruckshaw; and, from what then appeared to this deponent, he verily believes the said Samuel Bruckshaw was at that time in his perfect senses.

JAMES GEE.

Sworn at my chambers in Serjeant's-
   Inn, the 24th day of January,
   1772, before

     W. H. ASHHURST.

Numb. XI.

	Between Sam. Bruckshaw, Plaintiff,
In the King's Bench	and
	Jn. Hopkins and Jn. Exton, Defts.

WILLIAM SELLERS, of Tuxford, in the county of Nottingham, innholder, Edward Thornton, of the same place, brickmaker, and John Fell, of the same place, mercer, severally make oath and say, and first the said William Sellers for himself saith, That some time about the latter-end of June, 1770, the Plaintiff was brought in a chaise by two men to this deponent's house, loaded with irons on his hands and legs, which much surprized this deponent, as the said Plaintiff had, about a fortnight before, spent the evening and lay at this deponent's house. And this deponent, William Sellers, saith, That the said Plaintiff requested to be taken before a magistrate, who might enquire into the cause of his confinement, but there was none in that neighbourhood; but this deponent told the Plaintiff there was a constable near, which the Plaintiff desired might be sent for, which he accordingly was; and that the said constable (who was the said Edward Thornton) loosed one of the irons from the Plaintiff's leg, for him to go into the garden; and this deponent saith, that the said Plaintiff appeared to this deponent to be as perfectly in his senses as any man whatever. And this deponent saith, the Plaintiff was conveyed from this deponent's house by the said two men who brought him there, with irons on his legs. – And this deponent, Edward Thornton, saith, That some time about the latter-end of June, 1770, being sent for to the house of the said William Sellers, he accordingly went, and found the Plaintiff loaded with irons on his hands and legs, but which this deponent, at the request of Plaintiff, loosed from one of his legs, for him to go into the garden; and that the Plaintiff desired the deponent to demand of the two men who had the said Plaintiff in custody, their authority for treating him and conveying him in this way; and that thereupon the said two men produced some order, which this deponent believes was signed by the defendants, but which order, upon the face thereof, did not appear to be made on the complaint, or on the information, of any person whatever. And this deponent saith, that the Plaintiff appeared to this deponent to be as perfectly in his senses as any man whatever – And this deponent, John Fell, saith, That some time about the latter-end of June, 1770, he saw the Plaintiff at the house of the said William Sellers, loaded with irons, and that the Plaintiff appeared to this deponent to be as perfectly in his senses as any man whatever. And all the deponents say, that the Plaintiff was conveyed, with irons on his legs, from the house of said William Sellers, in a chaise, by two men who brought him there; and that, from the manner of the said Plaintiff's being treated and conveyed, they should have supposed him to have been a felon, had not the said two men who had the Plaintiff in custody given another reason, to wit, that he was insane; the contrary of which these deponents believe to be true, as the said Plaintiff did not discover the least marks of insanity.

Sworn at Tuxford aforesaid,	*William Sellers,*
the 12th day of April,	*Edw. Thornton,*
1773, before me,	*John Fell.*

WILLIAM LOWTHER,
a Commissioner, &c.

(Examined)
J. DODGSON.

Numb. XII.

In the King's Bench

Between Sam. Bruckshaw, Plaintiff,
and
Jn. Hopkins and Jn. Exton, Defts.

JOHN NIELD, late of Bottoms, within the parish of Mottram Longendale, in the county of Chester, but now of Stealy-bridge in the parish of Ashton Underline, in the county of Lancaster, barber, and Ralph Heaward, of Stealy-wood, in the said parish of Mottram Longendale, clothier, severally make oath and say, and first, the said John Nield says, That he was sent for in a few days after the Plaintiff came to the house of John Wilson at Scout-mill, which he believes might be in or about the months of June or July, which was in the year of our Lord 1770, to shave the Plaintiff, who was there confined, and whom he found in a garret, chained down in a bed without curtains, and that the Plaintiff had nothing on but his shirt, and that he had irons on one leg; and this deponent, John Nield, saith, that he frequently shaved Plaintiff during his confinement at Scout-mill, which was for many months, and that the said Plaintiff was very often in chains, and that from the Plaintiff's being thus treated, this deponent looked on him to be a madman; but he soon found when he became acquainted with Plaintiff, that he was a sensible and reasonable man, and as perfectly in his senses as any man whatever; and that he would as readily have lain in a room with Plaintiff, as with any other person. And this said deponent saith, that Scout-mill is a most horrible, obscure place in itself. And this deponent saith, that the behaviour of the Plaintiff was very different from the behaviour of others who were confined at Scout-mill, who were really mad, and whom this deponent shaved. – And this deponent, Ralph Heaward, for himself saith, That he saw the Plaintiff in or about the month of August, which was in the said year of our Lord, 1770, at the house of John Wilson, at Scout-mill aforesaid, where Plaintiff was confined many months; and this deponent saith he often saw, and had frequent conversations with, the Plaintiff, and he had several times irons on his legs, and that the Plaintiff always behaved and acted like a reasonable man, and in a peaceable and orderly manner.

Sworn at Ashton Underline aforesaid, this 21st day of April, in
the year of our Lord, 1773,
before me,

John Nield,
Ralph Heaward.

THO.TAYLOR,
a Commissioner, &c.

(Examined)
J. DODGSON

Numb. XIII.

WE whose names are hereunto set and subscribed, according to the date affixed therewith, did see and converse with Mr. Samuel Bruckshaw during his imprisonment at Scout-mill, and from the result of such conversation never had the least reason to believe him disordered in his mind.

Witness our several hands and respective names, this 31st day of March, 1771.

(I believe the 3rd day of the present instant March was the first time I saw or conversed with Mr. Bruckshaw.)

		John Cradock
	Feb. 4,	*Cornelius Kenworthy*
	March 15,	*Dan. Woolley*
1770,	Aug. 12,	*Ralph Heaward*
	June 30,	*John Nield* (shaved me all the time.)
	July	*John Kershaw*
	Ditto	*Joseph Kenworthy*
	August 29,	*James Buckley*
	Ditto,	*John Lingard*
1771,	Jan 16,	*James Burchall*
	Feb. 4,	*Tho. Townson*

Numb. XIV.

WE whose names are hereunto set and subscribed (according to the dates affixed therewith) did see and converse with Mr. Samuel Bruckshaw, and from the result of such conversation never had the least reason to believe him disordered in his mind. – Witness our several and respective names, this 30th day of April, 1771.

1770.	June 27,	*John Morley,* constable of Sheffield, with me most of the afternoon. S.B.
		his *William X Nelson* Mark. Drove me 40 miles. S.B.
	June 27,	*Edward Thornton.* Constable of Tuxford, with me at Breakfast, &c. S.B.
	June	*George Inskip,* Drove me in a returned chaise from Barnbymoor to Tuxford on the 12th, and on the 27th from Tuxford to Worksop in irons. S.B.

[Wilsons in their passions repeatedly expressed themselves to me in these words: "We could have more money for killing thee than curing thee; thou never will be better as long as thou livest; thou'rt an incurable, and sure to live a charge upon thy brother." Once during the aforesaid 82 days close confinement in the smoaky garret, Wilson rushed suddenly upon me, and with a case-knife[99] made a push at my breast. And once in their breaking in garret he pulled the bed-clothes off me, and his son held me down upon my back, while he, in an unmerciful manner, beat me with a six-foot staff, which bruised me much upon several parts of my body; and for several hours after I really believed that my legs were broke.]

The following Transcript from Judge BLACKSTONE'S Commentaries, suitably concludes this Pamphlet.

"THE impartial administration of justice, which secures both our persons and properties, is the great end of civil society; but if that be entirely entrusted to the magistracy, a select body of men, and those generally selected by the Prince, or such as enjoy the highest offices in the state, their decisions, in spite of their own natural integrity, will have frequently an involuntary bias towards those of their own rank and dignity: it is not to be expected from human nature that the *few* should be always attentive to the interest and good of the *many*. In settling and adjusting a question of fact, when intrusted to any single magistrate, partiality and injustice have an ample field to range in: here, therefore, a competent number of sensible and upright jurymen, chosen by lot from among those of the middle rank, will be found the best investigators of truth, and the surest guardians of Public Justice. For the most powerful individual in the state will be cautious of committing any flagrant invasion of another's right, when he knows that the fact of his oppression must be examined and decided by twelve indifferent men not appointed 'till the hour of trial; and that, when once the fact is ascertained, the law must of course redress it. This, therefore, preserves in the hands of the people that share, which they ought to have in the administration of public justice, and prevents the encroachments of the more wealthy and powerful citizens."

THE END

BELCHER's

ADDRESS TO HUMANITY:

CONTAINING,

A LETTER TO DR. THOMAS MONRO;

A RECEIPT TO MAKE A LUNATIC, AND SEIZE

HIS ESTATE;

AND

A SKETCH OF A TRUE SMILING HYENA.

———————————

And many a plague fucceed, and many a woe,
And long, long, long, of Hell the bellows blow.
From the Author's Galaxy. [1]

———————————

SOLD BY ALLEN AND WEST, NO. 15, PATERNOSTER-ROW;
AND BY THE AUTHOR, AT HIS HOUSE, NO. 9, LOWER
THORNHAUGH-STREET, BEDFORD-SQUARE, LONDON.

PRICE SIXPENCE.

1796.

Also may be had of Allen & West,
Peace and Reconciliation;
To which is added.
A Letter to Mr. Fox.

Interspersed with Considerations on Universal Suffrage;
on the Coalition of Mr. FOX and Lord NORTH, and the
Propriety of a Coalition with Mr. THELWALL; a Prediction
of Emigration and Depopulation, should not a Repeal
of the late obnoxious Acts and a Reform take place; and
Anecdotes of the unexampled Persecution of the Author,
the subject of the *Address to Humanity,* &c.

In the Press.
Belcher's Cream of Knowledge,

Skimmed from the Milk of Human Savageness, and ma-
tured in the School of Adversity.
The Soul's dark cottage, batter'd and decay'd,
Lets in new light through chinks that time hath made.
WALLER.[2]

This Work will not be published in periodical
Numbers, but each portion will be in itself complete.

Advertisement.

*SHOULD my injuries, of the most crying kind imaginable, of which the following
pages are a sketch, be the means of turning the thoughts of men in power to atrocities
far beyond words to express (which, through the practices of the law, are not yet at an*

end respecting me), I shall have the consolation that my sufferings have not been in vain. At all events, sacrificing my feelings to a faint hope of public good, I hope that, without impiety, I may say with Sir John Scott, who has my thanks, Liberavi animam meam; *or rather, that it has always been free, and sometimes smiled, even in the bosom of horror.*

W.B.[3]

A Letter to Dr. Thomas Monro.[4]

SIR,

BEING, by your assistance, together with that of another real Gentleman of the Faculty, restored from legal death, and the most insupportable situation possible to a man of feeling, that of imputed, accompanied with the disabilities of real, insanity; and having been advertised in the news-papers of my provincial residence, whilst I was just as much in my senses, as I am at present, and at the same time furnished one of those papers with a series of essays, &c. &c. after mature deliberation I am induced now to make known some circumstances of my own case, a relation of the whole of which would fill a folio.

After the incredible conduct of a man who, after taking a handsome fee, and making several false promises, doomed me, as far as was in his power, to an entire broken heart; with an outrage to common sense, and the wonder of the Attorney General, who declared it was a *d–d odd thing;* though Christian charity forbids a literal interpretation of the term *d–d;* after this, I am the more obliged to you, and because, almost the moment you saw me, you, with that intuitive sagacity which is visible in your countenance, pronounced me perfectly in my senses, and, soon convinced that I had given all the proofs of sanity possible to be given, readily consented to give a speedy certificate of it.

Yes, I declare on my soul, that it was impossible to doubt, as no one who knew me did, or could doubt of my sanity; and no one unacquainted with the affair ever thought of my being otherwise. Notwithstanding which, a man, who calls himself the friend of the unfortunate, took money, &c. of me, and resisted all this demonstration; and was, I have reason to believe, privy to a dark anonymous statement to the Attorney General, whether demonstration itself, it could be called no less, was evidence of my sanity; and whether the restoration of my estate would be the consequence of a *supersedeas?*[5] Good God! yet for such complication of injustice, treachery, and tyranny, no special Acts of Parliament are enacted, no fine, imprisonment, pillory and transportation provided.

You, Sir, particularly expressed your wonder (wonderful indeed has been my fate) at my being able to settle my mind to the composition of a series of literary works in such circumstances, which I will now explain to you with the utmost sincerity and truth. That serenity of mind and peace, surpassing your understanding though of the very first rate, was chiefly owing to the conviction of a superintending Providence;[6] and that misfortune is no more than a reasonable tribute to the misery of the world. Nor let this be deemed cant and hypocrisy, which I abhor, by those ignorant of the consolation of religion to devout minds deprived of every other. To the aid of religion I added also that of philosophy and metaphysics, a kind of a medium between both, and attended closely to the resources of my mind, when pressed and strained to the utmost, at which times I usually found my imagination assisted, as it were, by collision, when suffering under the most unutterable anguish.

During my irremediable confinement, I was driven to the verge of desperation and real lunacy, through want of sleep, occasioned (I speak as if on oath) chiefly by the thinness of the partitions of the apartments, whereby I was disturbed by night with snoring and coughing, and by day with ranting and raving; so that I know not what I would not have given for an hour's peace, and am now astonished that I survived all.

The poet says that, at the point of death,

> both worlds at once we view,
> When standing on the threshold of the new.[7]

Having thus closely attended to the operations of my mind when urged to the brink of insanity, as to form an idea of its reality, the best account I can give of it is, that in real derangement the *mind is rather out of the body* than the body out of the mind, according to the expression, "out of one's mind." I shall not, however, say all, lest I should be deemed a fanatic, after having in a manner learned to live in mental fire, and experienced the reality of religion which enabled its martyrs to endure real flames. Flames I never endured; but when as perfectly in my senses as I trust I am at present, I have been bound and tortured in a strait waistcoat, fettered, crammed with physic with a bullock's horn,[8] and knocked down, and at length declared a lunatic by a Jury that never saw me; and, what would make a man tear his flesh from his bones, all through affected kindness. Another dreadful aggravation is, that every degree of resentment against the authors of their ruin, is considered as a presumption of remaining insanity in the sufferer, who has hardly any chance of restoration without their consent, though he adduces thousands of proofs that the whole was a scene of iniquity thus countenanced and encouraged. And so dead is society to these notorious breaches of it, that hardly an instance has occurred of legal redress obtained, even for the loss of property, the least part (though mine has amounted to thousands of pounds) of the incalculable and inexpressible injury.

The Attorney General, (Mr. Gurney was my other own Counsel; but I pay all, as I suffered all.), who has my thanks for making the motion, being fond of the ejaculation *Liberavi animam meam*, would use it with increased propriety, were he officially to attack a system of outrage that beggars description, and commences with depriving the sufferer of his property, the means of redress; a system controlled by no provisional guard in the nature of a Grand Jury;[9] but a person, body, and often mind, is at the mercy of interested or offended relations, who thus have it in their power to inflict, without the charge of any crime, a punishment in comparison of which, transportation for life, or death itself, would be mercy.

To what particular cause I ascribe my persecution, of a kind the *more* severe, because attended with indignity and contempt, instead of honour, its proper companion, is not material to the public: but they may be assured that these kinds of enormities are practised; and I am content to be branded with the appellation of liar, if I have exaggerated this sketch. But as if I were doomed to be the object of contradictions, I was found a lunatic, whilst composing remarks on Johnson's Lives of the English Poets, inserted in the Gentleman's Magazine, and afterwards published by Hookham, under the title of the Art of Criticism:[10] and was declared *non compos*,[11] and unable to attend to my affairs, which a respectable attorney kindly took into his hands, for me with a salary he procured under the seal, at a time when I contributed to Young's Annals of Husbandry,[12] and used a farm of 100 acres entirely myself, who was at last extremely unwilling to part with his perquisites. I was afterwards still deemed a lunatic for years and years, when none except those acquainted with my history ever thought of such a thing; and a certain person alluded to declared I was the most extraordinary one he ever knew, yet took my money and books with a grin, and then bilked me.[13] And to crown all, whilst endeavouring to prove myself not a lunatic, and become a fresh prey to savages, I was summoned on a coroner's inquest about fifty yards from my own house, on which I thought it best to serve, and did accordingly.

Of rapacity and brutality, and all that is shocking to human feelings, a mad-house, that premature coffin of mind, body, and estate, is to an imputed lunatic, the concentration. A trade to which seventeen years of the prime of my life has been sacrificed: a trade known to all, and disregarded by all, the connivance at which is a horrible disgrace to government and to society; which, whilst I forgive where forgiveness is due, it shall be the object of my life to expose to detestation and abhorrence. Yes, on this subject I have an especial right to speak – I owe it to God, my country, and humanity to speak, and I will speak, and, if possible, make my hearers *ears*.

Mr. Erskine lately swore he would not die a slave.[14] I hope that he will not: yet in a nation in which such outrages as I have experienced are practised with impunity, and their prosecution discountenanced, no man is safe from living and dying in a strait waistcoat, in which I have lain whole winter nights bound, and cold from want of bed-clothes, a sufficiency not being allowed me, whilst as perfectly in my senses as I am now. Would to God that he, since those whose duty it is to investigate them shun them, would dart his lightning on scenes on which day has never shone! that miscreants to whom I bid defiance, may not for ever fatten on unspeakable calamity. If the publication of my case is dangerous, so is likewise silence. Should I at last perish, let it be in the face of the day.

It sometimes happens that obscure persons, through extraordinary circumstances, become the instruments of good. And I will hope that the present Lord Chancellor,[15] whose readiness in doing me justice, heretofore an entire stranger to it, as far as he was applied to, has my sincere thanks, and whose humanity and integrity in his high office are universally acknowledged, will strike at the root of this enormous evil, and thereby record his name on the roll of the benefactors of mankind.

A Victim to the Trade of Lunacy.

Postscript.

You, Sir, as I have observed, having expressed your wonder at my writings, the offspring of such very unpropitious circumstances, I take this opportunity of recommending to the favour of the public, my poetical effusions (effusions, I say, the versions of Scripture itself being not servile) in the Galaxy, the composition of which was an alleviation of my misery, and at times the source of pleasure; for barren is the rock interspersed with no patches of verdure. A work which having been long buried in the same living grave with its master, may possibly now partake of his resurrection.

Had I known how dreadfully this couplet of the Galaxy*–

> *And many a plague succeed, and many a woe,*
> *And long, long, long, of Hell the bellows blow –*

would have been verified in me, I should have been overwhelmed with despair, totally beyond the philosophy of any human being; so true it is that

---

*(The *Galaxy*, containing near 300 quarto pages of sacred and miscellaneous poetry and prose, having been, as might be supposed, blasted in the bud by very bitter winds, may be now had at No. 9. Thornhaugh-Street, Bedford-Square,[19] for half-a-crown, not one third of its value, if some good judges may be depended on. However, such a book of poetry, warm from the brain of a Lunatic, ought to excite the curiosity of a nation celebrated for humanity; especially as the receipt shall be wholly applied to a Clergyman and his Family, actually starving in prison.)

ignorance of the future, that anticipating Lethe, is the best boon of human life.

My favourite author, Cowley, says that those safe-landed no more regard the wind; yet though I do not belive Locke's doctrine of material traces worn in the mind, I find Pope's assertion, that of all sciences the hardest is to forget, more truly verified.[16]

I perfectly remember that when, on the 8th of October, 1778, I was overwhelmed with astonishment at being carried to Hackney,[17] to take my abode with idiots and real or supposed madmen, some of them just as mad as myself, these lines of Milton occurred to me:

> Hail, horrors! hail
> Infernal world! and thou profoundest hell,
> Receive thy new possessor, one who brings
> A mind not to be chang'd by place or time.[18]

For had I been the devil, I could hardly have been used worse.

The Trade of Lunacy;
or,
an approved receipt, To make a Lunatic, and seize his Estate.

WATCH for some season of vexation, and then, by proper insinuations and a pitying tone of voice, work up the patient to a due pitch of passion; then lay on blisters;[20] and before his agitation of spirits has time to subside, hurry him away violently to a mad-house, so denominated, that is to say, one of the graves of mind, body, and estate, much more dreadful than the Bastille and Inquisition.[21] There, as an earnest of taking possession of all his property, the means of redress, pick his pockets of every thing, totally confound his understanding by the strangeness of his treatment, and lay him in an apartment of which the partitions are so thin that he be kept awake by coughing, snoring, and raving; and then allege as a proof of madness, that he sleeps ill; but do not destroy him quite, unless bribed high, but give him opium to enable him to endure farther tortures and at the same time render him delirious. And should his stomach reject the plenty of physic with which you must be sure to ply him, the use of a bullock's horn will be very proper. Use him also with all manner of savage indignity; and be sure not to forget the strait waistcoat, nor also handcuffs and fetters occasionally, they being no less powerful arguments in the hands of mad-house-keepers, than cannon in those of state-tyrants. When the physicians, by appointment of Parliament, visit the house,[22] take particular care they do not see the patient alone; but the master of the house must be sure to be with them himself, lest something improper should possibly transpire.

In the mean time, with all imaginable secrecy and kindness, and with tears in your eyes, sue out a commission of Lunacy against the unfortunate patient.[23] And should his patience far exceed Job's,[24] so as to erase human feelings from his mind, and he be not totally undone; suffer nobody whatever to come near him, nor let him be seen by the Jury, to whom you may allege what you will against him without danger of contradiction; as the managers, commissioners, attornies, counsel, and possibly the leaders of the jury, will be of your choosing, and at your disposal; whilst doctors, lawyers, committees, rent-gatherers, mad-house-keepers, ruffians, and various other respectable brutes, make plenty of work for each other, among whom the property of the unfortunate patient should be liberally scattered.

So shall the trade of Lunacy prosper, and become more and more honourable and respectable.

N.B. The friends and guardians of a lunatic need very seldom be afraid that the state of his mind will be regarded as an object, unless they mean that it should; but may depend on it that their will and choice will determine whether he is in his senses or not.

Sketch of an Helleborean Savage, or Smiling Hyena,[25] famous in a Province over which the Devil is said to do his business, by which the Author was severely bitten, and Sir John Scott induced to declare it was a D——D ODD THING.

THIS animal is a non-descript of a mixed species. Form obtuse – body black – head grey – teeth and prowess on the decline – visage smiling, especially at the sight of shining metal, of which its paws are extremely retentive – heart supposed to be a kind of tough white leather.

N.B. He doth ravish the *rich* when he getteth him into his den.

FINIS.

Notes

Introduction

1 Tobias Smollett, *The Life and Adventures of Sir Launcelot Greaves*, 1760–1, ed. David Evans, Oxford: Oxford University Press, 1973, pp. 185–6.

2 On treatment, see Allan Ingram, *The Madhouse of Language: Writing and Reading Madness in the Eighteenth Century*, London: Routledge, 1991, chapters 2 and 3.

3 On private madhouses and their regulation, see especially Roy Porter, *Mind-Forg'd Manacles: A History of Madness from the Restoration to the Regency*, London: The Athlone Press, 1987, pp. 136–55, and William Llewellyn Parry-Jones, *The Trade in Lunacy: A Study of Private Madhouses in England in the Eighteenth and Nineteenth Centuries*, London: Routledge & Kegan Paul, 1971.

4 For fuller details, see *Dictionary of National Biography*. There is a biography of Cruden by E. Olivier, *The Eccentric Life of Alexander Cruden*, London: Faber, 1934, and also a full summary and assessment in Roy Porter, *A Social History of Madness: Stories of the Insane*, London: Weidenfeld & Nicolson, 1987, pp. 126–35. The 'shovel' reference is to *The Adventures of Alexander the Corrector*, London: for the Author, 1754, pp. 5–6.

Hannah Allen

1 'Esay' is the book of Isaiah, but xxxviii. 14, Hezekiah's thanksgiving after recovery from his sickness. The second quotation in full is: 'To whom ye forgive anything, I forgive also: for if I forgave anything, to whom I forgave it, for your sakes forgave I it in the person of Christ; lest Satan should get an advantage of us: for we are not ignorant of his devices' (10–11). Hannah Allen's writing, especially in the opening section, 'To the Reader', is biblically heavily allusive. I have tried to identify the major points of reference.

2 The comparison of soul and body to music and the instrument producing it probably derives from Pythagoras, though modified through Christian adoption. Various medical writers, such as Bartholomaeus Anglicus and Philip Barrough in the sixteenth century, recommended music as a potential cure for the melancholy soul. Allen was writing at a time when the image of the body was undergoing radical revision, with humoral theory and its doctrine of balances giving way to an understanding based on circulation and energies. Her contemporary Thomas Willis was one of the most influential English writers in this field.

3 Bandogs are particularly fierce guard dogs, usually tied or chained.

4 David collected the bones of Saul and Jonathan for proper burial in response to visitation of famine upon Israel (II Samuel xxi. 12–14). Heman was the sage, Heman the Ezrahite, who took credit for composing the 88th Psalm, which includes the lines 'Thy wrath lieth hard upon me, And thou hast afflicted me with all thy waves.' (7) Hezekiah was king of Judah. His lamentations at the threats of Sennacherib, king of Assyria, are described in II Kings xix. Job, whose story is narrated in the book of the same name, had long stood as a model for patience under unexplained suffering in spite of his desire, in the depths of his despair, for death: 'Then thou scarest me with dreams, And terrifiest me through visions: So that my soul chooseth strangling, And death rather than my life.' (vii. 14–15)

5   The speaking of Jehovah to Moses from the Burning Bush is told in Exodus iii. 2–3.

6   Leviathan was the dreadful dragon of the sea, mentioned variously in the Old Testament and a persistent allusion in Christian writing in England.

7   The reference is to Christ's words to those following him to Calvary, warning them of worse times to come: 'weep not for me, but weep for yourselves, and for your children . . . For if they do these things in a green tree, what shall be done in the dry?' (Luke xxiii. 29–31)

8   The Apostle is Paul, and the verse is from II Corinthians v. 7.

9   The reference is to Philippians iv. 7: 'And the peace of God, which passeth all understanding, shall keep your hearts and minds through Christ Jesus.'

10   While 'briss' is suggestive of bristle, it probably refers to an eyelash.

11   'Rock of Ages' is from Isaiah xxvi, 4: 'in the Lord Jehovah is the rock of ages' in the Hebrew, but 'is everlasting strength' in the Authorised Version.

12   The reference is to II Peter iii. 3–4: 'there shall come in the last days scoffers, walking after their own lusts, and saying, Where is the promise of his coming?'

13   See Psalms lxix. 12: 'They that sit in the gate speak against me; And I was the song of the drunkards.'

14   At the Last Supper, Christ told the disciples: 'ye shall weep and lament, but the world shall rejoice: and ye shall be sorrowful, but your sorrow shall be turned into joy.' (John xvi. 20) He continued: 'And ye now therefore have sorrow: but I will see you again, and your heart shall rejoice, and your joy no man taketh from you.' (John, xvi. 22)

15   The reference is to Proverbs xiv. 32: 'The wicked is driven away in his wickedness: But the righteous hath hope in his death.'

16   See Psalms lviii. 9: 'Before your pots can feel the thorns, He shall take them away as with a whirlwind, both living, and in his wrath.' The psalmist is describing the vengence the Lord will take against the wicked.

17   Snelston is near Ashbourne, some twelve miles north-west of Derby. Uttoxeter Woodland is only around seven miles from Snelston, just over the border into Staffordshire.

18   Aldermanbury, in the City, runs up from Gresham Street, past the Guildhall, towards London Wall.

19   In this passage the prophet is discussing God's capacity to heal those with whom he has been wrathful.

20   Richard Bolton (1572–1631) was a puritan divine, preacher and writer from Blackburn in Lancashire. His works, which included *A Discourse about the State of True Happinesse*, published in 1611 and extending to many editions, were extremely popular and widely read. A 'much enlarged' third edition appeared in 1614.

21   The verses, addressed to Job, concern the bullrush that 'withereth before any other herb. So are the paths of all that forgot God; And the hypocrite's hope shall perish.' (Job viii. 11–13)

22   Cain and Abel were the first two sons of Adam and Eve. When Cain killed Abel he became an exile from the Lord. The story is told in Genesis iv. Judas, of course, was the betrayer of Christ.

23   The full quotation is: 'For if we sin wilfully after that we have received the knowledge of the truth, there remaineth no more sacrifice for sins, but a certain fearful looking for of judgment and fiery indignation, which shall devour the adversaries.' (Hebrews x. 26–7)

24   These depressing passages are answered in the 'Promises' that conclude the pamphlet.

25   Tamworth is near Lichfield, on Staffordshire's border with Leicestershire.

26   Nuneaton is between Leicester and Coventry, just within Warwickshire.

27   St Swithin's Lane in the City runs up from Cannon Street to King William Street and the Royal Exchange.

28   The Oxford English Directory gives 1683, the date of the pamphlet, as the earliest use for 'Chemist: One who deals in or retails medicinal drugs'.

29   'Wainscot' is wooden panelling, originally made from timber of a superior quality, such as oak.

30   Newgate prison, near St Paul's and the River Fleet, held the most desperate and serious criminals. Many were condemned and awaiting execution, for which they would endure the public journey to Tyburn west of the City, near where Marble Arch now stands. The

practice ended only in 1783, after which, and until as late as 1868, public executions were carried out at Newgate.

31 Opium, particularly as tincture of laudanum, was available for purchase in the seventeenth century, but its vogue really began in the eighteenth, when its use and abuse became widespread.

32 Apothecaries were forerunners of chemists, though they might also sell a range of such commodities as spices and preserves as well as medicinal drugs and preparations.

33 While there is a long history of fearing death by spider, there are no recorded instances of anyone having been poisoned by smoking one.

34 This abruptly inserted letter by Hannah Allen is perhaps addressed to 'Lady Baker', who is later reported as having been 'pleased to write me several Letters'.

35 The narrative here moves into the third person for a short stretch, possibly drawing upon a different account or memoir, perhaps by Mr or Mrs Walker.

36 '*Dead Dog*' is probably an allusion to II Samuel xvi. 9. After Shimei, of the house of Saul, has cursed and flung stones at David, Abishai, one of David's 'mighty men', says to the king, 'Why should this dead dog curse my lord the king? let me go over, I pray thee, and take off his head.'

37 The verse is not quoted, possibly on grounds of propriety, as in Colossians iii. 5 St Paul advises: 'Mortify therefore your members which are upon the earth; fornication, uncleanness, inordinate affection, evil concupiscence, and covetousness, which is idolatry.' Here, perhaps, is the slightest hint of a side to Hannah Allen's nature which she does not wish to spell out, but which gives greater force to her feelings about her late husband.

38 Pashur was son of Immer the priest and was responsible for putting the prophet Jeremiah in the stocks. His doom was prophesied on the next day by Jeremiah: 'The Lord hath not called thy name Pashur, but Magor-Missabib. For thus saith the Lord, Behold, I will make thee a terror to thyself, and to all thy friends.' (Jeremiah xx. 1–4) 'Magor-Missabib' is literally 'terror on every side'.

39 The reference is probably to I John v. 16–17: 'If any man see his brother sin a sin which is not unto death, he shall ask, and he shall give him life for them that sin not unto death. There is a sin unto death: I do not say that he shall pray for it.'

40 Christ told his apostles: 'And whosoever shall not receive you, nor hear your words, when ye depart out of that house or city, shake off the dust of your feet.' (Matthew x. 14) (There are similar verses at Mark vi. 11 and Luke ix. 5.)

41 Christ's teaching of the 'foolish man, which built his house upon the sand' is in Matthew vii. 26–7.

42 Christ's words are most bluntly recorded at Mark iii. 28–30: 'Verily I say unto you, All sins shall be forgiven unto the sons of men, and blasphemies wherewith soever they shall blaspheme: but he that shall blaspheme against the Holy Ghost hath never forgiveness, but is in danger of eternal damnation: because they said, He hath an unclean spirit.' Variations are at Matthew xii. 31–2 and Luke xii. 10.

43 Letting blood by opening a vein, a minor operation normally performed by a surgeon, had for many years been standard treatment in a wide range of ailments, particularly those thought to arise from any kind of excess present in the body.

44 The 'Leads' would be an attic area without any kind of ceiling, thus giving directly on to the bare roof with its leaden strips that ensured waterproofing.

45 Smithfield is to the north-west of St Paul's, near Newgate Street, and was a notorious area, especially with its market, for thieves and prostitutes.

46 Aldersgate Street runs directly north from St Paul's to the Barbican, just to the east of Smithfield.

47 Barnet is some twelve miles from the city, and at that time thoroughly rural.

48 Eight shillings (now forty pence) was a considerable fare, reflecting the distance to Barnet.

49 Highgate, between Holloway and Finchley, is approximately halfway to Barnet.

50 An apostate is one who renounces his or her religious faith.

51 Julian the Apostate was Roman emperor from 361 until 363. Half-brother of Constantine

the Great, who had taken the empire over officially to Christianity, Julian had lost his faith after the massacre of his family in 337. When he became emperor he returned to the old religion and removed all privileges from the Christian church.

52   Richard Baxter (1615–91) was one of the most famous and influential of Nonconformist divines, both through his itinerant preaching and through his many writings. He had only been permitted to enter the City of London since 1672 when the Act of Indulgence gave some degree of toleration to leading Nonconformists. In 1685 he was to be fined 500 marks for sedition by the infamous Judge Jeffreys, and was imprisoned for the eighteen months it took for the fine to be paid.

53   'And he smote the men of Beth-shemesh, because they had looked into the ark of the Lord, even he smote of the people fifty thousand and threescore and ten men: and the people lamented, because the Lord had smitten many of the people with a great slaughter.' (I Samuel vi. 19)

54   There is no biblical quotation here, but Allen's words echo Isaiah vi. 5: 'Then said I, Woe is me! for I am undone; because I am a man of unclean lips, and I dwell in the midst of a people of unclean lips.'

55   Old Jewry is not far from St Swithin's Lane. It runs almost due north from Poultry to Gresham Street, towards Moorgate.

56   A horn-book was originally a sheet of paper on which was inscribed the alphabet, and possibly also numbers and the Lord's Prayer, protected by a thin layer of horn. It came, therefore, to mean any kind of primer for teaching young children.

57   The full quotation is: 'For we know him that hath said, Vengeance belongeth unto me, I will recompense, saith the Lord. And again, The Lord shall judge his people. It is a fearful thing to fall into the hands of the living God.' (Hebrews x. 30–1)

58   The argument is based on the least of several evils. Four lepers were at the gate of Samaria during its besieging by the Syrians, 'and they said one to another, Why sit we here until we die? If we say, We will enter into the city, then the famine is in the city, and we shall die there: and if we sit still here, we die also. Now therefore come, and let us fall unto the host of the Syrians: if they save us alive, we shall live; and if they kill us, we shall but die.' In the event, they found the Syrians fled, having been made by the Lord to hear 'the noise of a great host', and so they feasted in splendour in the tents of the Syrians. (II Kings vii. 3–8)

59   'Pettinacious' is not a recognised word, but is similar both to 'pertinacious', meaning persistent or stubborn in holding to one's opinion, and to 'pettish', meaning subject to fits of offended ill humour, either of which would be appropriate here.

60   An arbour can mean an orchard, but here is clearly a bower of retreat within the orchard made from trees trained over a trellis.

61   Michaelmas is the feast of St Michael, 29 September.

62   Peter is writing of the 'lively hope' given by the resurrection of Christ 'Wherein ye greatly rejoice, though now for a season, if need be, ye are in heaviness through manifold temptations.' (I Peter i. 3–6)

Alexander Cruden

1   Cruden had received, after persistent applications, the Royal Warrant for the then vacant office of 'Queen's Bookseller' in 1735. It was to this queen, Caroline, wife of George II, that Cruden dedicated and presented his *Concordance* on 3 November, 1737, seventeen days before her sudden death. His shop was situated under the Royal Exchange, between the Poultry and Cornhill.

2   Bethnal Green was then still a village about a quarter of a mile north-east of the City of London.

3   Constables had served their function as officers of the peace since the late sixteenth century – the earliest use of the word is 1597.

4   Sir John Barnard, Lord Mayor of London and therefore enjoying jurisdiction over the

City, was also one of the opposing candidates – and the sitting member since 1722 – for election to the House of Commons for the City of London in 1754 when Cruden decided to stand. In the event, Cruden withdrew his candidature, insisting that he would only serve if elected unopposed. Barnard continued to represent the City until 1761.

5   Dr James Monro (1680–1752) was physician to Bethlem Hospital between 1728 and his death. His eldest son, John (1715–91), succeeded him until his own death. It was John, ironically, who certified the release of Cruden from confinement in a Chelsea madhouse in 1753.

6   The full quotation from St Paul is: 'Finally, brethren, pray for us, that the word of the Lord may have free course, and be glorified, even as it is with you: and that we may be delivered from unreasonable and wicked men: for all men have not faith.' (II Thessalonians iii. 1–2)

7   Lord Harrington was William Stanhope (*c.* 1683–1756), diplomat, general and MP. Secretary of State for the North between 1730 and 1742, and again from 1744 until 1746, he was created Baron Harrington in 1730 and 1st Earl of Harrington in 1742.

8   Piccadilly, west of the City, was even then a fashionable area, having been subject to considerable building speculation during the late sixteenth century.

9   Wild Court runs between Wild Street and Kingsway, a little south of Holborn.

10   This Latin line means 'She herself may burn: she delights, however, in the torments of the lover'. It is, however, a version of lines 209–10 of Juvenal's sixth satire, 'ardeat ipsa licet, tormentis gaudet amantis et spoliis': 'She may be on fire herself, but that doesn't lessen Her gold-digging itch, her sadistic urges' (tr. Peter Green, Penguin, 1967).

11   John Oswald actually owned the house where Cruden had lodgings, though his immediate landlord and landlady were the Grants.

12   Chancery Lane runs from north to south between Holborn and the Strand.

13   Gray's Inn, between Gray's Inn Road and Holborn, is slightly north of Chancery Lane.

14   Swallow Street is between Piccadilly and what is now Regent Street. The Presbyterian meeting-house, under Dr John Guyse, was actually in Broad Street.

15   A blackmore – or blackamoor – was a negro.

16   This was presumably St Andrew's, Holborn, which had been rebuilt in 1686 by Sir Christopher Wren.

17   Spring Gardens are just off what is now Trafalgar Square, and were originally popular recreational gardens. As Ludgate Hill is a continuation of the Strand and Fleet Street towards St Paul's, Cruden is being taken in entirely the opposite direction to Spring Gardens.

18   See Allen n.32.

19   The strait waistcoat was by this time in fairly wide use, especially in private madhouses, though it is uncertain when or by whom it was invented. Tick is a strong and hard linen material.

20   The Penny Post, which carried all letters for one penny, had been introduced in 1680.

21   Mercury was commonly prescribed for gonorrhoea. Excessive use was known to affect the mind, and indeed could be fatal.

22   Serjeant-Major Cruden was in fact Cruden's cousin. His rank at that time was a commissioned one, similar to the modern adjutant.

23   Cruden was a strict Sabbatarian (that is, one who insisted on the observance of the Sabbath day) as well as being implacably opposed to swearing of any kind.

24   The 'White-house' or the 'Blind Beggar's House' was a large mansion on the green. It had been built during the reign of Elizabeth I by a London citizen, John Kirby, and had belonged, among others, to Sir William Ryder, Deputy Master of Trinity House during Samuel Pepys' time. Pepys deposited valuables there during the Great Fire.

25   A chariot was a light vehicle kept for personal use, unlike the heavier coach which would normally be hired for specific journeys. Only the wealthiest would keep their own coach.

26   This draws on Psalms cxxiv. 7: 'Our soul is escaped as a bird out of the snare of the fowler.'

27   These are the words of the Lord, answering Job out of the whirlwind and advising him to 'Gird up thy loins like a man.' (Job xxxviii. 3)

28 Negro servants, fashionably, were given classical names, just as slaves transported to America were.

29 A cornet was one of the junior commissioned officers in a troop of cavalry, whose duties included carrying the colours. Half-pay might be received by an officer when not on actual service, or when retired.

30 Southgate is just north-west of Bethnal Green, on the way to Islington. Cruden was on good terms with the now widowed Mrs Coltman of Elm Hall, whose son he had tutored when first coming to England.

31 This was William Cruden, a pious and prosperous merchant and member of the town council in Aberdeen. He was to die in 1739, and Cruden's mother, Isabel, a year later.

32 Holborn is part of the main thoroughfare that bisects the City from the west end to St Paul's in the east.

33 Samuel Reynardson, like William Crookshank, worshipped at Guyse's Meeting House.

34 Green tea is roasted almost immediately after it has been gathered. It is often artificially coloured.

35 Hackney is immediately to the north of Bethnal Green.

36 Stoicism was founded by the Greek philosopher Zeno of Citium in around 310 BC, and advocated approximation to God through complete submission to his will. Suffering was held to be a matter of indifference in the pursuit of virtue. Cruden, however, believed in using such means as God permits to come to hand in the achieving of deliverance.

37 The King's Bench was the supreme court of common law in the kingdom.

38 This was probably William Stukely, the London physician and gout specialist. He had published *Of the Spleen, its Description and History* in 1723.

39 A Bill of Exchange was a written order for a sum to be paid at the cost of the writer.

40 Bath was a fashionable spa town throughout the century. Several eminent physicians, such as George Cheyne, Cruden's contemporary, had their practices there.

41 The original 'good and faithful servant' is found in the parable of the talents (Matthew xxv. 21).

42 Mile End is a little to the south-east of Bethnal Green. At that time it was another small village near London. Note that this day's entry is the second 23 April in Cruden's journal, Saturday being mistakenly entered as the 23rd as well as Sunday.

43 Bethlem Hospital was in Moorfields, just outside London Wall, and therefore stood between Bethnal Green and the City.

44 Admission to Bethlem would be at the recommendation of the parish having responsibility for the individual concerned. St Christopher's would have been the parish of St Christopher le Stocks in Cornhill, so named because of its proximity to the former City stocks. It was destroyed in the Great Fire, rebuilt by Wren in 1671, and finally demolished in 1781 to allow an extension to the Bank of England. Its churchyard survived until 1934, when the Bank required another extension.

45 Cruden went to the east, initially, to Mile End, before almost doubling back south-west along Mile End Road to Whitechapel. Perhaps he felt that the more direct route, which would have brought him into the City at Bishopsgate, further to the west, was dangerously close to Bethlem. From Whitechapel he followed Whitechapel Road into Aldgate. Leadenhall Street, turning off Aldgate, would have brought him along Cornhill to the Royal Exchange, where his shop was. The entire walk was probably around five miles.

46 Strictly speaking Sheriff's officers were bull-dogs, but the name was – and still is – applied to a variety of officials or attendants with responsibility for policing or apprehending.

47 Grocer's Hall, meeting-place of the Grocer's Company, is opposite the Bank of England, between Princes Street and Grocers' Hall Court, occupying the same site since 1427. Sir John Barnard, the Lord Mayor, was a member of the Grocers' Company.

48 Guildhall is near Aldermanbury, not far from the Grocers' Hall. Coffee-houses, of which there were above two thousand in London in any one time, provided not only refreshment but accommodation, and meeting-places for like-minded people. Some even offered private mailing services. It was North's that Cruden made his headquarters for his election campaign in 1754.

49 See Allen n.30.

50 Downing Street is probably now Down Street at the far end of Piccadilly, close to Hyde Park Corner.

51 The story of Joseph, eleventh of Jacob's twelve sons, is told in Genesis xxxvii–l. Mr Crookshank, who also worshipped at Guyse's Meeting House, refers to Joseph's achieving authority under Pharoah. Cruden has in mind Joseph's earlier experience of being cast into a pit in the wilderness by his jealous brothers, prior to their selling him into slavery (Genesis xxxvii).

52 Apart from a brief period, Hyde Park had been a public park since early in the sixteenth century. After the Restoration in 1660 it became a fashionable rendezvous and recreational area. St James's Park was enclosed as a park during the reign of Henry VIII.

53 This would presumably be Richmond-upon-Thames, to the south-west of London.

54 Great Ormond Street is to the south of what was to become Russell Square, running to the east from Southampton Row.

55 A groat was originally worth four pence, but had ceased to be issued in 1662.

56 Ware is in Hertfordshire, some twenty miles north of London. One of the positions Cruden occupied after leaving Aberdeen was Greek and Latin usher – or under-master – at a school there.

57 St Paul's School was founded in 1510 by John Colet. John Leland, John Milton and Samuel Pepys were all educated there, though the school was destroyed in the Great Fire of 1666. The Duke of Marlborough was a pupil at the rebuilt school.

58 The Royal College of Physicians was founded in 1518 by Thomas Linacre, physician to a succession of Tudor monarchs. From 1689 until 1825 it occupied its own impressive building in Warwick Lane.

59 The *St James's Evening Post* was published, usually four times each week, between June 1715 and July 1755.

60 Lincoln's Inn Fields, behind Lincoln's Inn, between Kingsway and Chancery Lane, were an open area used for various recreational activities and, according to the 1735 Act of Parliament that enclosed them, also for illicit and disorderly purposes.

61 'He' in the text is Christ, who has just ordained and named his apostles.

62 A Baron was one of the judges of the Court of the Exchequer.

63 A projector was someone who engaged in speculative schemes, usually for making money.

64 Myrmidons are unscrupulous hired ruffians, though the term derives from a race inhabiting classical Thessaly, renowned for their warlike ferocity. Achilles went to the siege of Troy accompanied by Myrmidons.

65 Ahitophel was one of David's counsellors, a man of great sagacity but little trustworthiness. He advised David's third son, Absalom, how he might destroy his father, but committed suicide when he saw that the rebellion had failed (II Samuel xv–xvii). John Dryden's poem, *Absalom and Achitophel*, published in 1681, reworked the biblical story in terms of the Duke of Monmouth's rebellion against Charles II under the influence of the Earl of Shaftesbury.

66 Bashaw, or later Pasha, was the title given to high-ranking Turkish officers. It had come in England to be synonymous with imperiousness.

67 Commissioners of Lunacy would be appointed to investigate whether an individual was indeed a lunatic as alleged, though such a commission was normally set up only when substantial property was involved.

68 '*Res Medica*' are 'things medical'.

69 Gracechurch Street is a continuation of Bishopsgate down towards the Monument and London Bridge.

70 Westminster Hall, apart from being used for state trials, was normally divided among the courts of Common Pleas, King's Bench, Lord Chancellor's, the Master of the Rolls, and others, who shared space, too, with shops and stalls selling books, sweetmeats, coffee and a variety of goods.

71 A tallow-chandler made and sold candles of tallow, or animal fat.

72 Cruden's ambitions to become a don at Marischal College in Aberdeen had been ruined by his infatuation and subsequent confinement in the tolbooth, or town prison, which also made it necessary for him to leave 'his native place'.

73 The allusion is to the riddle posed by Samson in Judges xiv. 14: 'Out of the eater came forth meat, And out of the strong came forth sweetness.'

74 Revealed religion is that made known by divine agency.

75 A black theta. Theta, the eighth letter of the Greek alphabet, signified death in ballots held in order to decide a criminal sentence in ancient Greece.

76 The Stationer's Company has its origins in the fifteenth century, though its charter was awarded in 1557. It kept a register of printed books from early in the sixteenth century, entry being made compulsory in 1662 and continuing for copyright purposes until 1911. Stationers' Hall, which was rebuilt in 1674 after the Great Fire, is just inside the City near Ludgate. A livery-man is a freeman of the City entitled to wear his company's livery.

77 This, clearly, could have been John Monro who was to release Cruden from his later confinement in the madhouse at Chelsea.

78 Some of the great English trials, including those of the Earl of Surrey and of Lady Jane Grey, in the sixteenth century, took place in the Guildhall. The Sheriff's Court would have been the equivalent of a County Court, dealing with civil actions.

79 The two cited quotations are actually 'Say not thou, I will recompense evil; But wait on the Lord, and he shall save thee' (Proverbs xx. 22) and 'This poor man cried, and the Lord heard him, And saved him out of all his trouble.' (Psalms xxxiv. 6)

Samuel Bruckshaw

1 'Provoco ad Populum' means 'I appeal to the people.'

2 Frederick Bull (c. 1714–84), MP for the City of London, was retiring Lord Mayor in 1774. One attraction for Bruckshaw, however, would have been Bull's support for John Wilkes and his association therefore with principles of popular liberty. In 1780 Bull, still an MP and an alderman, played a prominent part in the Gordon Riots in support of Lord George Gordon, leading one of the protest marches into the City.

3 A divan was an Oriental council of state or court of justice. Like most things Oriental, and especially Turkish, the word carried associations of arbitrariness and corruption.

4 See Cruden n.37.

5 A nonsuit arises when the plaintiff withdraws his or her action, though this might happen when the judge orders a stoppage because of the plaintiff's failure to establish a legal cause or to produce sufficient evidence.

6 See Cruden n.62.

7 'This I will, thus I command' is a quotation from Juvenal's Satire VI, line 223. The next line is 'Be my will sufficient reason. '

8 The 24th Geo. IId. Chap. 44 is 'An Act for the rendering Justices of the Peace more safe in the Execution of their Office; and for indemnifying Constables and others acting in Obedience to their Warrants'. This became law in 1751. Under the terms of the Act, which is relatively short and uncomplicated, Bruckshaw, when he began his subsequent legal action, proceeded correctly in relation to the crucial first clause, which instructs that 'no Writ shall be sued out against . . . any Justice of the Peace for any Thing by him done in the Execution of his Office, until Notice in Writing . . . shall have been delivered to him . . . at least one Calendar Month before the suing out or serving the same'. Where Bruckshaw would seem to have been vulnerable, however, is in relation to the final clause, clause VIII, setting down that 'no action shall be brought against any Justice of the Peace for any thing done in the Execution of his Office . . . unless commenced within six Calendar Months after the Act committed'.

9 'Procul á Jove' means 'far from Jove', that is, at a distance from the source of power.

10 A Dedimus is a writ empowering someone who is not a judge to perform an act in place of a judge, from the words of the writ dedimus potestatem, meaning 'we have given the power'.

11 Sir William de Grey (1719–81), having been made attorney-general in 1766, became Lord Chief Justice of Common Pleas in 1771, the year of the case cited. He was made 1st Baron Walsingham a year before he died. For Guildhall, see Cruden n.78.

12 William Murray (1705–93) was one of the leading legal figures of the century. Since 1756, when he was created Baron Mansfield, he had been Chief Justice of the King's Bench and a member of the cabinet. He became 1st Earl of Mansfield in 1776.

13 A *Special* jury is one consisting only of persons of a certain station or who occupy premises of a certain rateable value. Later, Bruckshaw refers to the possibility of a jury of merchants.

14 George Jeffreys (1648–89), created 1st Baron and Lord Chancellor in 1685, was the notorious judge, and from 1683 Chief Justice of King's Bench, who during the 'bloody assize' of 1685 hanged or transported hundreds of the West Country supporters of the Duke of Monmouth's rebellion against James II. Sir Dudley Ryder (1691–1756) rose to become Lord Chief Justice of King's Bench in 1754. Knighted in 1740, his reputation had been made in parliament where he brought forward a bill in 1741 for the impressment of the Porteous rioters in Edinburgh. He was also responsible for the remorseless prosecution of the '45 rebels.

15 'Condign' means merited, especially by crimes.

16 Bourne is a small town between Stamford and Spalding, just on the edge of the Fens. The much larger Stamford has the advantage of lying on the Great North Road from London to Edinburgh, now the A1.

17 A wool-stapler buys wool from the producer and sells it, graded for quality, to the manufacturer.

18 See Cruden n.13.

19 For a trader, taking one's freedom was to join the company established in the particular community that guaranteed the rights and privileges appropriate to that trade. It would also have involved a payment, which Bruckshaw was obviously not prepared to make.

20 A fine in this context would be a final agreement.

21 An assignment is the legal transference of effects with, as here, trustees appointed with power to act within a limited time.

22 Factors buy or sell on behalf of another. In this case they apparently made every effort to sell stock at less than market price.

23 The *St James's Chronicle* (or the *British Evening Post*) began in March 1761 and ran uninterrupted until August 1866, when it amalgamated with *The Press*, continuing then until 1884 as *The Press and St James's Chronicle.*

24 An 'aguish' disorder would have been a feverish condition, with fits of shaking and hot and cold sweating.

25 Inns, like coffee houses, were commonly used as receiving addresses for mail.

26 Shalloon was a closely woven woollen material generally used for linings.

27 Tuxford is a village on the Great North Road in Nottinghamshire between Worksop and Newark.

28 A capital messuage is the one of several dwellings with their land and appurtenances under a single ownership that the owner actually occupies. The word messuage probably derives from the French *ménage*, meaning household.

29 This was a set meal provided at a fixed price by an inn.

30 A 'serjeant' was an officer responsible for arresting offenders and for summoning persons to appear before a court.

31 See Cruden n.3.

32 A *mittimus*, from the first word of the writ, meaning 'we send', is a warrant directing a keeper to hold a named individual in custody.

33 The Recorder was then a person with legal knowledge appointed by the mayor and alderman to record the proceedings of their courts.

34 There are no Thickbrooms in the current area telephone directory.

35 See Allen n.32.

36 Presumably the mayor is using 'tax' in the sense of 'challenge' or 'dispute', though the context of his remarks makes the general drift unclear.

37 A bludgeon was a short stick or truncheon, with one loaded, or thicker, end.

38 A justice of the peace of the quorum was one, usually of special qualifications, whose presence was necessary to constitute the validity of a bench.

39 The Lord-lieutenant of a county is appointed by the sovereign as chief executive authority and head of the magistracy.

40 A moidore, although a Portuguese gold coin, was nevertheless current in England with a value of 27 shillings. A guinea was worth 21 shillings.

41 A chaise was a light travelling carriage. The Wilsons would have taken a post-chaise, which was changed at each stage of a longer journey.

42 The Wilsons were travelling on the Great North Road. Witham Common was the first stage, halfway between Stamford and the second stage, Grantham.

43 The intention had presumably been to leave the Great North Road at Grantham and travel west to Nottingham, thence directly north-west through Ashbourne and Macclesfield to Stockport and Ashton-under-Lyne, skirting the Derbyshire Peaks on the south. Going on mistakenly to Newark obliged them to divert through Worksop and Sheffield, and then to cross the moors between Stocksbridge and Hadfield via the remote Woodhead, arriving at Scout Mill from the east. It is this part of the journey that Bruckshaw later regards as 'a very improper road for a chaise'.

44 This would have been an ecclesiastical visitation by one or more higher officers of the church in order to examine the state of the parish or diocese.

45 Sir John Fielding's men is a reference to the small professional police force founded in London in 1753 by the writer and magistrate Henry Fielding and his half-brother John, also a magistrate. This force was designed to pursue and arrest criminals no matter where in the kingdom they fled to.

46 While a 'Pallator' is obviously some kind of ecclesiastical servant or server, possibly a 'cope-bearer', I can find no trace of the word elsewhere.

47 A John Wilson of Ashton-under-Lyne took out a licence to run a private madhouse on 12 October 1780, according to the Manchester Quarter Sessions Petitions Order Book, ten years, therefore, after the events in Bruckshaw's narrative.

48 A turnpike-road was one on which turnpikes, or barriers, were erected for the collection of tolls which would ensure the maintenance of the road. These were therefore generally in better condition than other roads, which could be appalling, especially in winter months.

49 A ridge-tree, or ridge-piece, is the beam at the point of the roof on which the rafters rest.

50 Dropsy is an accumulation of water or fluid in the body, and can be a sign of the failure of a major organ, especially heart and kidneys. Wilson's offering dropsy as an explanation for swelling could suggest that they also provided a discreet termination service for unwanted pregnancies.

51 The quotation from Laurence Sterne's *A Sentimental Journey through France and Italy* (1768) is from a section in which the narrator, 'Yorick', is trying to imagine the miseries of confinement.

52 Luzley is to the north-east of Ashton, on the road to Mossley.

53 The identity of this person is unknown.

54 The quotation is from *Hamlet* V.i.271, where Hamlet is demanding from the enraged Laertes what he would have done for his dead sister Ophelia. 'Eisel' is vinegar. Bruckshaw might not see the irony of quoting a character who spends part of the play feigning madness.

55 Fabrigas against Mostyn was heard in Common Pleas, Michaelmas Term, 14 Geo.III. It was an 'Action of trespass and false imprisonment by the plaintiff, a native Minorquin, against the defendant, who was Governor of Minorca'. In this case, the jury found for the plaintiff and awarded damages of £3,000, though part of the challenge involved whether the trial should take place in Minorca, Fabrigas being 'a mere native of the island', or in London. The Duke of Richmond was Charles Lennox, the 3rd Duke (1735–1806), a significant political figure and later member of government. He was an ardent reformist and also supported the American colonists in parliament.

56 Dey was the title of the commander of the Janissaries – or personal bodyguards – of Algiers who deposed the pasha in 1710 and took over rule of the country

57 Bearbinder Lane was presumably in the legal area of London between Holborn and the river.

58 An *affidavit*, meaning 'he declares' from the Latin verb *affidare*, is a written statement formally sworn by a deponent or witness.

59 Staple Inn, just off Holborn opposite Gray's Inn Road, was one of the minor inns of the court, from 1529 owned by Gray's Inn, but by the eighteenth century disused as a legal school and its chambers occupied by attorneys, solicitors and clerks.

60 See Cruden n.69.

61 Lawrence Lane runs from Gresham Street down to Cheapside.

62 Bread Street, called after the medieval market, runs between Cheapside and Cannon Street.

63 A *Latitat* writ, meaning 'he lies hid' from the Latin verb *latitare*, was one that supposed the defendant to lie hidden and summoned him to answer in the King's Bench by the 'returnable' date.

64 A Writ of Inquiry is simply a writ directing that an inquiry be held.

65 See Cruden n.12.

66 Serjeant in this context was a Serjeant at Law, a member of a superior order of barristers from which the Common Law judges were always chosen.

67 In law, the venue is the locality where an action is laid and to which the jury therefore should be summoned to come. The venue is in the parish of St Mary-le-Bow in Cheapside.

68 The quotation is from John Gay's *Fables*, published in 1727, 'The Shepherd's Dog and the Wolf', lines 33–4.

69 Hoxton Square is out of the City in Shoreditch, just to the west of Bethnal Green.

70 Fleet Square is a continuation of the Strand into Ludgate Hill.

71 St Paul's Churchyard runs to the south of the cathedral, connecting Ludgate Hill with Cannon Street.

72 King Street runs south from Gresham Street to Cheapside and Poultry.

73 Wood Street runs from the centre of Cheapside up to Gresham Street. There were compters in both Wood Street and Poultry. These were sheriff's prisons which held people for debt. Raincock and Bolton apparently held corporation office with regard to the compters.

74 The Temple, home of the legal fraternity, is alongside what is now Victoria Embankment.

75 Lincoln's Inn Hall, to the west of Chancery Lane, was used by the Court of Chancery from about 1737.

76 A *subpoena*, from the Latin *sub poena* meaning 'under penalty', is a writ demanding the presence of the named person to answer a charge against him, or of a named witness, under penalty for failure to do so.

77 To pray a *talis*, from Latin phrase *tales de circumstantibus* meaning 'such persons from those standing about', is to seek from those present in court additional members of a jury to fill a deficiency among those originally summoned.

78 A process is the formal commencement of any action at law, such as would have been necessary for the original arrest of Bruckshaw.

79 Money against Leach, which was heard in King's Bench, Trinity Term, 5 Geo.III, was an 'Action of trespass and false imprisonment, for breaking and entering the home of the defendant in error . . . and imprisoning him for five days without reasonable or probable cause'. As with Fabrigas against Mostyn, the jury found for the plaintiff and awarded damages, though part of the action involved suspicion of printing and circulating the subversive journal the *North Briton*, founded by John Wilkes.

80 Bruckshaw, having had his action declared void, has had to pay the defendants' costs as well as his own.

81 A 'common-hall' in this context is a public meeting.

82 See Cruden n.70.

83 A crier in a court of justice is an officer who makes public announcements, though here he clearly acts in other capacities as well.

84 Highgate is in north London. See Allen n.49.

85 The *postea* endorsement, from the Latin meaning 'afterwards', sets out the proceedings that took place at a trial and the verdict that was given.

86 Sir William Blackstone (1723–80), first Vinerian Professor of English Law at Oxford and

from 1763 solicitor-general to the queen, was the author of the influential *Commentaries on the Laws of England*, published between 1765 and 1769. This was not the Mr Justice Blackstone before whom Bruckshaw's case was heard at Lincoln.

87   The Court of Common Pleas heard civil actions brought by one subject against another.

88   A petition is a formally written application – here to the monarch – soliciting the redress of an injury.

89   Henry Howard was Earl of Suffolk, having succeeded to the title in 1757. He was Secretary of State from 1771, and died in 1779. Cleveland Row continues Pall Mall towards Green Park (or Upper St James's Park, as it was sometimes called).

90   Bruckshaw is quoting Matthew v. 40, which is about turning the other cheek: 'And if any man will sue thee at the law, and take away thy coat, let him have thy cloke also.'

91   Bruckshaw is mocking the step-by-step logic of theological reasoning.

92   This is a paraphrase of Romans iv. 18: 'Who against hope believed in hope, that he might become the father of many nations, according to that which was spoken, So shall thy seed be.'

93   A churchwarden is a lay officer elected to assist the incumbent of a parish with a variety of parochial duties. Overseers of the Poor were appointed annually to undertake administrative responsibilities in connection with relief of the poor of a parish.

94   A wool-comber carded or combed wool by hand and was therefore engaged in a manual occupation, while wool-stapling was a trade.

95   This is likely to have been the parish of St Lawrence Jewry, the church in Gresham Street.

96   Bloomsbury Square, which was formed in about 1665, is just to the east of the British Museum. A fashionable address, it was outside Lord Mansfield's house during the 'No Popery' riots of 1780 that a huge bonfire was made of books, furniture, manuscripts and works of art.

97   Bredbury is just to the north of Stockport, on the way to Manchester.

98   Check is a fabric with a pattern of small squares.

99   A case-knife is one carried in a case or sheath.

William Belcher

1   *The Galaxy, Consisting of a variety of sacred and other poetry* by W. Belcher 'and others' was published in 1790.

2   *Belcher's Cream of Knowledge* was also probably published in 1790. I have not been able to trace *Peace and Reconciliation*. The quotation is from the seventeenth-century poet Edmund Waller, 'Of the last Verses in the Book', published in 1686: 'The Soul's dark Cottage, batter'd and decay'd, Lets in new Light thro' chinks that time has made' (lines 13–14). See also n.7 below.

3   Sir John Scott (1751–1838) was then Attorney-General, and was to become Chief Justice of Common Pleas in 1799 and Lord Chancellor in 1801. He was created 1st Earl of Eldon in 1821. He was one of the most significant, if also conservative, legal figures of the period and was attacked by Shelley in the *Mask of Anarchy* in 1819 for his role in the Massacre of Peterloo. *Liberavi animam meam* means 'I have freed my soul.'

4   Thomas Monro (1759–1833) was the youngest son of John Monro whom he succeeded as physician to Bethlem Hospital in 1792. Clearly he had the gratitude of Belcher for his part in his release, but he lost his post at Bethlem after the Parliamentary Committee reports of 1815 and 1816, being succeeded by his son Edward Thomas Monro. (He in turn lost his place after a report by the Commissioners in Lunacy in 1852.) Monro was also a talented watercolourist.

5   A writ of *supersedeas*, from the Latin, meaning 'you shall desist', commands the suspension of legal proceedings.

6   Belcher is making passing allusion to St Paul's words, quoted in Allen n.9.

7   The quotation is from the same poem by Waller, 'Of the last Verses in the Book': 'Leaving the old, both Worlds at once they view, That Stand upon the threshold of the New' (lines 17–18).

8   The use of a bullock's horn was commonplace for the forced administration of medicines.

9   A Grand jury consisted of between twelve and twenty-three persons. Its purpose was to inquire into the validity of indictments prior to their being submitted to trial by jury. Grand juries were abolished in 1933.

10 *The Lives of the Poets* by Samuel Johnson was published 1779–81. *The Gentleman's Magazine* was founded and run by Edward Cave in 1731, lasting in some form up until 1914.

11 *Non compos mentis* is the Latin for 'not master of one's mind'.

12 Arthur Young (1741–1820) was a well-known agricultural theorist. He became secretary to the Board of Agriculture in 1793. His periodical *Annals of Agriculture* was published from 1784 until 1809.

13 To bilk is to defraud. Its earliest use as a verb is given in the *Oxford English Dictionary* as 1651.

14 Thomas Erskine (1750–1823) was one of the most brilliant defence barristers of his time, appearing for, among others, Horne Tooke in 1794 and James Hadfield, indicted for attempting to assassinate George III, in 1800. In 1806 he was created 1st Baron Erskine and made Lord Chancellor, though he resigned the following year. He held libertarian principles and was sympathetic to the French Revolution.

15 Alexander Wedderburn (1733–1805), created 1st Baron Loughborough in 1780, was the current Lord Chancellor. He was made 1st Earl of Rosslyn in 1801.

16 Belcher is misquoting from Cowley's 'Elegie upon Anacreon, Who was choked by a Grape-Stone' (published 1656): '*Rumour* they no more should mind Then Men safe-landed do the *Wind*' (lines 55–6). John Locke's influential theories about ideas are developed in Book II of the *Essay concerning Human Understanding*, published in 1690. Locke is particularly concerned with attacking the notion of 'innate' ideas. The reference to Alexander Pope is to his poem *Eloisa to Abelard*, which was published in 1717: 'Of all affliction taught a lover yet, 'Tis sure the hardest science to forget!' (lines 189–90).

17 Hackney is just to the north of Bethnal Green. One known madhouse there was Brooke House, but as that was owned by the Monro family it is unlikely to be the one in which Belcher was confined.

18 The quotation is from *Paradise Lost*, I, 250–3. The lines are spoken by Satan.

19 No. 9 Thornhaugh Street (or Lower Thornhaugh Street, as it is given on the title page) was a very exclusive address. Bedford Square, which had been formed between 1775 and 1780, was part of the Bedford estate and included among its residents the Lord Chancellor and, from 1814, Lord Eldon. Thornhaugh Street is now just off Russell Square, which was formed in 1804 (called after the family name of the Dukes of Bedford) to the north of the British Museum.

20 The application of blisters – or rather of dressings designed to raise blisters – was one of the standard treatments for madness, based on the theory that excesses within the body needed to be able to escape.

21 The Bastille, the state prison in Paris, was destroyed at the beginning of the Revolution, 14 July 1789.

22 See Introduction for discussion of the inspection of private madhouses.

23 A commission of lunacy is a warrant issued to investigate whether a person is a lunatic or not. See also Cruden n.67.

24 See Allen n.4.

25 Helleborean refers to plants of the *Helleborus* species, which were much in use as treatments for mental illness. The hyena is defined by Dr Johnson in his *Dictionary*, first published in 1755, as 'An animal like a wolf, said fabulously to imitate human voices.'

Further Reading

Anthologies

Hunter, Richard and Macalpine, Ida (eds), *Three Hundred Years of Psychiatry, 1535–1860*, London, 1963.

Ingram, Allan (ed.), *Patterns of Madness in the Eighteenth Century: A Reader*, Liverpool, 1997.

Peterson, Dale (ed.), *A Mad People's History of Madness*, Pittsburgh, 1982.

Porter, Roy (ed.), *The Faber Book of Madness*, London, 1991.

Other Selected Works

Busfield, Joan, *Managing Madness. Changing Ideas and Practice*, London, 1986.

Bynum. W.F., Porter, Roy and Shepherd, Michael (eds), *The Anatomy of Madness: Essays in the History of Psychiatry*, 2 vols, London, 1985.

Doerner, Klaus, *Madmen and the Bourgeoisie: A Social History of Insanity and Psychiatry*, 1969; trans. Joachim Neugroschel and Jean Steinberg, Oxford, 1981.

Foucault, Michel, *Madness and Civilization: A History of Insanity in the Age of Reason*, 1961; trans. Richard Howard, London, 1967.

Fox, Christopher (ed.), *Psychology and Literature in the Eighteenth Century*, New York, 1987.

Gilman, Sander L., King, Helen, Porter, Roy, Rousseau, G.S. and Showalter, Elaine, *Hysteria beyond Freud*, Berkeley and Los Angeles, 1993.

Ingram, Allan, *The Madhouse of Language: Writing and Reading Madness in the Eighteenth Century*, London, 1991.

Macalpine, Ida and Hunter, Richard, *George III and the Mad Business*, London, 1969.

Olivier, Edith, *The Eccentric Life of Alexander Cruden*, London, 1934.

Parry-Jones, William Llewellyn, *The Trade in Lunacy, A Study of Private Madhouses in England in the Eighteenth and Nineteenth Centuries*, London, 1971.

Porter, Roy, *Mind-Forg' Manacles: A History of Madness in England from the Restoration to the Regency*, London, 1987.

Porter, Roy, *A Social History of Madness: Stories of the Insane*, London, 1987.

Scull, Andrew, *Museums of Madness*, London, 1979.

Showalter, Elaine, *The Female Malady: Women, Madness and English Culture, 1830–1980*, London, 1985.

Usher, Jane, *Women's Madness: Misogyny or Mental Illness?* Hemel Hempstead, 1991.

Index

Entries are confined to major topics and to names of significant figures.